# FAST FORDS OF THE "GEORGIA SHAKER"

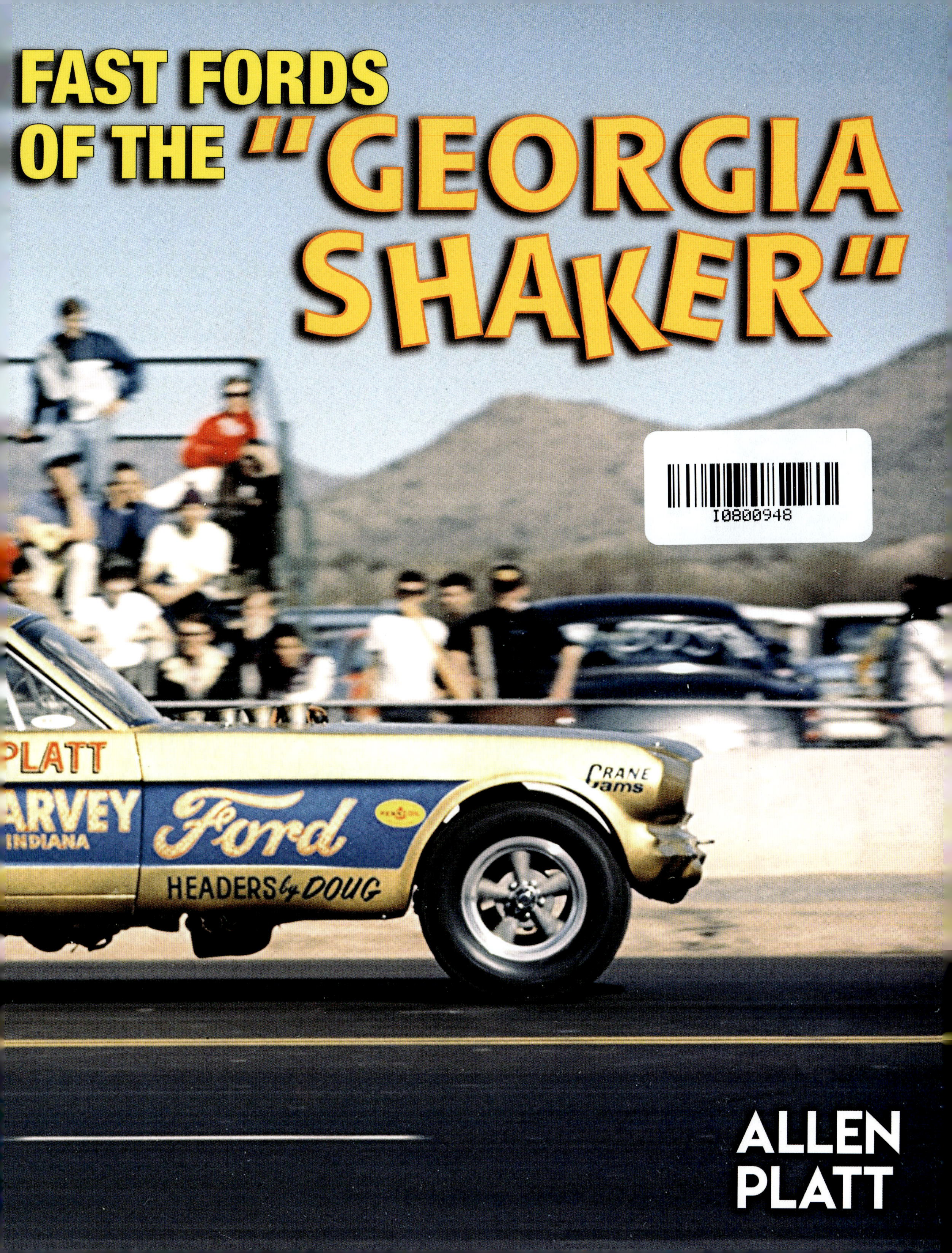




ALLEN PLATT

CarTech®

CarTech®, Inc.
838 Lake Street South
Forest Lake, MN 55025
Phone: 651-277-1200 or 800-551-4754
Fax: 651-277-1203
www.cartechbooks.com



Photos included are courtesy georgiashaker.com collection unless noted otherwise.

Edit by Wes Eisenschenk
Layout by Monica Seiberlich

ISBN 978-1-61325-397-7
Item No. CT625

Library of Congress Cataloging-in-Publication Data

Names: Platt, Allen, 1963- author.
Title: Hubert Platt : fast Fords of the "Georgia Shaker" / Allen Platt.
Description: Forest Lake, MN : CarTech, Inc., [2019] | Includes bibliographical references and index.
Identifiers: LCCN 2018061554 | ISBN 9781613253977 (alk. paper)
Subjects: LCSH: Platt, Hubert, 1931- | Automobile racing drivers--United States--History--Biography. | Drag racing--United States--History. | LCGFT: Biographies.
Classification: LCC GV1032.P63 P53 2019 | DDC 796.72092 [B] --dc23
LC record available at https://lccn.loc.gov/2018061554

Written, edited, and designed in the U.S.A.
Printed in China
10 9 8 7 6 5 4 3 2 1



PUBLISHER'S NOTE: In reporting history, the images required to tell the tale will vary greatly in quality, especially by modern photographic standards. While some images in this volume are not up to those digital standards, we have included them, as we feel they are an important element in telling the story.

DISTRIBUTION BY:

*Europe*
PGUK
63 Hatton Garden
London EC1N 8LE, England
Phone: 020 7061 1980 • Fax: 020 7242 3725
www.pguk.co.uk

*Australia*
Renniks Publications Ltd.
3/37-39 Green Street
Banksmeadow, NSW 2109, Australia
Phone: 2 9695 7055 • Fax: 2 9695 7355
www.renniks.com

*Canada*
Login Canada
300 Saulteaux Crescent
Winnipeg, MB, R3J 3T2 Canada
Phone: 800 665 1148 • Fax: 800 665 0103
www.lb.ca

# HUBERT PLATT

CarTech®

INDIANAPOLIS RACEWAY PARK
DOUG'S HEADERS
HUBERT PLATT
GEORGIA "SHAKER"
CRANE CAMS
PAUL HARVEY Ford
INDIANAPOLIS INDIANA
RACEMASTER
Casler RACING TIRES

# TABLE OF CONTENTS

Acknowledgments ........ 6
Foreword ........ 7

**CHAPTER 1:** Poor Boy ........ 8
**CHAPTER 2:** New Beginnings ........ 19
**CHAPTER 3:** Nalley-Nicholson Race Team ........ 26
**CHAPTER 4:** Brand Loyalty? ........ 32
**CHAPTER 5:** Keeping Up with the Factory ........ 42
**CHAPTER 6:** The One-Piece Body Mustang ........ 69
**CHAPTER 7:** The Factory Comes Knocking ........ 75
**CHAPTER 8:** The Switch to Super Stock ........ 87
**CHAPTER 9:** Cobra Jets ........ 97
**CHAPTER 10:** Ford Drag Team ........ 111
**CHAPTER 11:** The Pro Stock Years ........ 142
**CHAPTER 12:** The Reunion Years ........ 164

Index ........ 190

# ACKNOWLEDGMENTS

In the early 1990s, Dad and I started going to drag racer reunions and people would always say, "Someone should write a book about the Georgia Shaker." We would always nod and smile and say, "That would be great!" We never thought once that the someone would be me. Then, when Dad turned 80, I started to record some of his old stories. I even had the wherewithal to make a chronological list of all of his race cars while we were on a road trip to the races and he was driving (yes, he could drive seven hours or more on a road trip in his 80s). This list of race cars that Hubert helped me make was the backbone of this book, without it there would have been a lot of speculation. So thank you, Dad, for helping me get started on the right foot!

I took the advice you gave to me as a boy, which was, "If you are going to do something, do it right!" and with that in mind I left no stone unturned in making this book as accurate as possible. I would like to thank Ford drag racing fan Lloyd Wolfe for the flash drive with more than 200 newspaper and magazine stories, ads, and clippings that he had collected all about Hubert's racing career. This proved to be invaluable, as it confirmed and added facts such as ETs and speeds to many of Dad's stories.

Thanks to my mom, Bee Platt, for the huge scrapbook she made in the 1960s, and especially for not throwing it away and allowing me to keep it after the divorce.

To my uncles, Ponnie Flegel and Ray Platt, thanks for telling me the stories Dad didn't. Thank you to Bruce Brantley for your memories from the early 1960s, they are priceless. Thanks big time to Doug Thorley, Larry Yates, Dick Brannan, and Larry Coleman for helping me sort out the stories from the mid 1960s.

I would also like to thank Bob Swaim, Jon Brantmeier, Jerry Coley, and Rusty Gillis for the historical facts about the 1969–1970 Ford Drag Team. Thanks to Herb McCandless for the detailed info about the United States Racing Team, your memories are golden. Thanks to Willie "Camrod" Campbell for giving me the inside scoop on your relationship with Hubert. Getting so many first-hand stories from the people who lived it helped make this book what it is.

Thank you to the collectors who own the surviving *Georgia Shaker* race cars: Tim Holland, Mike Kerr, Brent Hajek, Bob Perkins, and Gary Schwartz. The personal relationships you guys had with Dad and your willingness to bring his old cars out during his reunion years opened many conversations between he and I and helped educate me on them. For that and for brightening Dad's golden years, I thank you.

Thanks to the following photographers: Paul Hutchins, Marvin Smith, Bob McClurg, Doug Boyce, Michael Goyda, Bill Cook, Martyn Schorr, Steve Reyes, and especially fans who gave us never-before-seen photos. Thanks to all the fans who come up to me at every drag race and car show and tell me that my dad was your hero; this warms my heart, thank you for the love. Also thanks to the fans who told me their "I was there that day" stories; they really helped refine many of the stories I was already writing.

Wes Eisenschenk at CarTech Books, thank you for having patience with a first-time author and for all of your help.

A very special thank you to my lovely wife, Anna. Your dedication to helping me with this project was second to none. You have been my strength and motivation when I didn't think I could do this, pushing me in the right direction with encouraging words in your loving and caring way. I couldn't ask for a better partner, and I'll never forget how happy Hubert was when I married you!

Lastly to my father, Hubert, to say you were a cool dad and that going to the drag races with you as a kid was fun is a huge understatement. There was never a dull moment being your son. Now that you're gone, I'm so grateful for the legacy you have left for me to carry on. I do it with passion. I love you. Long live the *Georgia Shaker*.

# FOREWORD

## by Linda Vaughn "Miss Hurst Golden Shifter"

Being from the South and particularly being a Georgia girl, I had heard of the wild Platt brothers who had been tearing up the Georgia drag strips since the early 1960s. I got my first chance to meet Hubert at Yellow River Dragstrip in Covington, Georgia, with my friends Phil Bonner and Jimmy Newberry.

Hubert was something else, and I just loved watching him cuss and work. The boys would race the cars, come back to the pits and raise hell, rebuild the car, and go at it again. Those were great times—the music, the racing, and the people played far less games than today.

At that time, I lived in the Montego apartments in Atlanta, less than a mile from Hubert's home. I remember Hubert and his buddy Randy Payne beating on my door at least once in the middle of the night, saying that they were working on the race cars and had run out of whiskey. I'm not a whiskey girl, but I gave them my daddy's Jack Daniel's and off they went. I went to see them race the next day, and they actually won; surprising, considering they had been up all night!

Through the years, I got to know Hubert and it turned into a great friendship. We just really bonded. I fell in love with him and treated him like a brother. When I would see Hubert anywhere in the country at the drag races, I knew that was my Georgia family. My mother traveled with me, and she fell in love with Hubert as well. They loved to joke around and cut up. Once at a World Finals after-party in Tulsa, Oklahoma, Hubert brought some white lightnin' that was so strong you could put it on a snake bite and it would heal it. I mean you could run a Top Fuel Dragster off the stuff! Hu-baby had a couple of sips too many, and my mom had to take care of him the rest of the night; what a hoot!

Hubert used to tickle me; he was a comedian, but he was also a hell of a competitor. I was so proud of him and the way he raced, he was just a damn good race driver. Hubert had a smile for everybody and I don't know anyone who didn't like him, except maybe some of the match racers 'cause he whipped their asses!

We remained friends all through the years. We worked car shows together and had a lot of fun the last 20 years before he passed away. When I think about Hubert today, most of all I miss his laughter and his smile and him picking on me. I really miss that a lot. He was a great driver and a great friend. He was the "Georgia Shaker."

CHAPTER 1

# POOR BOY

Just two years into the Great Depression wasn't the most opportune time to start a family, but that is exactly what Clarence and Elizabeth Platt did. On December 8, 1931, the young couple's first son, Hubert, was born. Less than one year later, their second son, Huston, arrived in November 1932. The couple went on to have four more children: Buddy, Mabel, Ray, and Joe.

The Platts made their home in the small fishing community of Little River, South Carolina, just below the North Carolina border. Clarence "Poodle" Platt was a carpenter and brick mason who was known as a local tough guy and builder. Elizabeth "Libby" Platt was a seamstress.

The Platts were a family of little means, but they had a roof over their heads and food on the table. Times were hard through the Great Depression and then World War II, and there wasn't a lot of luxury in their lives.

*It wasn't easy raising a family of six children through the Great Depression and World War II, but to their credit, Clarence and Elizabeth Platt's two eldest sons would grow to be fine men. They would reach hall of fame status and leave their marks on automotive history and the sport of drag racing.*

In 1946, 14-year-old Hubert started his day before the sun rose. He crawled out of a warm bed shared with two younger brothers and made his way to a cold kitchen. There, he started a fire in the small wood-burning stove. His mother soon followed to make coffee for her husband and breakfast for the family.

In these quiet early morning hours, Hubert sat on the front porch watching the cars go by and people going to work, and he would dream. Unlike most 14-year-old boys who dreamed of toys or playing sports, Hubert dreamed of only one thing: having a big, long, shiny convertible car. In his dream, he was driving with the top down, a beautiful female by his side, his foot on the gas, and his hair in the wind. He didn't have any place in particular he was going, just somewhere fun and exciting.

Hubert didn't just want this, he craved it. He wanted it enough that he dropped out of the eighth grade and started to pursue it immediately.

### Off to Work

Poodle and Libby reluctantly agreed to allow their oldest son to quit school and begin to work, not that they had much influence on the strong-willed Hubert. In their own words, he was "hardheaded."

At first, Hubert went to work with his father as a carpenter's helper, but this was short lived. Poodle was a bit rough; he was a tough, no-nonsense kind of guy who was especially hard on his eldest son. This was more than young Hubert could bear, so he set out in search of something that would give him a little freedom from his overbearing father. Over the next couple of years, Hubert worked every kind of odd job there was from cutting grass and raking leaves to washing cars. Finally, he landed his first real job at the local A & P grocery store as a bag boy.

Hubert enjoyed the attention he got at the A & P as a cute and charming bag boy, and he certainly enjoyed receiving tips from the ladies whose bags he would carry out. He quickly learned there was more money to be made than just the 40-cent minimum wage he earned per hour. In fact, he preferred hustling with a smile for tips more than any other part of the job.

*Hubert poses with his arm around younger brother Huston. The pair looked like a couple of tough kids. Certainly, they had the fastest bicycle on the block.*

Hubert had taken an interest in dressing and looking nice, and he was beginning to develop a real sense of style. Working steady made it possible for him to afford to dress the way he wanted in pleated and creased pants, nice shirts, and shiny shoes. He found that the sharper he looked, the more tips came his way.

## Hubert's First Ride

Hubert began to save his money, and it wasn't long before he had the grand sum of $125. He used it to purchase his first car: a 1939 Ford. The car was more than 10 years old and was a little rough, but Hubert didn't care. He was happy to have some wheels.

He became the first person in his family to own an automobile. His father never drove a car, and his mother wouldn't drive or own a car of her own until many years later when Hubert bought her one.

Whenever Hubert was asked about his first car, he'd say, "I ran it a little hard." Needless to say, that was an understatement. When Hubert was at the wheel, he had two speeds: stop and wide open. The 1939 Ford Coupe was equipped with a 221-ci V-8 fitted with a Stromberg carburetor that was rated at 85 hp. Like all the 1939 Fords, it had a sliding gear 3-speed transmission, single dry plate clutch, shaft drive, and a 3/4-inch floating-gear axle with 4.33:1 ratio. Hubert pushed the car to its limits and beyond.

*Hubert spent a good amount of his money on clothes. From his sweater vest and pleated pants down to his argyle socks, he was a sharp-dressed young man who always took pride in his appearance.*

***A Mechanic Is Born***

As with most high-mileage, 10-year-old cars that are being abused, the 1939 Ford quit running. When Hubert took it to a local garage to get the locked-up engine fixed, the mechanic told him that it would cost $150 dollars to do the repairs. Knowing he had only paid $125 for the entire car, Hubert decided there was only one thing he could afford to do: take it home and fix it himself.

Teenage Hubert was by no stretch of the imagination a mechanic, but he dove into this repair headfirst. He completely disassembled the small V-8 and found that all three of its main bearings were spun in the cast-iron block. That was no easy repair even for a professional, but the will of a young man who wants to get back behind the wheel and on the streets is strong.

After long hours and late nights of trial and error, Hubert got the little V-8 running again. This gave him a newfound confidence to try new things that may have seemed impossible at one time. Hubert had worked his way up to the position of assistant manager at the A & P, but the experience and success he had rebuilding the engine on the 1939 Ford made him begin to think he might be cut out for much more than a career in groceries.

## "I Used to Haul Liquor"

In the late 1940s, post–World War II America was experiencing an economic boom. Unlike 10 years earlier in the 1930s, jobs were now plentiful. GIs returning home could find well-paying employment, and they began to buy new cars and homes. The middle class was growing at a faster-than-ever pace as more families started to enjoy the "American Dream."

This economic upswing helped many businesses grow and expand. Even some unlikely trades, such as the illegal liquor business, saw incredible growth. The Carolinas have a rich history of producing a powerful liquor made from corn mash, better known as moonshine, to the delight of drinkers all throughout the South. Through a friend of a friend, Hubert met a man named Skeeter, who told him how someone with a fast car and a lot of nerve could make a great deal of money in the evenings by making several trips a week delivering the illegal elixir.

There were lots of folks who liked to sip the shine, but next to none had the courage to go deep into "Hell Hole Swamp" to purchase a jar. The name said it all, Hell Hole Swamp's reputation was as bad as it sounded. It was a place where you never let your guard down and you constantly looked over your shoulder. Hubert was young and courageous, and the lure of easy money was more than he could pass up. He took the side job, but not without first conducting some research.

Hubert began to watch the local police in the evenings, and he noticed that they ate at the same diner every night at the same time and were there for about an hour. There was his window of opportunity. He would have one hour to leave the swamp with a load, speed all across the county, and make his drops; it was a drive that took more than two hours at a normal pace.

Hubert's car held up to 20 cases of fruit jars filled with moonshine and a helper in the passenger seat for quicker off-loads. Loaded to capacity, the hot rod Ford would run 120 mph, and it needed every bit of that to complete the deliveries before the law got back on patrol. Hubert's carefully timed plan worked well, and before long he had a regular routine going.

Things were going smoothly with Hubert's side hustle, but what wasn't going well was keeping a steady helper. Hubert employed the services of young black men who would take the trip for only a couple dollars. The extra pair of hands made for speedier off-loads, but many of those hired hands quit after the first white-knuckled ride. A steady helper who could handle racing across the countryside wide open with the fearless driver and his load of illegal liquor proved to be a thing that was hard to come by.

## Keeping Up Appearances

Although his new line of work had its ups and downs, Hubert was enjoying the fruits of his labor. He bought a new car and of course his fancy clothes. Hubert knew these things would look suspicious based on his salary; it was time to look for a better day job.

On the Carolina coast, there were many fishing docks where men could find employment. There were lots of different jobs to be had as well, from fishing and processing to boat repair. Hubert had never learned to swim, so going out on a boat and fishing for days on end was out of the question. He didn't even like the thought of it; out at sea was no place for him.

Instead, Hubert landed a job with a company that did maintenance dredging in Georgetown Harbor. The ocean tides continually brought silt into the channel, which required regular maintenance dredging to allow larger ships to come into Winyah Bay to the Georgetown Paper Mill. Hubert worked on a barge with a huge crane on deck.

The rig had a great deal of mechanical equipment that would break down, and it was with this outfit that

## Watch Out for That Mule!

"Oh, please, Mr. Hubert, pull over and let me outta this car before you get the both of us killed!" Hubert ignored the terrified pleas from yet another helper who couldn't handle the job. There was no time to make any unnecessary stops. The young man continued to beg and plead, but it fell on deaf ears. Hubert kept his foot to the floor and sped down the road.

"Oh, Mr. Hubert, there's a curve up ahead. You'd best slow down!" Hubert knew this road like the back of his hand and knew he could take the upcoming curve at more than 100 mph. Hubert had no plans to slow down.

They were flying headlong toward the curve when a mule stepped out onto the road. The helper screamed, "Stop, Mr. Hubert! Watch out for that mule!" Hubert told the man to shut up and steered hard into the curve, clipping the mule's rear end as they flew past it.

The mule's tail busted out the driver-side glass, cutting Hubert's hand just as it lost control of its bowels, but Hubert never lost control of the car or left the road. He continued at the 100-plus-mph pace with his white coveralls covered in blood and the mule's lunch, a terrible looking and smelling affair. His helper was passed out cold in the passenger's seat, drenched in sweat.

When they arrived at the next drop point, the helper came to, bolted out of the car, and ran into the woods as fast as he could. Hubert never saw him again.

Hubert learned to weld. He was a natural. Welding came easy to him, and he did it beautifully. It was a skill that would serve him his entire life. Hubert would be quoted many times for saying "I can weld anything from the crack of dawn to a broken heart."

### Sharks!

In the early 1950s, 18-year-old Hubert and his 17-year-old brother Huston were a far cry from the teenagers of today. They did play some baseball as youths, but Huston was the better ballplayer of the two and Hubert lost interest quickly. Other kinds of games became much more attractive to them both.

For these two boys, the equivalent of today's social media and video games was a deck of playing cards and a pair of dice. The very-competitive brothers would stay up all hours of the night playing poker and craps and trying to beat the other out of his money. At the same time, they were trying out and perfecting every "under the table" and "up the sleeve" trick they knew or could think of.

What these late-night battles produced was two card sharks who knew every trick in the book. They could pull them off seamlessly with the adept sleight of hand of a sideshow magician. The two also perfected their skills at playing off on one another in a group. Both could count cards, and either brother would fold with precision timing to aid the other in winning.

Their skills didn't stop with card games. They excelled with dice and were also quite the hustlers at the local pool halls. The brothers had a true and natural knack for gambling and games of chance.

### The Preacher's Daughter

Hubert was friendly and charming, and he had many close friends. One was Paul McCants, a restaurant owner in Georgetown, South Carolina. McCants was a

*This adorable teenage couple couldn't imagine the excitement the next two decades had in store for them.*

***Soon-to-be newlyweds, Bee and Hubert are looking quite dapper for teenagers in their Sunday best. Hubert always said he picked a preacher's daughter because he was a "straight arrow!"***

little older than Hubert, but the two were fast friends and Hubert frequented the restaurant. In the summer of 1950, McCants introduced the young bachelor to his niece, Beatrice "Bee" Flegel.

Bee was a preacher's daughter from nearby Andrews, South Carolina. She was visiting for the summer after having just graduated from high school. Hubert and Bee began to date, and on March 17, 1951, they were wed at the Georgetown Justice of the Peace. Bee was a month shy of her 18th birthday; Hubert was 19.

The newlyweds settled down in Georgetown. With Hubert's newly acquired welding skills, he was able to land a more lucrative job working at International Paper. It was the largest paper mill in the world and was credited for saving Georgetown in the late 1930s.

International Paper was a huge plant that paid its employees a good wage. Hubert and Bee were able to rent a house on Winyah Bay near the mill. Bee's younger brother, Ponnie, came to live with them.

Hubert also upgraded his ride. First he bought a 1950 Olds, then he moved on to a 1951 Crown Victoria. He installed an Olds engine in the Crown Vic and drag raced it on the streets, always looking to be in the mix with the fastest and flashiest cars around.

### *The Hut*

One might think that marrying a preacher's daughter would settle a young man down, but not so much for Hubert. He was known to frequent a secret place in the secluded woods behind the International Paper mill. This small, one-room shack was known to its patrons as "The Hut." The Hut was an illegal gambling house with a bad reputation. It had a single-lane dirt road that was hardly wide enough for one car leading in and out.

Legend has it that many a man's paycheck was lost in The Hut after a payday's poker game. Men who dared would go on Friday after getting paid to try their luck in the high-stakes poker game. This was just Hubert's game.

Much to the displeasure of his young new wife, he would often go on Friday night and sometimes not

## Side Hustle on the Side Hustle

Bee's younger brother, Ponnie, often worked serving as a gopher for the men gambling in The Hut during the weekends. At his day job, he made 75 cents per hour or $30 a week, but his weekend hustle proved to be far a more lucrative gig. Ponnie would sometimes make upward of $100 to $150 per weekend.

His job at The Hut included running to pick up beer from the store, barbecue from the Whistling Pig, and moonshine from the widow in town who sold it by the jar out the side window of her house. The old widow got away with running her small operation because she'd paid off the local law. Ponnie would run out at all hours of the night and bring food and drink back to The Hut so the men could play uninterrupted.

Ponnie often found himself sleeping in the car between errands and while waiting for Hubert. On more than one Sunday night when the weekend's game was coming to an end, he would be awakened by Hubert making a mad dash to the car while yelling for Ponnie to start it up. Hubert would yell, "Let's get out of here! These guys are mad because I'm leaving with all their money, but I've got to get home and back to work in the morning!" Hubert would jump in the car and they'd race down the narrow dirt lane in a cloud of dust.

return until Sunday evening. The only perk was that he had often tripled his paycheck.

### Two Special Deliveries

Hubert occasionally picked up a case or two of shine under the cover of darkness in the wee hours of the morning before work. He would keep it in the trunk all day while he was at work and then make his drops on his way home, some real moonlighting.

On February 8, 1952, Hubert got a message at lunch that he was needed at home. His pregnant wife had gone into labor. He raced home to pick her up and rushed her to the hospital. Once she was safe and sound in the delivery room and he was sent out to the waiting room, the expectant father remembered the other little package sitting in the trunk of his car.

He rushed out of the hospital waiting room to make his deliveries before the doctor could make his. He raced at top speed to his drop points and was back seated in the waiting room before the doctor came in to tell him his firstborn had made it safely into the world. He now had a daughter, Carolyn Lynette, who they called Lynette.

### The Big Race

With the new addition to his family to support, Hubert took on a second job. After welding at the mill all day, he worked as a part-time salesman at night and on weekends at Gaskin Motors, a Chrysler dealership in Georgetown.

In the 1950s, people were very loyal to their brand of car. It was considered fighting words to put down another person's brand. Around the breakroom tables and water coolers at International Paper, there was a constant conversation, an argument if you will, about which brand had the fastest car. After months of bickering, the man who oversaw the games at The Hut decided to organize an illegal street race.

"The Big Race" was to take place on a Saturday in the spring of 1953. The plan was to race as many cars as wanted to compete and could come up with the $100 entry fee. The winner would take all (minus the organizer's fee). The race was to go on Highway 41 north from the Highway 17 split to Jamestown. This 40-mile stretch through the Francis Marion National Forest was a paved road with no houses; it was perfect for the race.

Hubert was not going to miss out on this for anything, but he knew his 1951 Crown Vic was no match for some of the 1953 Oldsmobiles that would be in the race. The 1953 Super 88 Olds with the rocket V-8 was a favorite to win among the bookies. Hubert knew what he was going to have to do to win. He "borrowed" a brand-new 1953 Firedome DeSoto with a 276-ci V-8 rated at 160 hp from the Chrysler dealership where he worked. He showed up on race day ready to go. So did nine other cars and racers, all with high hopes of winning bragging rights as well as the large cash purse.

There were so many entries they decided to draw numbers from a hat to determine the starting order. Hubert drew number eight, putting him in the back of the pack. As the first pairs of cars took off out of sight, it seemed that there'd be no way to catch the leaders. Hubert wasn't discouraged though, he took off and began to catch and pass the cars in front of him.

One by one, Hubert and the new DeSoto passed the others through the forest. It was the fastest and best-handling car he had ever driven. When the pack reached Jamestown, Hubert and the DeSoto were out in front, winning the 40-mile race by 10 car lengths to the second-place Olds Super 88. With the winnings, Hubert bought the beautiful two-tone blue DeSoto.

Winning the Big Race through the rural forest boosted Hubert's confidence and his popularity. As with most people in the spotlight, Hubert found that some people loved him and some hated him. This big win may have gained him as many non-fans as it did fans. Some would become jealous and think of him as just a cocky show-off.

### Amusement Company Cover-Up

Always on the lookout to make more money, Hubert took a new side job with the Rose Amusement Company, which supplied jukeboxes and slot machines to pool halls and juke joints all across Georgetown and its surrounding counties. Hubert's job was to visit the different establishments on nights and weekends to collect the contents of the coin boxes as well as fix any jammed machines. Hubert saw it as far more; it was the perfect opportunity to expand his moonshine-hauling operation.

In the mid 1950s in the very segregated South, a black man would never enter a white bar and likewise no white man would ever enter a black bar. Anyone who stepped out of bounds into the wrong establishments or even into the wrong part of town looked shockingly out of place. Under the cover of the Rose Amusement Company, Hubert could go freely in and out of any neighborhood.

With his new job, Hubert had direct contact with the managers and barkeeps of the black establishments. He was able to explain that he had the means to bring moonshine directly from the source discreetly with his

*Hubert was right at home in a sharp uniform. With his outgoing personality and hard work, he quickly rose to the rank of sergeant.*

weekly visits for the coin collections. In no time, he was supplying all of the black bars on his route with shine and making a nice profit for his efforts.

Although his operation was subtle and went unnoticed, Hubert's spending on new cars and clothing did not. It added to the animosity of some of the upstanding citizens of the community. People began to talk, and the authorities were tipped off.

## The Army or Bust

The saying goes "crime doesn't pay" and no one is immune, not even slick Hubert. He soon found himself in front of a judge with an ultimatum: "Jail or the army." He picked the latter and immediately was forced to enlist in the US Army.

Two of Hubert's younger brothers, Huston and Buddy, were also old enough to serve. They decided to enlist with him, although Buddy wasn't accepted because of a heart condition.

This abrupt decision came as a huge surprise to Hubert's wife, who knew nothing of the courtroom ultimatum or even the run-in with the law that led to it. Hubert convinced her that he and his brother were answering their patriotic call of duty, and he kept his secret. Bee never understood how he could voluntarily leave her at home with a three-year-old daughter to join the US Army, but Hubert knew all too well how much worse the alternative would have been.

Hubert was 23 years old when he completed basic training at Fort Jackson, South Carolina. He then embarked on a surprisingly exciting military career. Hubert was a leader and quickly rose to the rank of sergeant. He was stationed at Fort Belvoir, Virginia, and moved his wife and young daughter into a trailer park 13 miles northeast of the base in Alexandria, a suburb of Washington, DC.

*Hubert looks happy. That's understandable, considering he could have been in a much worse place had the judge not given him a choice.*

While living in Alexandria in the final year of his enlistment, Hubert purchased his next ride. Most 25-year-old men with a pregnant wife and a five-year-old daughter would be shopping for a station wagon or a four-door sedan, but Hubert came home with something else. He bought a black 1957 Chevy Bel Air two-door hardtop with a 283-ci V-8, solid-lift cam, 9.50:1 compression, and twin Carter 380-cfm 4-barrel carburetors rated at 270 hp with a 3-speed manual transmission.

*Hubert enjoyed living off base and having his wife and daughter with him while he was fulfilling his army duties, but Virginia seemed a long way from South Carolina. This made wife and new mother Bee homesick.*

***Trying to prove he could make a lap around the base in an unrealistic amount of time after a night of drinking proved to be a poor choice. Hubert learned the hard way that there is a limit to how far you can push a car. He was lucky to have no more than a bruised ego when he walked away unharmed from this crash on the military base in Virginia.***

With this new ride, Hubert got his first taste of a real drag strip and became hooked. He had heard about some races that were held on the weekends for small cash prizes and trophies, so he decided to go see for himself. Manassas Drag Strip was 25 miles west of the army base, and Hubert ran his black Chevy there several weekends in the Stock classes. He loved the competition and the speed!

## The Shine Gets Hubert Out of a Jam

Hubert couldn't confine his love for speed to just the track. After a night of drinking with fellow GIs, he could not resist the urge to prove his prowess behind the wheel by showing how fast he could make a lap around the large army base in the '57 Chevy.

Hubert pushed the '57 until the worst happened. The rear wheels came off the pavement and onto the muddy shoulder. At 90 mph, the rear end broke loose. The car flipped onto its roof and slid 50 yards in the ditch before coming to a stop. The insurance company declared the car totaled with its crushed roof. Hubert came out of the crashed without a single scratch. His only injury was a bruised ego.

He immediately replaced the wreck with an almost identical black 1957 Chevy two-door hardtop that also had a 283-ci with twin 4-barrel carburetors. The only difference was this new car had a dealer-installed 4-speed on the floor.

Although this wasn't a problem with the insurance company, Hubert found himself in hot water with the commander of the base. He was looking at a stint in the brig for this offense. If it wasn't for his close friendship with the army cook, who was a fellow sergeant, it may have been worse.

Bee was pregnant with their second child when Hubert bought this black 1957 two-door hardtop coupe to replace the almost identical one he wrecked while stationed in Virginia. A 283-ci V-8 with two 4-barrel carburetors wasn't exactly what you'd call a family car, but it was what Bee had grown to expect from Hubert.

*A young Hubert was briefly stationed in the Marshall Islands in the North Pacific, where he was part of a demolition team. He was a slim soldier with his 28-inch waist, and he wouldn't fill out until his 30s.*

The cook was also close friends with the base commander and knew he had a taste for white liquor. He arranged a deal where Hubert could make a quick trip home to Little River, South Carolina, pick up two cases of moonshine (one for the commander and one for the cook), and bring them back to the base in exchange for the dismissal of his charges.

Hubert was given a 24-hour leave to make the 800-mile round trip. It was no problem for Hubert to make the 6-hour one-way drive there and back in the allotted time, but what was a problem was trying to explain to his parents why he hadn't brought his wife and five-year-old daughter along and why he had to make such a quick turnaround.

## Back to Carolina

Toward the end of Hubert's two-year enlistment (September 1955 to September 1957), he was to be deployed overseas. During his deployment, his pregnant wife and daughter returned to her home of Andrews, South Carolina.

Hubert did a short stint in Hawaii while on his way to the Marshall Islands in the North Pacific. He was stationed at the Eniwetok Nuclear Test Site as part of a demolition team. The team performed such duties as dismantling bombs and handling nuclear warheads; tasks not suited to the faint of heart. Hubert had a cool head and said he was never rattled by his duties.

When he was discharged from the army, Hubert returned home to South Carolina. There, he was greeted by his six-week-old son, Hubert Jr., affectionately called "Hubie," a combination of both parent's names.

### *Backroads Daredevil*

Hubert took some time off to decide if he should reenlist in the army or pursue something else. As the

*Looking more like a leading man in a movie rather than a moonshine runner from the South, Hubert's good looks, charm, and Southern hospitality never failed to open doors. These traits were key to his success.*

*Hubert's 1957 Chevy has a deep shine and is unbelievably clean to be in a county full of dirt roads. The car sits in front of the more than 100-year-old Oak Ridge Church in Andrews, South Carolina. The church still stands today and is open for business every Sunday. Bee's father, Reverend Martin Flegel, was a deacon and copastor here for many years.*

saying goes "an idle mind is the devil's workshop," and in no time Hubert found himself running his 1957 Chevy wide open all through the Carolina back roads.

Hubert was on a personal mission to redeem himself after the crash on the base in Virginia, which he felt was a slight on his reputation behind the wheel. He began to bet any nonbelievers $100 that he could get the '57 up to 100 mph, lock down the brakes, slide the car around the other direction, downshift, and go back the other way without ever leaving the pavement. It was a seemingly impossible feat on roads cutting through the forest that were notoriously narrow with a ditch on either side.

Hubert proved it could be done time and time again to the disbelief of local gamblers. They would shine their flashlights on the road to check and see if the skid marks ever left the pavement. They never did! Hubert was an ace at this game, and many $100 bets found their way into his pocket. His reputation was again intact.

### It Would Be Best to Go

After two years in the army, Hubert's shine-hauling days were well behind him, but late in the summer of 1958, he crossed paths with an old associate who was looking for 10 cases of the stuff. Never one to resist the lure of easy money, Hubert was convinced it would be worth one more trip to Hell Hole Swamp. While in the swamp picking up the 10 cases, he decided to pick up a case for himself. The 24 fruit jars of the elixir would make perfect gifts to hand out to family and friends for the upcoming holiday season.

At the drop point, the purchaser's helper, who was hauling the cases into the woods, mistakenly carried Hubert's extra case out of the car. Hubert told him to go back and retrieve it, explaining that there were 11 cases and the extra case was his. Unfortunately, this man never liked Hubert; he was a jealous type who didn't care for the flashy cars and clothes Hubert always sported. It angered him when he got back in the woods and discovered that Hubert had been right and there were in fact 11 cases. He was embarrassed in front of his boss when he had to return the extra case to the car trunk, and that made his hate and resentment for Hubert grow even more.

As Hubert drove away, an anonymous call was made to the local authorities detailing the black '57 Chevy and its contents. Hubert stopped in town at The Cafe, a local hangout, and soon noticed two police officers walking around his car. One of the officers he recognized as Prescott Brown, an older officer Hubert had known for years and who had a reputation for looking the other way. The second officer was a rookie Hubert had never seen before.

The rookie pushed the quarter panel of the '57 Chevy and said he could hear the shine sloshing in the jars!

*Hubert always kept his cars immaculately clean. He had his initials "HCP" hand painted on both doors of this 1957 Chevy Bel Air. With its clean lines and long tail fins, it was one the most iconic cars of the 1950s.*

Prescott explained to Hubert that they had received a tip and were going to have to search the car. Hubert pleaded with Prescott, confessing quietly that he did have a case in the car and asking if there was anything he could to do to possibly be allowed to go. Prescott said that with the young rookie watching there could be no under-handed payoffs. Hubert watched helplessly as the rookie searched the car and found the case of shine. The car was impounded, and Hubert was arrested.

After a night in jail, Hubert's uncle was allowed to pay the $302 bail, and he was released. The car, however, was not so lucky. Under South Carolina state law, the car was seized. It was a huge blow to Hubert to lose the beautiful car that he loved so much, especially when he only owed seven more payments on it.

Standing before a judge again, Hubert was issued a very stern warning. The judge told him, "You lost your car this time; if we catch you again, we're going to put you under the jail." As if it wasn't enough to lose the car, the local newspaper ran a story telling of the entire event on the front page. This added to Hubert and his wife's humiliation.

This statement prompted Hubert to decide to leave South Carolina and the watchful eye of the law. After the humiliating newspaper story, Bee was quick to agree. The couple made their plans to move the family to Georgia.

### *A Need for A New Ride*

The whole ordeal left the young Platt family without a way to leave. Although Hubert had some non-fans, he still had some real friends, one of whom worked at the local Ford dealership. He told Hubert that he had a way to help him out of his car troubles and he invited Hubert to come down after hours. Hubert went, and waiting for him in the back garage was a shiny, new 1958 Ford Custom 300 Tudor Sedan.

The salesman explained that the car had been ordered by the police department for highway patrol, but it had been refused for being the wrong color. At the time, South Carolina state patrol cars were tan, and this car was dark brown. Hubert knew what the salesman had in mind, and after seeing the 332-ci Special V-8 Police Interceptor, he was sold! He bought the would-be police car on the spot!

# CHAPTER 2

# NEW BEGINNINGS

Hubert, his wife, Bee, six-year-old, Lynette, and one-year-old, Hubie, put South Carolina in the rearview mirror and headed west 300 miles to Atlanta, Georgia, where Hubert had family. They settled in a small rental house on Dresden Drive in Brookhaven, a suburb 10 miles northeast of downtown Atlanta.

Hubert went to work at Moorehead Machine Shop, which was another 10 miles north on Peachtree Road in Norcross. This business was owned by Hubert's Uncle Lewis, who was married to Hubert's mother's sister. Hubert worked as a welder but also learned to run machinist equipment, such as a milling machine and a metal lathe. Hubert was a quick study and became quite skilled with these machines in a short time.

Hubert was making decent money working for his uncle, and as always, he was looking for some excitement. He decided to try out what he called "round and round racing."

Oval track racing on dirt or pavement is deeply rooted in the South's history. Spectators filled the grandstands at local tracks every weekend all throughout the South. Hubert loved driving fast, and he wanted a piece of this action. He and a friend put their money in together and bought a used race car from Grand National legend Banjo Matthews.

The 1937 Chevy was a good race car and had potential for success, but every race it got caught up in the inevitable crash. Hubert and his friend would work to repair the race car just to have it smashed up again the following weekend. After only two months, Hubert tired of this and sold the car, retiring from "round and round" racing forever.

## Texaco

For his new job, Hubert had to commute to and from work through the city of Chamblee on Peachtree Road. In this little town just 3 miles north of his home was a small, abandoned gas station. Ever since Hubert had been going back and forth to Norcross, it had sat empty, dark, and deserted.

With his love of cars and all things automotive, Hubert could easily imagine himself as the proprietor of a gas station. He liked the idea of being his own boss so much that he looked into the property and found it was owned by Texaco. After a few phone calls, a meeting, and a short interview, the station was his.

Hubert reopened the little station through a "no money down" lease deal with Texaco. He basically signed for gas, oil, and parts and paid for it all at the end of the month plus a small rent. The station had two pumps, two bays for working on cars, an office, and a back room for storage.

Hubert employed his brother Huston as a mechanic and his 17-year-old brother Ray to work the pumps. Hubert's full-service Texaco provided engine building and head work for race cars as well as regular repairs for work trucks and family cars.

### *Gambling Station*

Directly behind the Texaco was Allied Van Lines, a huge trucking hub for the Southeast. The little station saw a lot of business from the Allied employees, and the Platt brothers soon became friends with most of the truck drivers.

Being hustling entrepreneurs, Hubert and Huston ran some pretty lively high-stakes poker and craps games out of the back storage room of the station while brother Ray watched the front. Much like The Hut, many-a-paycheck was lost in the back room of the little filling station.

One of the Allied office managers was obsessed with gambling, and he lost so much money that winter that Huston bought a brand-new convertible Pontiac with it. Huston ordered a special black-on-black paint with a red interior. He gave the salesman strict instructions that no one was to drive his car. He would come to the dealership on the day of delivery to unload it off the truck himself.

On the delivery date, Hubert drove Huston to the dealership to pick up his new car. When the brothers pulled up, they saw the semi tractor-trailer full of new 1960 model Pontiacs. Huston's black convertible was on the top rack of the trailer in front with a red, two-door hardtop behind it. Huston eagerly asked the truck driver to unload the first car so he could get his new car down. The truck driver informed him that he was only the truck driver and didn't unload cars. They had gotten there so early that the dealership wasn't open yet and the man who unloaded cars wasn't there either.

Hubert offered to move the car in back, and the truck driver agreed to allow him. Hubert unloaded the two-door hardtop and Huston unloaded his black convertible, adamant that no one but him drive his new car. Everything went fine until Hubert decided that he liked the two-door hardtop and wanted to buy it. Huston was furious; he couldn't believe that Hubert would steal his thunder and buy an almost matching new car on the same day as him. This was just one episode between the brothers that fueled the fire of sibling rivalry.

### "Real Drag Car"

Gambling became a regular thing in the back room of the Texaco. A lot of money changed hands, even the occasional watch or gold ring, but in the fall of 1959, Hubert won something that set him on the path he would follow for the next two decades.

One of the truckers lost a pretty big poker hand and owed Hubert a good bit of money. The truck driver offered Hubert a 1938 Chevy race car to settle the debt. Hubert quickly explained that a few months earlier he had sold his 1937 Chevy race car and wasn't interested. The trucker was quick to reply, "This is no round and round car; this is a real drag car."

This sparked Hubert's interest, and he agreed. What the trucker dropped off a few days later was far from a "real drag car." It was a gutted-out 1938 Chevy with a non-running V-8, a broken rear end, and bald street tires on the rear. Nevertheless, Hubert saw its potential. He rolled it into one of the Texaco's two small bays to begin its transformation.

The Platt brothers were excited about this project. Even though the Chevy needed a lot of work, it was more of a real drag car than the street cars they had been racing in the Stock classes. They knew that with some hard work it could be a competitive gasser. So, they rolled up their sleeves and got to work on the little coupe.

Huston had a natural knack for rebuilding engines and transmissions. He completely rebuilt the 283 V-8 that had been bored out to 301 ci and installed a bigger cam and high-performance pistons. Huston also freshened up the 4-speed manual transmission with a new pressure plate, clutch, and shifter.

The brothers had Bruce Brantley of Chamblee Carburetor & Electric rebuild the Rochester 4-barrel carburetor with a few tricks as well as the distributor. Bruce was a specialist when it came to high-performance ignition systems.

Hubert worked on the suspension, beefing up the welds on the leaf spring axle front end and adding some

*Facing page: In 1960, Hubert and Huston seemed to have the world at their feet. Not to be outdone, Huston had all the confidence and swagger of his older brother. He proudly posed with his custom-ordered 1960 Pontiac in front of Hubert's Texaco station, where he worked as a mechanic.*

*Hubert's first real race car, the B/Gas 1938 Chevy, carried many of the hallmarks of a late 1950s and early 1960s drag car and hot rod. From its whitewall slicks on red steel rims to its hot rod flames to its louvered hood, it had many of the elements that modern hot rodders try to emulate today.*

welded traction bars to the back. The broken rear end was replaced with a set of new 4.88:1 gears. A new set of rubber all the way around included 8-inch-wide whitewall drag slicks on 15-inch red steel wheels on the rear and slim whitewall tires on the front with solid stainless hubcaps.

The car was painted dark blue with white, red, and yellow flames all across the front fenders and onto the doors. In big white letters on the door was "B/G 301," stating the class B-Gas and the cubic inches. All the way down the hood on both sides it said "Hubert Platt Texaco" in large block letters. Just beneath that it read "Engine by Huston Platt."

After all the hard work that went into the car, Hubert had his first "real drag car," and it was a solid one at that. By way of a tow bar hooked to the front bumper, Hubert

***In the late 1950s and early 1960s, most stock race cars were driven to the drag races. When it came to the gassers, the tow bar was a much more practical way to get these modified, high-performance machines to the track. Most drivers would put street tires on the rear and replace them with the slicks when they got to the track.***

would drag his new race car to all the local tracks every weekend. He was happy and proud to be part of this somewhat-new and growing scene.

Hubert became obsessed with drag racing in his late 20s. With new tracks popping up all around Georgia, there was no shortage of places to race. There was Cumming, Dallas, Covington, Yellow River, Camp Wheeler in Macon, and the original Atlanta Speed Shop in Newton County. There were also tracks just across the border in Jackson, South Carolina, and in Phenix City, Alabama. Hubert became a regular at all of these tracks and more. He even drove up into Tennessee and down into Florida to race.

With his focus so heavily on drag racing and constantly trying to make improvements to the race car, the little Texaco station was less of a priority. It began to fail financially. Without 100-percent commitment from its proprietor, a small business couldn't make it. In August 1960, Hubert closed the little station just 14 months after opening it.

## Gasser Days

Hubert continued to race the 1938 Chevy around the Southeast with great success, becoming the B-class record holder. Drag racing was fun, but in no way did it pay the bills. So, in the fall of 1960, Hubert relied once again on his welding skills and gained employment at Lockheed Industrial Products. It was a private company owned by Lockheed that built ground support equipment for airplanes, such as passenger stairs, cargo ramps, etc.

Hubert spent his days welding at Lockheed and his nights working on the 1938 Chevy in the driveway of his rental house in Doraville, Georgia, a suburb of Atlanta. Hubert had moved to this house with a rent-to-own plan, but without the Texaco Station to work on his race car, it became clear to him that he needed a house with a garage. This rental house had no garage and would not do.

While Hubert looked for a house more suited to his needs, he saved money for a down payment. However, the desire to take his racing to another level was so strong that he saw no harm in using some of the savings to improve the race car. He was certain he would win the money right back.

Hubert ordered a set of Hilborn injectors for the 301 V-8. They cost $300, which seemed like an awful lot of money for some speed equipment, but the gamble paid off. He made the move to A-Gas and set the record on his first weekend out.

Racing seemed to come easy to Hubert. He was a natural behind the wheel and under the hood. His slick confidence and flair didn't hurt either. The fans loved him and loved to see him race.

Working at Lockheed provided Hubert with enough flexibility to support his racing endeavors. In fact, they were so supportive they even allowed him to take time off to race at Speed Week in Daytona, Florida, at the NASCAR Drag Racing Championships.

Hubert held the A- and B-Gas records at the same time in 1961. Legend has it that there were some weekends when he would race the 1938 in both A- and B-Gas competition *on the same day,* changing out the intake setup from the carburetor to the injectors between rounds. Anyone who has ever turned a wrench at the drag races knows that was no easy feat.

## Terminal Transport Sponsorship

In the spring of 1961, Hubert was racing the 1938 Chevy in A-Gas competition at the annual March meet at the original Atlanta Speed Shop Dragway in Newton County, Georgia. It was a who's who of Southeastern racers ready to kick off the 1961 season.

One team in particular stood out to Hubert: the Terminal Transport team sponsored by the Atlanta-based trucking company. It was a sharp-looking outfit with team members wearing matching white uniforms. They were trying to enter their 1955 Chevy with a 365-ci small-block with two 4s and a 4-speed, a regular C/G set up, in C-Gas but were having obvious trouble getting the car to run, much less compete. When they did get it cranked, it just popped and backfired loudly.

*Hubert had the A-Gas 1938 Chevy and the B-Gas 1957 Chevy looking sharp in matching Terminal Transport colors at Daytona International Speedway for the NASCAR-sanctioned drag races. Now with the support of the Terminal Transport's semitrailer, there was no need for the 1938 Chevy's tow bar or front bumper. Notice the 1957 Chevy's custom Corvette grille.*

Hubert said to his friend Bruce Brantley, who was there helping him tune the 1938 Chevy, "Let's go see if we can help these guys." Hubert felt sorry for them and offered his and Bruce's services, which the men eagerly accepted. Hubert and Bruce went to work on the ailing 1955 Chevy. Bruce changed the advance curve in the distributor, set the timing, and adjusted the carburetor linkage on the two 4s. In just a few minutes, Hubert and his friend had the car sounding better than ever. The crew was shocked and they asked Hubert if he would make a test run in the car. Hubert obliged them by setting the C-Gas track record.

The owner of Terminal Transport, Mr. Katz, was so impressed that he hired Hubert on the spot, making him a salaried employee in charge of Terminal Transport's racing division. This was a huge deal for Hubert. He quit his job at Lockheed and was able to focus full-time on drag racing.

In 1961, Terminal Transport spent $25,000 on drag racing. It sponsored a four-car team that now included Hubert's A-Gas 1938 Chevy, the C-Gas 1955 Chevy, a B-Gas 1957 Chevy, and a brand-new 1961 Pontiac with a tri-powered V-8. Hubert drove all three gassers and also raced the Pontiac in the Stock classes. All four cars were painted brown with yellow checkerboard on the doors and hood and tan checkerboard on the roof.

Terminal Transport was a trucking company that hauled freight and new cars from the GM plant in Doraville, Georgia, so it had no problem getting the race cars to the track. The team showed up at the races with a road tractor pulling a four-car carrier. In a time when guys got their race cars to the track with tow bars, this kind of thing was unheard of. It is believed that Hubert and the Terminal Transport team were the first drag racers to bring their cars to the track with a semi tractor-trailer setup.

On May 1, 1960, Terminal Transport knew it had made a good choice in Hubert when he set two national records in one day. In the 1938 Chevy, he set the A-Gas speed record at 108.7 mph, then he went on to set the ET

*The Terminal Transport Racing Team was ahead of its time in many ways, including having a multi-car team with brightly colored matching paint jobs.*

*A row of Gassers sit ready to do battle on June 3, 1961, in Covington, Georgia, at the Newton County drags. They are (from left to right): National Champ "Ohio" George Montgomery's light blue A/G 1933 Willy's, Hubert Platt's Terminal Transport* Double T Special *B/G 1957 Chevy and matching A/G 1938 Chevy, D. L. Maddox's red B/G 1939 Chevy, the Barnett Brothers' A/G Willy's, and David Brinkman's A/G 1932 Chevy.*

Hubert Platt, shown in the center, being presented the coveted Index of Performance award for breaking two class records with the same car during the Official SEDN Record meet on June 24th and 25th. Clifford and Bunnell, the strip managers, are making the presentation. Platt, with the help of his sponsors, the Terminal Transport Company, and the Double T-Racing Team, set the Fuel Injected Chevie powered '37 Chevie Coupe up for B-Gas on Saturday and promptly broke the E.T.

*It would be almost two decades before semi tractor-trailers would become commonplace in motorsports. It was simply unheard of in 1961, making the "Double T Racing Team" a standout at any event.*

record of 13.48 in the Stock class with the 1957 Chevy at the Ashville-Hendersonville Dragway in Danville, Virginia.

In June, the team had the 1938 Chevy set up for B-Gas on Saturday, when Hubert broke the previous record of 12.70 with a 12.34. He already held the speed record at 108.95 mph. On Sunday, the 1938 Chevy was set up for A-Gas and set a new record of 12.12 followed by a 12.14 to back it up.

The July 1961 issue of *Southeastern Drag News*, an independent racing and hot rod publication, featured a large picture on the cover of Hubert in the 1938 Chevy coming off the starting line in the A-Gas final round. The headline read "Hubert Platt Wins Index of Performance Award at Covington on June 25th." The coveted index of Performance Award was given for breaking two class records with the same car during an official SEDN record meet. This was the first time Hubert had a picture of one of his race cars on the cover of a newspaper or magazine.

## Things Heat Up at the New Home

In the summer of 1961, Hubert and his family found the house they had been looking for: a three-bedroom, one-and-a-half-bath, brick rancher with a full basement garage. It was the first house on the street, and the garage door was on the lead end of the house, putting the race car shop as far away from the neighbors as possible. The bank set Hubert up with a 30-year mortgage with pay-

Southeastern DRAG NEWS

S. E. D. N.

.20 cents

VOL. 3. – NO. 7 AN INDEPENDENT RACING & HOT ROD PUBLICATION JULY, 1961

HUBERT PLATT WINS INDEX OF PERFORMANCE AWARD AT COVINGTON ON JUNE 25TH

One of the hottest contests for an Official SEDN Record at any of the events this year was the record attempts and the elimin-
ation run between David Brinkman, from Augusta, Georgia, and Hubert Platt from Atlanta. While Platt was busy setting the B-
Gas E.T. record with his Fuel Injected Chevie-powered '37 Chevie, on June 24th (see story in this issue) at Covington, Dave
Brinkman broke the A-Gas E.T. Record with a run of 9.13. Dave backed it up with a 9.15, driving his Chevie-powered '32 Chev-
ie coupe. Platt set his machine up for A-Gas and finally managed to drop the E.T.record to 12.12 backed it up with a 9.14.
The final proof came when Hubert Platt barely edged Brinkman out in the A-Gas Trophy run on June 25th.

OFFICIAL SOUTHEAST RECORD MEET JULY 29th & 30th

SATURDAY NIGHT DRAGS Featuring Street Machines Only

Sponsored by the BROWARD AUTO CLUB

*The 1938 Chevy was a strong contender that won many races and held the A- and B-Gas record throughout 1961. It also gave Hubert his first taste of front-page headlines.*

ments of $88 a month. Hubert immediately began to take on side projects and work on other people's race cars in the basement for extra income.

Only six weeks after moving into their new house, Bee was on her way home from the grocery store with nine-year-old daughter Lynette and almost four-year-old son Hubie when she was passed on the road by a fire truck with full sirens and lights blaring. Like all young mothers, Bee told the children to "wave at the firemen" as they began to follow along behind the truck. The fire engine made the exact next two turns Bee and the children took toward the house, and Bee joked, "They must be going to our house." When they turned the last corner, Bee saw the devastating sight of the entire roof of her new home engulfed in flames.

Hubert had been working on a customer's Corvette drag car when a lit cigar got away from him and ignited a fire in the engine compartment. Before he could get it under control, it blew up in his face. The flames shot up and caught the exposed floor joist of the house above. The new wood went up like matchsticks. The worst part was the house was so new that Hubert hadn't yet purchased homeowner's insurance. He had to pay for the home to be rebuilt out of his own pocket. It took four months to rebuild, and the family was able to move back in by Thanksgiving.

*The brick rancher was 11 miles northeast of downtown Atlanta and just what Hubert was looking for. The pyramid shape of new brick above the garage door is evidence of the repair after the fire.*

# CHAPTER 3

# NALLEY-NICHOLSON RACE TEAM

In drag racing, there is a way of tuning the entire car for maximum performance and not just the engine. The trick is to get the power to the rear wheels and to the ground. To do this, mechanics use a dynamometer, a chassis dyno where the rear wheels are on rollers to measure horsepower and torque outputs.

"Dyno" Don Nicholson earned his nickname by being the first to master the dynamometer. Don was so good at tuning on the dyno at Service Chevrolet in Pasadena, California, that Chevrolet gave him one of the first 1961 Bubble Top Bel Airs with a 409 4-speed. He thanked them by winning the National Hot Rod Association's (NHRA) inaugural Winternationals in the Top Stock Eliminator Class.

With Chevrolet's continued support, Don went back to back, winning again in 1962. This gave him national recognition and a winning reputation, and he began to get offers from all over the United States. The most attractive offer came from Nalley Chevrolet in Atlanta, Georgia. It was headquarters for the Southern Engineering and Development Company (SEDCO), which was a front for Chevy's secret racing program. Atlanta was also appealing because it was drag-race central, and with so many local tracks, there was lots of money to be made match racing.

In April 1962, Nicholson accepted Nalley's offer and moved to Atlanta. Nalley Chevrolet put him in charge of the dyno shop and gave him a new factory drag car and a fully funded race program.

### Fast Friends

It is unclear where the two met, but presumably Hubert and Don first crossed paths at the drag races. The two became immediate friends. They hit it off so well that Don offered Hubert a job at Nalley and invited him to become a part of the factory race team. Don gave Huston Platt a job as well and swayed Hubert with the promise of his own factory drag car.

Hubert quit Terminal Transport and sold the 1938 Chevy, which marked the end of his gasser racing. The Nalley-Nicholson Dyno Shop built engines to stock or to the owner's specifications. Huston balanced and built most of the engines, Hubert built the cylinder heads, and Don built engines and tuned on the dyno. Don also custom-built tube headers for customers and all the race cars at the shop.

Hubert and Don were both passionate about drag racing. When they weren't at work in the dyno shop, they could be found in each other's home garages working on various projects and sharpening their skills. Working off each other's ideas, they honed their craft. With the two men constantly working on cars together, their wives, Bee and Patty, as well as their young daughters, Lynette and Cindy, became great friends. They spent countless days, evenings, and weekends together at their homes and at the drag strips. These families really did eat, breathe, and sleep drag racing.

### *Lil' General*

As a new addition to the Nalley Race Team, Hubert was given the first 1962 Biscayne drag car to ever come to Atlanta. In Hubert's own words, it was "an ugly brown color." The car was Anniversary Gold or a darker version of it. Despite the "ugly" color, the car was a state-of-the-art 1962 factory drag car with a 409 big-block, 4.3125 bore with 3.50 stroke, 11.00:1 compression with two 4-barrel Carter AFB carburetors, an aluminum intake manifold, and a forged-steel crankshaft.

This car competed in the Super Super/Stock (SS/S) class, which allowed a high-lift performance cam. The cam gave the engine more than its 1 hp per cubic inch rating of 409 hp and 420 ft-lbs of torque, which was distributed through the 4-speed transmission to the positive traction rear end. The brand-new Biscayne was also radio, heater, and back seat delete, all marks of a factory-built drag car.

Hubert named the car the *Lil' General* and had the "Forget Hell" Confederate soldier painted on the door. It boasted "Dyno Tuned By Don Nicholson" in huge letters

*The 1962 Chevrolet 409 Biscayne was a state-of-the-art factory drag car with radio, heater, and back seat delete. The SS/S indicates this car raced in the Super Super/Stock class, which allowed a high-lift performance cam.*

*In the late 1950s and early 1960s, teams took to wearing white to try and give drag racing a more professional aesthetic. They also hoped to distance themselves from the negative stereotype that drag racers were bad boy, greasy hoodlums. The all-white look was a more acceptable public image, which helped convince mainstream America that attending a drag race could be a family outing. Hubert Platt (center) and Don Nicholson (right) look very professional as they accept their trophy.*

## Chief Helper Slick

Hubert had a very close friend, more of a sidekick really, who he nicknamed "Slick." Ronald "Slick" Chesser was a big man, so big that the story has it he could drop a quarter through his wedding band. Slick was the happy-go-lucky type and the perfect right-hand man to Hubert's outgoing personality. The two together were the life of the party everywhere they went. Neither had ever met a stranger.

With his massive size that rivaled that of TV's Hoss Cartwright on the classic show *Bonanza,* Slick doubled as a bodyguard for Hubert. Time and time again, Hubert's fast cars and quick tongue got him in trouble with different people at the drag races, many times making them mad enough to fight. They always reconsidered the moment they saw Slick standing behind Hubert. A true friend, Slick always had his back.

all the way down the quarter panel. Above the side windows on the roof it said "Pilot Hubert Platt." Painted on the front fender were the class and number: "SS/S 120."

Hubert had some success with the *Lil' General*. With Don's tuning, Hubert won several class trophies around the Southeast.

### Corona Cream Biscayne

The Nalley-Nicholson stable of race-ready rides was deep. Hubert campaigned four different Chevys under the Nalley-Nicholson banner in 1962. There was a second Biscayne SS/S 910 that was an attention grabber in bright yellow (Corona Cream) with gold interior, gold steel wheels, and big red block letters all the way down the side that read "Nalley-Nicholson Dyno Shop."

The yellow Biscayne was somewhat of a test car at the dyno shop. It was raced by Don and Hubert at different times, but neither used it as a primary car. Mr. Nalley decided to sell the car and had a buyer lined up to purchase it immediately following a Super Stock event that Hubert was driving the car in at Tampa Dragway in Florida.

***Hubert campaigned four different 409 Chevys while working at the Nalley-Nicholson Dyno Shop. One was this Corona Cream Biscayne that met its fate in a towing accident.***

The event was on Sunday. Normally, Hubert used his own vehicle to tow the car, but Bee needed the car that particular weekend, and he had to borrow Huston's 1962 Chevy to use as a tow vehicle. After a full day of racing, Hubert and Slick joined a group of fellow racers at a local steakhouse for dinner and drinks. They closed the place down, and a racer who lived nearby invited everyone back to his place for a nightcap. That nightcap turned into a two-day party. Hubert and Slick finally got on their way Wednesday and headed north toward Atlanta.

About an hour outside of Tampa, running 65 to 70 mph down the highway, the trailer lost a wheel on its right side. The loose tire sped past them and into the woods. The trailer began to swerve, doing what Hubert called the "Watusi." Hubert told Slick, "Hold on! It's about to roll over!" as the trailer went up onto its side. It broke the chains, and the race car went flying off. It landed upright on its wheels, undamaged.

As the two men were trying to get the car back onto the trailer, a state patrol officer pulled up and offered his assistance. Hubert said he was "as nice as he could be" and helped them get the car back onto the trailer. He even helped them search the woods for the trailer tire. Then, he showed them to the truck stop down the road where they were able to repair the trailer. Hubert offered to buy the state patrolman dinner, but he said that could be considered "bribing a police officer." They laughed at his joke, and he went on his way.

Hubert and Slick had dinner and decided to move the extra 4-speed transmission Hubert had in the back seat of the race car into the back seat of the tow car to transfer weight. They didn't get but a couple of miles down the road and up to speed when the trailer started to do the "Watusi" again. This time, it swerved so violently that it flipped over. The trailer and race car landed on the back roof and decklid of the tow car. The extra transmission flew up from behind the seat, hitting Hubert in the back of the head and almost knocking him unconscious.

When Hubert got the whole rig stopped, the same state patrol officer pulled up. When he saw the upside-down race car, trailer, and crashed tow car, he told the guys they were done. He called a wrecker and had the race car and trailer towed back to the truck stop.

Hubert arranged for Allen Hyder of Clay Hyder Trucking, a close friend, to have the car towed back to Atlanta the next day. He and Slick got back onto the road headed north to Atlanta in Huston's car with the crushed rear roof and busted-out back glass. Hubert recalled that it was a cold ride home.

When they returned to Atlanta in the early morning hours before dawn, they quietly backed the crashed Chevy into Huston's driveway and walked to Hubert's house two blocks away. When Huston awoke and found his car crashed in the driveway, he stormed over to Hubert's and demanded to know what happened. Hubert apologized and told him about the towing accident and how he had much bigger things to worry about than his car.

Hubert knew he would have to quickly find a replacement body for the wrecked race car that was to be picked up by its purchaser the following Monday at Nalley. Allen Hyder delivered the crashed race car to Hubert's house on Thursday evening. When he saw the race car in the light of day, Hubert said it was "tore all to hell." Hubert only had three days to make this right.

Drastic times call for drastic measures, and there was only one thing Hubert could do. He made a phone call to an old friend who had a way of getting new cars extremely cheap in a "don't ask, don't tell" situation. The friend came over and Hubert showed him the crashed race car. Hubert explained that he needed another car to match this one exactly: a 1962 Biscayne in Corona Cream with a gold interior.

The friend left, and within an hour he was back with an identical matching car. The only difference was that this car had a 327. Hubert and Slick worked all weekend. They took the body off of the wrecked race car, stripped it down to the frame, and replaced it with the body of the newly acquired street car. They fixed every part that was bent and broken and then cleaned and waxed the car until there was no trace of the accident. They junked the extra frame and the wrecked race car body.

Bright and early Monday morning, Hubert returned to Nalley with the car. Mr. Nalley questioned him about where the car had been all week and asked why it had taken so long to get back from the races in Tampa. He also wanted to know why they took the lettering off the side of the car. Hubert told Nalley that he knew the car was sold so they had spent the previous week preparing the car for the new owner. He figured that removing the lettering was the right thing to do. Nalley said the car looked better than ever. He was shocked that you couldn't even tell where it had been lettered. Little did he know that it was a different body entirely. He never found out. The new owner never found out, and no one was ever the wiser.

## Stiff Competition

The competition in 1962 was fierce for Hubert in his Biscayne and Don in his Bel Air. The 409 Chevys were strong, but so were the 1962 Catalina Super Duty 421s, as well as the 1962 Dodge/Plymouth 413 Max Wedges. Then there was the 1962 Ford Fairlane 406 G-Code with top racers Phil Bonner or Dick Brannan behind the wheel. There were also big names driving their own 409 Chevrolets, such as Ronnie "Mr. 4-Speed" Sox of Sox & Martin, Dave Strickler driving for Bill Jenkins, Hayden Proffitt driving for Bill Thomas, Bill "Butch" Leal, Dickie Harrell, and Lamar Walden.

### *Bounty Hunter*

In the summer of 1962, Chevrolet was celebrating its 50th year in production. To honor this occasion, it produced 20 Central Office Production Order (COPO) aluminum-nosed, 409 Super Sport Impalas. Chevrolet gave one of these special rides to Don to race at the NHRA Nationals at Indy in the B/FX class.

In the final round, Don beat Dave Strickler's *Old Reliable III* with an ET of 12.93. After the Nationals, Don

***For the second half of the 1962 race season, Hubert blazed the strips in this 1962 Super Sport Impala named the* Bounty Hunter. *Raising the hood a couple of inches in the rear was an early way to get cold air into the engine bay and increase horsepower.***

*The torque of the big-block Chevy 409 was hard to beat out of the hole, as Hubert graciously shows this factory Super Stock Dodge.*

returned his focus to his primary race car. He passed the hardtop Super Sport to Hubert, who named the car *Bounty Hunter.* He had the names of 14 competitors painted on the decklid as bounties. Hubert campaigned this car for the rest of the 1962 season.

## Second Fiddle

Hubert and Don's relationship off the track was a match made in heaven, but on the drag strip, it was the rivalry from hell. The two met time and time again in the final round of competition, and the spoils would go to Don. One such instance was on November 4 at Easy Street Dragstrip in Newton Grove, North Carolina. In the final round, Don took the Top Stock Eliminator title in his Bel Air, winning $500 and leaving Hubert with runner-up honors and a $300 purse.

As if the brotherly rivalry with Huston wasn't already enough, Hubert was now in constant competition with Don. Hubert knew if he was going to beat Don he was going to have to leave Don. It was clear that this was *Don's* Nalley-Chevrolet deal and *Don's* dyno shop, and he would always have the first and best choice of everything. Hubert was grateful for his job at Nalley and to Don for bringing him onto the racing team and getting his first taste of factory support, but he in no way liked playing second fiddle.

It was obvious that this was the beginning of the end, and the partnership would have a shelf life of a 1962 season.

## 1962 Winter Nationals Bubble Top

The 1962 Bel Air that Don raced at the Winternationals also became a test car at the Nalley shop. Don and Hubert used this car to try new things and test new ideas. Even though above the driver's window was painted with "Driver Hubert Platt," it was quite often Huston behind the wheel and getting his feet wet in Super Stock competition.

Huston was already a drag racer in his own right. He raced a blown small-block Chevy-powered rail dragster that was the original *Dixie Twister* owned by Bobby Renzler. The car was also sponsored by the Nalley-Nicholson Dyno Shop.

At the end of the year, Hubert was making plans for 1963 and his own factory deal with Chevrolet. He hoped to receive a new 1963 Z11 Impala from the second batch due out in January. In the meantime, on November 22, 1962, he took the bubble-top Bel Air (which they had been testing new Z11 parts on) to Florida to compete in the eight-car Super Stock showdown.

Hubert had a banner day. He ran through the competition in eliminations, even downing Don's old 1961 Chevy that was being driven by Dave Heath. It had been a long day, and Hubert was looking to leave Nalley on a high note. His hopes were made a reality when he defeated none other than "Big Daddy" Don Garlits with an ET of 11.77. Garlits was making one of his rare Super Stock appearances in his new 1963 Dodge Max Wedge sponsored by Massey Motors. This win was a nice cap to mark the end of Hubert's 1962 season with Nalley-Nicholson.

*You can almost feel the acceleration as Hubert is standing hard on the 409 in first gear! Helmets didn't become mandatory in the Stock classes until A/FX came around more than a year later.*

# CHAPTER 4

# BRAND LOYALTY?

*The original* Georgia Shaker *Z11 and six-year-old Hubert Jr. (Hubie) eagerly await a day at the races in 1963. This would be Hubert's last Chevy race car and the only Chevy to carry his* Georgia Shaker *moniker.*

With the beginning of a new year, Hubert had high hopes of receiving one of the 50 or so 1963 Impalas slated for drag racing with the special Z11 package. Unfortunately, he did not. The price for a new 1963 Impala was $2,774 plus the $1,240 Z11 package, which made this more than a $4,000 car.

Hubert never liked paying full price for anything. He prided himself on being a real wheeler-dealer, and he sought out a discount. He found one in North Carolina from a man who had bought a Z11 and could no longer afford to make the payments. Hubert came to his rescue and purchased the car, freeing the man from his financial woes.

After returning home to Atlanta, Hubert sold the *Lil' General* 1962 Biscayne to a man in Orlando, Florida. He decided it was time to make a go of it on his own, so he quit Nalley and the dyno shop and began to work for himself full-time out of his basement garage.

Hubert was still getting new speed equipment and parts from Don, and he was still hoping to get factory support of his own when without any warning Chevrolet pulled out of racing. Cut off from the factory parts and with dashed hopes of full factory support, Hubert forged on through the 1963 race season as an independent.

### The Original *Georgia Shaker*

Hubert was looking for an identity and a name that would stick. In the 1960s, people "in the know" with what was going on and making things happen were called "the movers and the shakers." This phrase was used to describe people who are active and influential in some field of endeavor. Hubert told Slick, "We're shaking around to all these different states, and I want people to know where I'm from. Let's call it the *Georgia Shaker*." Little did he know that he himself was soon to be known as the "Georgia Shaker."

The *Georgia Shaker* was a beautiful car painted Monaco Blue with a blue interior. It had large red and white checkered racing flags on the doors. Below the flags read "Balanced By Douglas Atlanta, Ga." All the way down the long quarter panels it read the "Georgia Shaker" in big white letters. On the roof above the driver's window was

*Even though the Z11 was the first car to use cowl induction, Hubert opted for a homemade aluminum hood scoop that forced air directly into the twin Carter carburetors. Some Super Stock classes would use shoe polish to write the car's weight on the window as well as the class and number. Hubert must have had to use a couple hundred pounds of ballast weight to make the Z11 weigh 3,600 pounds for this particular Super Stock class.*

*The Z11's aluminum hood and front bumper are looking a little worse for wear as Hubert poses with one of the Safety Safari. The aluminum hood could be easily dented by an unknowing helper closing it as if it were a steel hood.*

painted "Driver Hubert Platt," and on the fender it read "Headers by Nicholson" and "Prepared by Hubert Platt." There appeared no mention of the dyno shop.

The car had two contingency decals on it: a large, round Hurst floor shift on the side of the roof that had "The Choice of Champions" painted beneath it and a rectangular Champion Spark Plugs decal behind the rear tire.

It wasn't only a strong-looking race car, it was Hubert's strongest-performing race car to date. The factory underrated the power of the Z11 at 430 hp and 435 ft-lbs of torque. The tweaked-and-tuned car would actually produce something closer to 500 hp. It used the standard 409 block in which the bore remained the same at 4.312 inches, but with a Z11 stroker forged crankshaft, that increased the stroke by 0.150 inches from the 409. The 3.65-inch stroke crank made it a 427.

The *Georgia Shaker* used forged connecting rods with high-dome pistons, giving it a compression rating of 13.5:1. The 427 had different cylinder heads from the W design. The new heads had large oval intake ports that were raised over the 409s. It came with factory iron headers that were immediately replaced by custom tube headers built by Don. It had a performance solid-lift cam with 5.56 lift and 3.25 duration. Also new for the Z11 was a two-piece aluminum intake manifold that would be topped off with twin Carter AFB 4-barrel carburetors, fed by a high-pressure fuel pump. It also had a lightweight aluminum water pump.

Although the Z11 was the first to incorporate a breather with cowl induction, Hubert removed this and opted for a custom homemade aluminum hood scoop that forced cold air into the carburetors. The engine also had a deep sump oil pan. All this power was distributed through a BorgWarner T-10 4-speed transmission with an aluminum case and Hurst floor shift to a 4.56:1 positive-traction rear end. On the ground was a set of 9-inch M&H drag slicks on a 15x8-inch set of GM stamped steel wheels. On the front were a set of 15x5.5-inch chrome-reverse wheels.

Weight reduction was huge for 1963. The list of deleted parts was more than the prior year and included windshield wipers, the front sway bar, radio, heater, and interior sound deadener. The list of aluminum parts had grown as well. The car had an aluminum front end, including the hood, fenders, bumper, braces, brackets, grille filler panel, and hood support latch as well as a two-piece fan shroud. For weight distribution and traction, the battery was mounted in the trunk. This race-rated vehicle continually produced times in the 11s at more than 100 mph in the quarter mile at a curb weight of 3,400 pounds, 300 pounds lighter than the standard Impala.

### Winning Ways

The Z11 was a winner in April at Orangeburg Drag Strip in South Carolina when Hubert took top honors in the Super Stock field of eight, taking home a $250 purse. In July, Hubert raced at Knoxville Dragway in Tennessee, where he received the top speed of the day in a group of fast competitors with a 12.14 ET at 117.34 mph.

## The World's Fastest Go-Kart

In a time when many homes did not have a television set, newspapers were the main source of news. To see an actual film of news taking place, one would have to go to a movie theater, where twice a week a newsreel kept American and British moviegoers up to date on current events while introducing them to foreign cultures and traditions. *Movietone News* library is one of the most comprehensive news film archives in the world and ran in American cinemas from 1927 to 1963, and in the UK as *British Movietone News* from 1929 to 1979. The biweekly newsreel covered politics, sports, fashion, and human interest stories, generally ending on a light or humorous note, creating the format newscasters use to this day.

In the fall of 1963 Hubert was at Tampa Dragway racing the Z11 in A-Modified Production (A/MP). The *Movietone News* film crew was on hand that day to film a story featuring the World's Fastest Go-Kart. Captain Jack McClure was somewhat of a daredevil and an entertainer with his rocket kart powered by twin T-16 Turbonique engines. As the cameras rolled, the little go-kart blasted off, blowing down the fence behind the starting line with its jet propulsion. It flew down the track at breakneck speed.

The solo run was impressive, but to show fans a true side-by-side comparison of just how fast the go-kart was, the crew asked Hubert if he would race McClure in the *Georgia Shaker,* which had the low ET of the meet. He agreed. The two lined up, the flag man dropped his flag, and the little kart sped out in front. The acceleration of the go-kart was too much for the full-bodied race car. The kart took the win at 125 mph to Hubert's 118 mph.

When asked 50 years later if he remembered racing and losing to the go-kart, Hubert said, "Hell yeah! The damn thing would go over 120 mph."

The 2-minute, black-and-white newsreel is a neat little piece of history and the second known film clip of Hubert racing. It was surely the delight of many a British moviegoer in the early 1960s and can be viewed today on YouTube. The clip is called "GO KART - DRAG RACING - SOUND."

Two weeks later, at Sportman's Park Dragstrip in Farmington, North Carolina, Hubert recorded a track record of 11.86 ET at 119 mph. After winning the final round, his time was protested. After a tear down, the car checked out legal. This was the scene week after week at drag strips all through the Southeastern United States.

### The Comet Deal

Huston Platt had his own 1963 Z11, the *Dixie Twister,* but he was also racing an experimental big-block Chevy II station wagon. Hubert said it was "bad ass" and that it gave him the idea to build a Falcon or Comet wagon with a 427.

Hubert mentioned this idea to Lincoln/Mercury racing director, Fran Hernandez, who loved the idea. It appeared as though the two had a deal. Hubert was excited about the prospect of his very own factory deal and began telling everyone he would soon have factory support. Mysteriously, two weeks later, Don Nicholson had a new deal with Mercury. Hubert was quoted years later saying, "I should have kept my mouth shut!"

### Thunderbolt

In mid-1963, Hubert and Allen Hyder were spending a lot of time together and planning a partnership for the 1964 racing season. Allen, who had been racing Pontiacs, had recently acquired a 1963½ R-code 427 medium-riser Lightweight Fastback Galaxie from Ford that he named *White Lightning.*

In October and November of 1963, Hubert and Allen took turns in each others' cars, Hubert drove *White Lightning* and Allen raced the *Georgia Shaker* Z11. Hubert, as well as most of the Galaxie racers, was having limited success. It seemed that even the new lightened version of the big Galaxie was no match for the competition.

Dick Brannan had a great 1963 season, being the first to win in NHRA Super Stock with a Ford and setting multiple track records. However, he and "the powers that be" at Ford were also very aware of the Galaxie's limitations. They knew they had to do something new for 1964.

Rhode Island's Tasca Ford was a performance-based dealership whose owner, Bob Tasca, was always pushing the envelope of how much performance you could get out of a particular vehicle. Often the innovative Tasca was noted for trying things the factory wouldn't. He had been tinkering with a 427 low-riser in a 1963 Fairlane 500 two-door hardtop. Ford's marketing manager, Frank Zimmerman, got wind of this and liked the idea, and it was this car that opened up the conversation for the consideration of the Fairlane for 1964. The plan was to take the smaller Ford Fairlane, lighten it up, and stuff it with a 427-ci drag engine.

Chevy had the Z11 and was working on a mystery engine, and the Mopar guys had the Max Wedge and soon-to-come Hemi. Dick knew Ford would have to pull out all the stops to beat the competition.

Ford gave Dick the full support of Dearborn Steel Tubing Shop (DST), which had built the Lightweight Galaxies the year before. Dick Brannan had 11 vintage Burgundy Fairlanes sent to DST. The cars were taken apart and reassembled as drag cars. The next 100-plus units all in Wimbleton White arrived at DST in pieces and were assembled there; half were 4-speeds and half were automatics.

The little Fairlanes were quite the beasts when they exited DST. From then on, they would be called Thunderbolts, or T-Bolts for short, which would become Ford's first true star of the quarter mile.

The Thunderbolts came equipped with a 427 high-riser with a 4.23-inch bore and 3.78-inch stroke with 12.7:1 high-compression pistons. They each had a solid-lift cam, an aluminum intake, and dual Holley 4-barrel carburetors with large air-intake hoses bringing in cold air from the unused headlamp bezels in the grille. The mechanical fuel pump was assisted by a Stewart Warner 240A electric fuel pump. Exhaust exited through equal-length tube headers that had to be snaked through the front suspension because the engine compartment was so small. With all of this, the engine was rated at 480 ft-lbs of torque and 425 hp but was actually tipping the horsepower scale closer to 500.

The Fords used a Hurst floor shifter on a BorgWarner T-10 aluminum case 4-speed transmission, which transferred power to the 9-inch rear end with 4.56:1 gears. The rear end also sported 2x3-inch rectangular tubing traction bars connected to a crossmember that was also a driveshaft hoop. Out back was a set of 7-inch M&H slicks (per the NHRA 1964 7-inch limit) mounted on silver painted stock stamped steel wheels, 15x7 inches on the rear and 15x6 inches on the front, which had Firestone bias-ply tires.

As always, weight was a huge factor. These cars were delivered with no sound deadener, seam sealant, heaters, or radios. The carpet was replaced with a rubber mat. They went as far as to remove the rearview mirror, passenger-side windshield wiper, and sun visor as well as the armrest and even the rear window cranks.

The first Thunderbolt for Dick Brannan had a one-piece fiberglass front bumper and gravel pan combination, and the 125-pound truck battery was in the trunk. The racers at Chrysler spoke out, and the NHRA made Ford change to a metal front bumper, which was aluminum on the rest of the cars. Ford also had to change to a car battery that weighed less than 100 pounds.

The T-Bolts had an aluminum radiator, water pump, and inner fender wells that were covered by fiberglass fenders, hood, and decklid. The rear side glass and backlight were replaced with plexiglass. This entire package brought the weight down to 3,200-pound curb weight, which was a full 225 pounds lighter than the lightest Lightweight Galaxie.

In October, the first batch of 11 Burgundy Thunderbolts went to Ford Drag Council members. Dick Brannan received the first car, which he had already been testing. The list appeared as follows:

**Thunderbolt Owners and Drivers**

| | *Dealership* | *Driver* |
|---|---|---|
| 1. | Romy-Hammes Ford | Dick Brannan |
| 2. | Bob Ford | Paul Harvey |
| 3. | Tasca Ford | Bill Lawton |
| 4. | Bob Ford | Len Richter |
| 5. | Performance Associates | Les Ritchey |
| 6. | Russ Davis Ford | Gas Ronda |
| 7. | Mickey Thompson | Butch Leal |
| 8. | Al Means Ford | Phil Bonner |
| 9. | Ed Martin Ford | Bob Allen |
| 10. | Wickersham Ford | Clester Andrews |
| 11. | Mickey Thompson | Mickey Thompson |

The Thunderbolts didn't disappoint. Gas Ronda won the Super Stock title with a 11.78 at 123.40 mph in an all-Thunderbolt final round against Butch Leal at the NHRA 1964 Winternationals in Pomona, California. Butch Leal went on to win Super Stock honors at the NHRA Indy Nationals with an 11.76 at 122.78 mph, beating a 1964 Plymouth Hemi in the final. Gas had a stellar year in his Thunderbolt, as he went on to be the 1964 NHRA Super/Stock World Champion.

### *The Little Georgia Shaker*

By the end of 1963, Hubert had been a full-time drag racer for three years, and his skill as a driver had captured the attention of Ford. The automaker chose him to be one of the first independent drag racers with no dealership affiliation to receive one of the new Ford drag cars.

When Hubert got the call, he was thrilled. It was redeeming after losing the Mercury deal. Although this wasn't a factory sponsorship and it was only the car, it was Ford's way of possibly recruiting one of the top Chevy drivers.

Hubert was very superstitious; however, it didn't seem to bother him a bit when he was scheduled to pick

***Hubert displayed the newly painted* Little Georgia Shaker *Thunderbolt outside the Commonwealth Ford dealership. This is one of the earliest-known photos of this car. It is still sporting its factory steel wheels.***

up Thunderbolt 13 on Friday the 13th in December 1963. Hubert headed north with an empty trailer and a smile that quickly turned over when on pickup day there was a snowstorm in Detroit that stranded him for three days.

Hubert had a Wednesday night match race already booked for the Thunderbolt. He would have liked to have been able to take the car home and tweak on it in his own garage and possibly even have gotten to make some test passes, but with the storm delay, he had to go directly to Panama City Beach from Detroit. When the storm cleared, Hubert headed south and drove 1,000 miles to Panama City Beach, Florida. That Wednesday night, with the car directly off the trailer and Hubert not being used to the new ride, he missed a gear and bent the valves in the 427. His night was over, and he headed home.

Back in Atlanta, Hubert had the Thunderbolt painted Ford Guardsman Blue, which went well with the Medium Palomino (gold) interior. He replaced the stock steel wheels with a set of chrome Howard units. With the T-bolt being a full 13 inches shorter than the *Georgia Shaker* Z11 Impala, Hubert decided to call this car the *Little Georgia Shaker*, and had this painted down the length of the quarter panel. Hand painted on the side of the roof was a large Hurst logo that said "The Choice of Champions" beneath it. The original artist painted the Hurst logo by memory and put the red on the right side of the "H" by mistake. On the roof above the side window, it read "Driver Hubert Platt." Across the back windshield in white script was painted the quote "That's All She Wrote."

***Hubert and best friend Allen Hyder ran ads in drag news publications all across the country, soliciting for match races against the two-car Ford/Chevy team. The two were booked almost every weekend in 1964 up until Allen's untimely passing.***

### Hyder-Platt Racing Team

As Hubert and Allen Hyder had planned, they joined forces in 1964. Allen sold the *White Lightning* Galaxie to a man in Tampa, and Hubert let him drive the Z11 *Georgia Shaker*, which remained painted the same with Allen's name in place of Hubert's over the door. They now had a two-car Ford/Chevy race team. This was a move that drove some people crazy. Brand loyalty ran very strong in the 1960s, and a two-car team with two rival brands was unheard of, but both cars were fast, and Hubert wasn't one to discriminate.

On one of the team's first outings was south of Daytona Beach, Florida, at Spruce Creek Airport during the NASCAR-sanctioned 1964 Winternationals. Hubert and Allen both won their classes, Hubert taking the Super Stock honors in the *Little Georgia Shaker* Thunderbolt and Allen winning the A/SS title in the Z11 *Georgia Shaker*.

Hubert and Allen were having success. They ran ads in all the drag-racing newspapers in the country with pictures of the two *Georgia Shaker* race cars, soliciting for bookings to match races. They were getting weekly responses from the ads, and racing every weekend against each other in a Ford-versus-Chevy showdown or in a three-way match race with another Ford. Sometimes the foe would be the *Strip Teaser* Thunderbolt of Howard Neal. The Thunderbolts would go head-to-head in a best two-out-of-three match race with the winner to go on to the best three-of-five against the Z11 Chevy.

On March 16, 1964, at Union Hill Drag Strip in Nashville, Tennessee, Hubert marched through the Super Stock field of 13 competitors to take home the $250 top prize with the *Little Georgia Shaker*. He ran an 11.90 in the final round.

#### *Loss of a Best Friend*

Allen Hyder was tragically killed in a construction accident. When on a steep hill, a large construction tractor rolled over on him. He was killed instantly and pronounced dead at the scene.

This was a huge blow to Hubert. Just months earlier in October 1963, he had named his third child and

***Hubert received Thunderbolt number 13. The Rebel flags seen here on the door would soon give way to a Frank Vego Ford sponsorship. The M&H Tires logo on the quarters would be replaced with Chamblee Carb & Electric, which was Bruce Brantley's shop.***

## Louisa Drag Strip

The guys were strong, but not undefeated. In 2012, a fan put a silent 8-mm home movie on YouTube that shows a four-car match race at Louisa Drag Strip in Virginia.

In the grainy, faded home movie, you see two Mopars warming up, awaiting the arrival of the Ford/Chevy *Georgia Shaker* team. As the Hyder-Platt rig pulls into the pits, you see the large Chevy ramp-back truck painted Monaco Blue to match the *Georgia Shaker* with crossing red checkered flags on the door and the Impala perched on the back while towing the *Little Georgia Shaker* Thunderbolt on a trailer.

The shaky video shows the Thunderbolt lose the first round to future Funny Car pioneer "Pee Wee" Wallace in his 1962 *Virginian 784* Plymouth while the Z11 stormed to a win past a red Max Wedge Plymouth Savoy. In the final round, the Z11 couldn't hold off the top end power of the *Virginian*.

The silent video is a great piece of drag racing history, and it can be seen on YouTube under the heading "Vintage 8mm Film Louisa Drag Strip- Louisa, VA."

***The Hyder-Platt Racing Team was a very rare Ford/Chevy two-car team. Allen Hyder took over driving duties in the Z11 while Hubert handled things in the T-Bolt.***

*The Ford Thunderbolt was a strong competitor throughout the 1964 season. Hubert gained a sponsorship from Frank Vego Ford partway through the year. The dealership was only 1 mile from his home in Atlanta.*

second son Allen Platt after his partner and best friend, Allen Hyder. In the wake of Allen's death, Hubert sold the Z11 *Georgia Shaker* to famed drag racer Wally Bell from New York.

## "Away VE-GO"

One mile north of Hubert's home on Buford Highway was Frank Vego Ford. The Atlanta Performance Ford dealer had sponsored Phil Bonner's 1963½ Lightweight the previous year. Phil was now driving a Thunderbolt sponsored by Al Means Ford. Frank was without a driver, so he offered a sponsorship to Hubert and his Thunderbolt.

Hubert and Frank had a good relationship, and Hubert enjoyed the support of a dealership so close to his home. The *Little Georgia Shaker* now had painted on the door a small character of Frank Vego saying "Away VE-GO" with "Frank Vego Ford" in large letters. On the quarter panel behind the tire it now read "Chamblee Carb. & Elec. Chamblee, GA," a nod to Bruce Brantley's shop, which built all of Hubert's performance carburetors and distributors.

Out on the tip of the front fender painted in white was "Crane Cams" with a small character of a crane with a racing helmet and parachute boasting the high-performance cam this class of Super Stock/Stock was allowed to have. The car wore a couple of contingency stickers of Valvoline and STP as well. The car's number and class were both boldly stated in the rear side windows: "SS/S 876."

## The Beginning of the Grudge Matches

When Hubert received the Thunderbolt from Ford, he was quoted as saying, "I've had the rest, now I've got the best." Hubert did so well racing under the blue oval banner that most fans forgot he ever drove anything else.

Brother Huston, on the other hand, was a loyal bowtie guy who was dead set on racing a Chevrolet with or without factory support. Huston was racing a 1964 Chevelle Z11 427 billed as the "World's Fastest Chevelle." It seemed logical that the two should go head-to-head.

***The Little Georgia Shaker** leaped off the line at Phenix City, Alabama. Fans packed this drag strip every weekend to see Super Stock and match race action.*

*This primitive Christmas tree took the job of a flagman in 1964. The 427 puts a good wrinkle in the T-Bolt's 7-inch slicks.*

*The Ford Fairlane Thunderbolt was a good bit shorter than Hubert's Z11* Georgia Shaker *Impala, which led to it being named the* Little Georgia Shaker. *Chrome Howard Racing wheels gave the T-Bolt a custom look. (Photo Courtesy Michael Goyda)*

The brothers staged a series of match races throughout the Southeast where the two would race the *Little Georgia Shaker* Thunderbolt against the *Dixie Twister* Chevelle. Promoters advertised the matchups as a "Brother vs. Brother Grudge Match." Flyers would tell the tale of the two brothers that hated each other because of their rival Ford/Chevy loyalties. The Platts would even play this up by not speaking to each other in the pits. This was a money-making act that promoters throughout the Southeast welcomed.

## Mr. Stock Eliminator List

At the end of 1964 and the beginning of 1965, *Super Stock News* and *Drag Speed Illustrated*, devised a list of the four fastest Super Stocks in the Southeast. On August 1, 1964, Hubert in the Thunderbolt faced off against Dyno Don Nicholson in the Comet for the number-one spot.

The little Comet downed the Thunderbolt two straight to solidify Don's first-place seat, which he would hold throughout the winter. Challenge runs could only be made on qualifying strips. These strips were in Virginia at Roanoke and Emporia drag strips; in North Carolina at Concord, Kinston, Mooresville, Fayetteville, and Columbus County drag strips; in South Carolina at Blaney, Greer, and Spartanburg drag strips; and in Georgia at Forsyth County drag strip in Cumming. Throughout the winter of 1964–1965, the Mr. Stock Eliminator List remained as follows: 1. Don Nicholson (Comet), 2. Hubert Platt (Thunderbolt), 3. Huston Platt (Chevelle), and 4. Ronnie Sox (Plymouth).

Brothers Hubert and Huston were rarely seen without a cigar. Raised in the Great Depression, when most people couldn't afford cigarettes, cigars were seen as a status symbol of the wealthy. Their brand was Tampa Nugget Sublimes, and although Huston never lit his, smoking cigars was part of the Platt brothers big shot persona.

## Wild Ride

The small Fairlane was never intended to have anything larger than a 289-ci V-8 that came in its sports model. When stuffed with the big-block 427 pushing 500+ hp with a 4-speed transmission and only a 7-inch slick on the back, the Thunderbolt was more than a handful to drive. It scared many a skilled racer.

Hubert said he would get a death grip on the steering wheel and wedge his left elbow against the door panel as hard as he could before he would drop the clutch. He said it was the only way he could hold it straight. He was quoted many times saying, "You had to have more nerve than detective Dick Tracy to drive a Thunderbolt."

There were two people who learned this lesson the hard way. When Hubert sold his Thunderbolt, new owner Lee Malkemes renamed it *Malfunction* and booked a match race in North Carolina versus Ronnie Sox for his first outing. On his first run, he lost control at the end of the track and flipped over, totaling the car and breaking his neck in the process. The second driver was an associate of Phil Bonner's. While Phil was racing his new Falcon match racer, the associate took Phil's Thunderbolt out to the local track without his permission, lost control, and crashed the car. It was a total loss.

Dyno Don Nicholson held the number-one spot on this Mr. Stock Eliminator List for nearly two years running. His A/FX Comet was one of the strongest and most consistent drag cars in the country.

# CHAPTER 5

# KEEPING UP WITH THE FACTORY

Even though Ford was successful with the Thunderbolt, by mid-1964 the tides were already changing. The ongoing need to stay quick and competitive had Ford looking forward to the upcoming year and the arrival of the new fastback 2+2 Mustang. It started to prepare for this by testing a 1964 Falcon with a 427 high-riser set up for drag racing and driven by Dick Brannan.

Ford got word that Phil Bonner had started building himself a Falcon to stay more competitive on the lucrative match race circuit. The automaker demanded he stop, and it had the car brought to Dearborn Steel Tubing to complete the project, saying it didn't want a factory driver building his own car.

*At this point, Hubert couldn't have imagined the fame and fortune this little Falcon would bring to him over the next year. On the day this photo was taken, he set the low ET of the meet with a 10.43 at 134 mph.*

### The Smallest Georgia Shaker

Hubert wanted to keep up with the factory. Feeling left out of this process, he purchased a used 1964 Falcon with a 6-cylinder and took it into his single-car basement garage. He transformed it from an economy grocery getter into exactly what they were building in Dearborn: a real A/FX quarter-mile drag machine. When equipped with lightweight fiberglass doors, fenders, hood, and bumper, the car weighed in at 3,210 pounds.

Underneath the custom teardrop-shaped hood scoop, Hubert moved the top of the spring towers outward to accommodate the 427 big-block powerplant. Looking big and bad stuffed into the Falcon's small engine bay, the engine was crowned by two Holley 4-barrel carburetors, which were fed clean air through air ducts behind the grille, similar to the Thunderbolt.

The engine was just as the factory built it with a few exceptions. One exception was the Crane 300-8 flat tappet camshaft and kit along with a set of Doug's Headers. The engine also sported a custom enlarged oil pan made by Hubert. He mounted a Hurst shifter onto the Ford 4-speed transmission, moving the power to the rear suspension, which was the same double-shock setup consisting of four shocks on the rear end with welded traction bars that was used on the Thunderbolt.

*The Ford Falcon was just a bit shorter in length than Hubert's* Little Georgia Shaker *Thunderbolt, which is how the car got its name: the* Smallest Georgia Shaker.

*The* Smallest Georgia Shaker *Falcon's engine bay could hardly contain the 427 mill with 8-quart oil pan and Headers by Doug, which are clearly visible from the front. Notice the round fresh-air ducts behind the grille, which led to the twin Holley 4-barrels.*

*Hubert clearly looked the part of a professional. He was dressed all in white as he took on the responsibilities of owner, driver, and mechanic for the* Georgia Shaker *race team.*

*Because of the fast times and speeds the* Smallest Georgia Shaker *was turning, rumors began to spread that the car had a gutted interior. This photo proves that to be far from the truth.*

*The Goodyear racing slicks were doing their job as they bit the racing surface and launched the* Smallest Georgia Shaker *off the starting line to another 10-second run.*

All that power met the track on a set of Goodyear 10-inch slicks and Howard Chrome Wheels. Hubert removed the 1964 trim and replaced it with 1965 trim, and after a fresh coat of paint, no one was the wiser. It was now a 1965 Falcon.

Hubert was now working at Southern Precision Grinding, where he did engine balancing, head work, and cam grinding. The shop sponsored his car, helping out with the expenses of racing. It also supplied Hubert with a company truck: a new black 1965 short-bed Ford pickup. The shop name was lettered prominently on the door of the race car as well as "Crane Cams" and "Headers by Doug" on the fender.

When faced with naming the car, which was smaller than his *Little Georgia Shaker,* Hubert decided to call this one the *Smallest Georgia Shaker.* He had the name painted down the length of the quarter panel in white and red lettering on the beautiful metallic blue finish. The car was a real looker, as was Hubert's red 1964 Thunderbird tow car. The bright red Thunderbird towed the *Smallest Georgia Shaker* and racked up many miles taking the Platt family to the races.

***Hubert's Falcon was Ford blue, which endeared it to Ford fans even more. Every aspect of how his cars looked was almost as important to him as their performance.***

Hubert's daughter, Lynette, was 13 at this time, and she had little patience for her dad, who would make a long trip even longer by stopping in every little town along the way to wash the race car at the local gas station. End to end, the whole rig was immaculately clean, and Hubert was as sharp as ever in his white racing suit with a blue stripe down the leg and matching jacket that read "*Georgia Shaker* Atlanta, Georgia" on the back. As always, Hubert loved to keep himself and his cars very professional and slick looking, but this car was more than just a looker.

On the last weekend of January 1965, the *Smallest Georgia Shaker* won its class with a final round ET of 10.65 in Orlando, Florida, at an A/FX meet. Hubert took home a $500 purse. It performed exceptionally well, turning in times in the 10.40s and 130s mph. These numbers were impressive enough to start rumors about the little race car that quickly spread across the United States.

*Super Stock Magazine* reported as early as December 1964 that it had heard of a little Falcon that was making a living legend out of its owner. According to the rumors, Hubert had a 427 in an all-fiberglass, gutted shell of a Falcon with a tube chassis. To its surprise, an inspection of the car at the Daytona Winter Drags detected no difference between Hubert's Falcon and the ones of similar make belonging to Brannan and Bonner. Instead of gutted, as the rumors had stated, they found the car carried full upholstery and even the standard Falcon Sprint seats front and rear, carpet, and headliner.

Hubert went on to further impress the *Super Stock Magazine* writers by setting the low ET of the meet with 10.43 at 134.14 mph. The magazine ran a cover story on the *Smallest Georgia Shaker* in the June 1965 issue called "Southern Sizzler Hubert Platt's 427 Falcon."

***To Hubert, having a clean, good-looking rig was of the utmost importance. Even the trailer had whitewalls and hubcaps. This photo was taken at one of the Platt brothers grudge match races, as you can see the back end of Huston's*** **Dixie Twister** ***1965 Chevelle next to Hubert's T-Bird.***

**The Smallest Georgia Shaker** ***is ready for another day at the races. This car would soon undergo a serious transformation, getting an altered wheelbase and becoming the*** **Georgia Shaker III.**

## Danger in the Pits

When most people think of the dangers of drag racing, they typically fear a horrific high-speed crash or being trapped in a fire. For Hubert, the biggest danger of his racing career to date happened in the pits.

Hubert was performing regular maintenance at a match race and was underneath the *Smallest Georgia Shaker* Falcon. The car was resting on four jack stands as well as the floor jack for safety. Nearly 100 overzealous fans surrounded the car, eager to get a look at the A/FX racer's construction. They knocked it off the jack stands and jack, pinning Hubert to the ground. The lower shock mount struck him near the temple.

The fans were able to lift the car, and Hubert was dragged to safety and rushed to the hospital. The emergency room doctor told Bee that the point of impact was only 3/8 inch away from being fatal. The left side of Hubert's face was completely paralyzed. However, the condition wasn't permanent, and he made a full recovery several weeks later.

*The bright red 1964 Thunderbird looks custom with whitewall tires and chrome aftermarket mag wheels sitting in the "top driveway" of the Platt family home. The "bottom driveway" led to the single-car basement garage on the end of the house and was for race cars. The Platt's T-bird would double as a family car as well as a tow car for the* **Smallest Georgia Shaker.** *Note the trailer hitch.*

*Hubert gets the air pressure just right for ultimate traction on the* **Smallest Georgia Shaker** *Falcon. He's sporting a custom Hubert Platt T-shirt with a picture of the race car, which was pretty cutting edge for 1965.*

### *43 Jr.* Versus the *Smallest Georgia Shaker*

In 1965, NASCAR racing champion Richard Petty protested NASCAR's boycott of the 426 Hemi and took up drag racing for the season. The king of NASCAR and the *Smallest Georgia Shaker* crossed paths three times that year.

#### *Lassiter Mountain Raceway Match*

The first time was April 24, 1965, at Lassiter Mountain Raceway in Birmingham, Alabama. During the solo test runs each driver was allowed to make before the match race, Petty had his blue *43 Jr.* Hemi Barracuda sounding strong when it roared to a blistering 10.79. Hubert had a little trouble getting the *Smallest Georgia Shaker* warmed up and had an initial test run of 11.34.

Hubert knew he was going to have to get off the line first to keep from being overpowered by the Hemi. Because of this, he left early and red lighted the first two rounds, but he was consistent with a 10.82 followed by a 10.81. Knowing he could not red light again, Hubert was more cautious off the line. He pushed it hard to win the third round by only a few inches with a 10.62.

In the fourth round, Hubert won on a holeshot when Petty recorded his best of the night but lost with 10.60 to Hubert's 10.65. Now tied at two rounds each, the fans were on their feet for this Ford versus Mopar final. To the

*On April 24, 1965, at Lassiter Mountain Raceway in Birmingham, Alabama, Hubert went head-to-head with racing star Richard Petty. Petty was drag racing while boycotting NASCAR's ban on the Hemi. Hubert's* Smallest Georgia Shaker *won three straight after red lighting in the first two rounds against Petty's* 43 Jr. *Barracuda.*

*Looking calm and cool between rounds, Hubert and NASCAR star Richard Petty discuss the twin Holley setup on the* Smallest Georgia Shaker. *Mechanic Larry Yates stands behind Hubert.*

*Lassiter Mountain Raceway's left lane had a sheer rock cliff going up about 20 feet high. The solid rock barrier added to the tension and excitement of the runs.*

*The match race against Petty was one of the few times Hubert ran the* Smallest Georgia Shaker *with no hood. These are the only known photos of him racing the car without the hood.*

delight of the Ford fans, Hubert outran the NASCAR star while setting the low ET of the meet: a 10.52.

### *Aquasco Dragway Match*

A few weeks later in May, Petty would get his shot at redemption at Aquasco Dragway in Maryland. It was accredited for being the first quarter-mile drag strip on the East Coast. On this day, luck wasn't on Hubert's side. He blew the engine in a pre-race test run.

It looked like he was out for the day until some fellow racers came to his aid with the parts to help him rebuild his engine. They completed the rebuild in time for the first round, but in high gear the newly rebuilt engine came apart, giving that round and the match to Petty. Hubert was unable to continue.

### *Thunderbolt Raceway Match*

The third meeting came at Thunderbolt Raceway in Jacksonville, Florida. Petty thrilled the Mopar fans on hand when he won the first round with an 11.35 at 117.98 mph. In the second round, Hubert gave the Ford fans something to cheer about when he won with an 11.58 at 116.60 mph.

In round three, Hubert ripped to his low ET of the night with a 10.96, but he was a little quick off the line and lit the red light. In the fourth round, Petty pulled the same slip and red lighted himself, tying the match two to two.

While in the pits before the fifth round, Hubert noticed that the front suspension of the *Smallest Georgia Shaker* had broken during a wheel stand in the fourth round. It was damaged beyond what could be repaired at the track. The Falcon was done for the night and had to leave this contest in a draw.

*Advertisements such as this one from* Drag Times *magazine were a sure way to get fans out to the track in the days long before internet advertising.*

*In mid 1965, the* Smallest Georgia Shaker *Falcon was undergoing its transformation period. The modifications to the engine, suspension, and wheelbase happened over the course of about a month.*

*Step one in the transformation of the* Smallest Georgia Shaker *into the* Georgia Shaker III *was the addition of Hilborn injectors on a custom Weber intake. Notice the original placement of the fuel tank barely protruding out from the passenger side of the grille.*

## The *Georgia Shaker III*

It was a busy year for anyone trying to keep up with A/FX Professional Drag Racing, and the winds of change were blowing. Before Hubert could even sit back and enjoy his success with the *Smallest Georgia Shaker,* it seemed a new advancement had turned over A/FX: the altered wheelbase (AWB).

If Hubert hadn't felt left out before by the factory, he certainly did now. Dick Brannan and Phil Bonner were both testing and racing new rides for Ford. Brannan in the first 2+2 Fastback SOHC-powered Mustang and Bonner in an altered-wheelbase, SOHC-powered Falcon.

Hubert had no choice but to follow suit without factory help, so he returned to his single-car basement garage and began to dismantle his prized possession and livelihood. What emerged on the other side of this flurry of cutting, grinding, and welding would be his most iconic ride, simply named *Georgia Shaker III.* This name hinted to those who were paying attention that this was the same Falcon reborn.

*The second step in the transformation of the* Smallest Georgia Shaker *into the* Georgia Shaker III *was the addition of the axle front end. It was installed 2 inches forward of the original center. Soon to come were the altered wheelbase to the rear end, new name, and new paint job.*

*Larry Yates and Hubert worked together for more than a year and a half in 1965 and 1966. Larry is credited with helping Hubert build the* Georgia Shaker III *Falcon and the blue home-made long-nose* Georgia Shaker *Mustang.*

*In 1965, there were only a handful of altered-wheelbase drag cars in the country. Hubert Platt's basement build would produce times in the 9s at speeds of 140+ mph, winning a high percentage of its match races throughout the season.*

*Hubert was very proud of the car and eager to have the* Georgia Shaker III *photo documented. The car was taken to the red clay hills of Cumming Dragway in Georgia for this photo shoot. Some of the images were later used on the cover and in the article "The* Georgia Shaker III*" of* Drag Racing *magazine's November 1965 issue.*

Hubert Platt
Georgia Shaker
CRANE CAMS
HEADERS by

What took place in that basement did not happen overnight. It started with a Hilborn injector setup on a custom Weber intake made by Holman & Moody that allowed for the use of alcohol and nitro. Hubert then installed a Mooneyes gas tank. It was first mounted sideways by the radiator then moved out onto the front bumper.

Next, Hubert modified the front-end suspension, removing all original parts, A-arms, springs, shocks, towers, etc. He took a leaf-spring axle front end out of a Ford Econoline van, cut 6 inches from the middle, welded it back together, and installed it under the Falcon 2 inches forward from stock. This increased the wheelbase to 111.5 inches.

Hubert tested and raced the car a couple of times like this before going all in and radically moving the rear end forward 10.5 inches to alter the wheelbase even more. Now at 101 inches overall, it was 8.5 inches shorter than stock.

When Hubert went to order a set of the newly released Cragar S/S mags for the Falcon, the catalog didn't have them in a narrow width, which is what he wanted for the front. So, he phoned Cragar and had a pair custom made.

Hubert and his partner, Larry Yates, worked day and night on the car. They were not only under pressure to keep up with the Ford factory but also from Mopar, which had started a huge AWB program before Ford. It took a lot of drive and confidence to take on the factories when you were just an independent racer working out of a basement garage, but one thing Hubert had plenty of was confidence. He never doubted himself and what he was doing.

When the transformation was complete, a fresh lettering job sporting the new name "Georgia Shaker III" and "Hubert Platt" was applied in bigger letters. The Southern Precision Grinding sponsor was removed. Hubert was here to stay, with or without factory or local sponsorship support.

## Successful Transformation

One of the first outings for the completely modified *Georgia Shaker III* was on July 31, 1965, in Montgomery, Alabama, at Dixie Southland Dragstrip. Hubert won the best three-out-of-five competition with a final-round blast of 10.69 at 132 mph. He put down the *Kid Goat* Hemi Dart of Billy Jacobs, who was on his heels with a 10.70.

### West Coast Connection

The *Georgia Shaker III* began to produce 9-second ETs at 140 mph. By August 1965, Hubert was getting booked for match races all over. In a match race against Dickie Harrell in West Texas, Hubert had all the fans in the crowded stands on their feet as he did big wheelstands in first and second gear every run. On his last pass of the night, Hubert stood the little Falcon on its back bumper. The front end came down with so much force it smashed the headers, a price Hubert was willing to pay to put on a good show.

Hubert told his wife, Bee, "We're already over half the way to California, we should just go to Doug Thorley's and get new headers in person." She agreed, and west they went. This turned out to be a wise decision. Hubert and Bee were about to make friendships that would last their lifetimes.

Hubert and Doug became friends at first sight. Although Hubert had run Doug's headers for a while now, the two had never met. They had a real mutual respect for one another, each genuinely impressed with the other. From their slick appearances to their reputations and general personas, the two were cut from the same cloth. Their wives took to one another as well, becoming best friends even though they lived on opposite coasts.

Doug was not only impressed by Hubert but also by his car. Doug thought the *Georgia Shaker III* was the coolest race car he had ever seen. With the new headers installed,

*Doug Thorley often used his close friends in his advertisements, as you can see in this ad from 1965. Doug was very close friends with H.L. and Shirley Shahan. They, as well as Hubert, appeared in many of Doug's ads throughout the 1960s.*

the two were off to Lions Drag Strip in Long Beach, California, for some testing. Upon their arrival, Doug introduced Hubert to C.J. "Pappy" Hart, who ran the strip.

Pappy said that Hubert's reputation had preceded him. He had heard of the wild wheelstanding Falcon from the South and its even wilder pilot. He wasn't so sure about turning this loose on his track for safety's sake. Doug explained that Hubert was letting him drive because a few days earlier, while working on the car, Hubert's ring arced off the battery and burned his hand. Pappy, feeling much more comfortable with the local guy at the wheel, allowed the Falcon to run.

When Doug dropped the clutch and left the line with the front wheels in the air, he was instantly hooked. He loved the excitement of this little AWB drag car so much he immediately started to work on one of his own: a 1965 Chevy II Nova that Bee would name the *Chevy 2 Much*.

#### *Money Machine*

After Pappy saw the little Falcon in action, he allowed Hubert to make some test passes. When he saw the way Hubert handled the wheelstanding Falcon, bringing the front wheels off the ground in first, second, and third gear, he knew the West Coast fans would love the excitement created by this Southern thriller. He asked Hubert to stay until the next Saturday with the promise of a $500 match race. Hubert agreed, and he and Bee stayed on with Doug and Betty.

The following Saturday at Lions, Pappy booked Hubert a match race with a fuel altered that had a fiberglass body with no roof. Hubert ran the little Falcon on a nitro mixture and won the match race on the first three passes to the delight of the fans. They loved the quick jumping starts of the AWB machine, which seemed to leap off of the line at the drop of the green light with 6-foot-high wheelstands.

The following Monday, Hubert and Bee were preparing to head for home when Pappy made a personal trip to Doug's house with an offer for Hubert. Pappy told him that the past Saturday's match race was a huge success, and if Hubert would stay until the next weekend, Pappy could get him a match race in Fontana Dragway on Friday, one at Lions on Saturday, and then at another track on Sunday, each paying $500 to show. Hubert quickly agreed, knowing that was more money than he had ever made in a week.

To put this into the proper context, in 1965, the average US worker made less than $100 a week. Throughout the rest of his life, Hubert was often quoted saying "I wish I had all the money I made with the Falcon. It made me two fortunes."

### The Grudge Match Continues

When Hubert transformed the *Smallest Georgia Shaker* into the *Georgia Shaker III*, Huston was working on his own AWB ride. Huston acquired a very rare AWB 1965 Fastback Chevy II from Bill Thomas Race Cars. With these new AWB cars on alcohol and sometimes nitro, the brothers continued booking match races coast to coast. Fans and promoters alike were always eager to witness the antics of the wild brothers from down South who never failed to fill the stands and entertain the crowds.

*Hubert was best known for the wheelstanding Ford Falcon, the Georgia Shaker III. Hubert said "I took that car to California, and it made me famous." It became Hubert's most iconic ride.*

*This is the cover of a rare program for a Platt brothers famous grudge match held at Delmar Dragway in Delmar, Delaware. Inside, the program states that this was to be a rematch of the October 31 battle that ended in a tie when the* Dixie Twister *sustained damage to the front when it make contact with the guardrail in the third round.*

### "Run Whatcha Brung"

Since the beginning of organized drag racing, there had been class racing. In 1951, the NHRA established Unmodified Stock and Modified Production. The classes, the rules, and restrictions grew from there, and by the 1960s there were more classes than you could keep up with from Stock to Nitro Dragsters.

In the South in the early 1960s, a promoter not affiliated with a sanctioning body could rent a track or an airstrip and put on a race. The classes that would be at one of these races depended on who or rather what cars showed up. Many times, there would not be enough cars to fill the ladder of a certain class, especially when the A/FX cars started morphing and things quickly got really confusing.

Promoters knew it was all about filling the grandstands and entertaining the fans, so when there were

***The Platt ladies represent for their husbands' good friend Doug. Annlyn, Huston's wife, is on the left, and Bee, Hubert's wife, is on the right. The bouffant hairstyles were all the rage in the mid 1960s.***

*The* Georgia Shaker III *Falcon gave Hubert his first taste of national recognition in Southern-style "Run Whatcha Brung" drag racing. Hubert is accredited for introducing this style of drag racing to Southern California in 1965 with this car.*

*Hubert always paid attention to detail, not just in the performance of his cars but in looks as well. The dashboard of the* Georgia Shaker III *had hand-painted pinstriping, much like the So-Cal custom show cars of the time.*

*Jumping off the cover of this magazine, the* Georgia Shaker III *was one of the most radical national touring drag cars in 1965.*

uneven classes, they would throw class rules out the window and race the cars that had shown up. It was an anything goes kind of thing. The faster cars would generally give a head start or a couple of car lengths to the slower vehicles to put on a good show. This Southern-style racing was called "Run Whatcha Brung." Some promoters even billed the races as such, and it eventually became a class.

Many times, the *Georgia Shaker III* was the only AWB injected car at a local event. Hubert would end up racing one of the dragsters or fuel altereds on hand. It was all to entertain the fans and keep them coming back to see who would be the fastest next week.

### Home-Built Long-Nose Mustang

Although Hubert had worked hard to keep up with the factory guys, it wasn't over yet. Dick Brannan and Phil Bonner both had successful Falcons, but they were now also testing and racing the new and incredibly popular 2+2 Fastback Mustang. They both had short AWB versions and the radical-looking long-nose AWB versions, both powered by SOHC.

Seeing how many cars the factory had given these guys really upset Hubert. He felt left out. Hadn't he done

*Hubert found and purchased this brand-new 1965 2+2 Sports Roof Mustang, which had been rolled by its unlucky new owner. Hubert's younger son Allen, not even two years old, is admiring the wreck.*

enough on the national stage, with tons of fans, magazine covers, and promoters calling every week wanting him at their track? He didn't understand it, but he didn't give up either. He loved this life, and his drive and ambition led him to continue to fight the factory in the A/FX war.

Some may say this was crazy. For the factory, building a drag car was not a big deal. It would send a brand-new body in white off to a race car shop such as Dearborn Steel Tubing or Holman & Moody and a team of specialists would use an unlimited supply of performance parts to build and complete a project. For an independent builder like Hubert, it didn't go quite like that. First, he had to search garages, body shops, and junk yards for a brand-new car that may have met an early demise.

In the early fall of 1965, Hubert found just the thing: a 1965 Mustang 2+2 Fastback that had been rolled. It had substantial damage to its roof, hood, front fenders, one door, and one quarter panel. The damage was so extensive that the car had been declared totaled. Much like Dr. Frankenstein, Hubert took the lifeless, mangled Mustang to his basement laboratory and began its transformation.

Hubert and Larry Yates worked day and night for eight straight days, producing one of the coolest home-built drag cars of all time. They started by gutting the car, straightening the body, and altering the wheelbase. First, they moved the rear wheels 2 inches forward. Then, they stretched the frame by lengthening the front end with 2x3-inch rectangular tubing, moving the front wheels a full 12 inches forward. The car received a full roll cage for safety, but it only had a windshield, with no side glass or back windshield.

The Holman & Moody cars had almost completely fiberglass bodies. Hubert's Mustang had an all-steel body

*Hubert's home-built long-nose Mustang was every bit as beautiful as the cars built at Holman & Moody at the time. Hubert seemed to be getting the same performance from the Wedge as the factory cars were from the SOHC.*

*In late fall of 1965, a packed crowd was on hand at Lions Drag Strip in Long Beach, California, to witness one of the first West Coast outings of the home-built long-nose Mustang. Lions Drag Strip was the premier place to see the most cutting-edge drag cars in Southern California, which was a hotbed of drag racing activity on the West Coast.*

*Hubert sits poised and ready in his silver fire suit. The Mustang was equipped with a full roll cage, which was much safer than the five-point roll bar in the Falcon.*

*The custom elements of this radical 1965 drag car are many. From the stretched front end to the shaved taillights, fans were in awe that this brand-new 1965 Sports Roof Mustang had been transformed into a Funny Car.*

*The original setback of the big-block 427 was just a few inches into the cowl. The engine would be relocated and set back much farther in the months to come.*

*The second setback of the engine required shorter stacks on the 427 Wedge to clear the cowl and the bottom of the windshield. The Mustang ran in the low 9s at more than 140 mph in this configuration.*

The long-nose Mustang had an axle front end much like the Falcon. With such a crude front suspension, the cars were a handful to drive.

*It was all business for Hubert in the home-built 1965 long-nose Mustang. The only necessities in the gutted interior were the seat, steering wheel, three pedals, Hurst floor shift, and the three gauges (a Sun tachometer, oil pressure, and water temperature).*

*With the new motor placement, the driver's seat had to be moved back to accommodate for the new transmission location. The large sheet metal firewall could be removed to access the engine from the interior.*

*Hubert was a standout and fan favorite at Lions Drag Strip in Long Beach. Hubert would say, "I got famous out at Lions in California."*

*The Ford versus Chevy match races between Hubert and Dickie Harrell were legendary. Hubert is shown here with his trademark cigar and the long-nose Mustang now sporting a "Dick Walters Ford" sponsor graphic.*

with a fiberglass front end that had the fenders and hood extended 14 inches to compensate for the modifications. Like this, it weighed in at 2,360 pounds. It later received an upgrade of fiberglass doors, which reduced the weight even more. All the fiberglass work was done by A & A Engineering.

Hubert's Mustang had a leaf spring–style axle front end. It had a Mooneyes fuel tank in front of its set-back 427 Wedge powerplant, which was pushing 650 hp, with a C-T Super Stock crankshaft, Hilborn injectors, and a Vertex Magneto. The engine was originally set back so far that the cowl was notched out to the back of the stock vent for clearance of the back four injector stacks. It had a 4-speed transmission with a Hurst floor shift, giving the power to a Ford rear end with 4.11:1 gears and welded rectangular-tube traction bars. On the ground were a set of 10.5-inch Goodyear slicks.

The Mustang was painted bright Ford Blue like the *Little Georgia Shaker*, the *Smallest Georgia Shaker*, and the *Georgia Shaker III* before it, but it was named simply *Georgia Shaker*. White and red lettering let everyone know it was "Cragar Equipped" and also was sporting a "Crane Cam" as well as "Headers By Doug." There was also one large decal boasting a

ORANGE COUNTY
GOLD CUP RACE – AT LIONS
SPECIAL SALUTE TO ALL RACERS FROM ORANGE COUNTY
16 FUELERS QUALIFY TO RUN FOR TOTAL FUEL PURSE OF $2000!!
★ FEATURE MATCH RACE ★
HUBERT PLATT'S
"FUNNY" MUSTANG
WILL RACE
DOUG HEADERS
"CHEVY TOO MUCH"
PLUS THE USUAL TOP GAS, JR. FUEL, ALTEREDS, COMP. ELIM., & A/GAS SUPERCHARGED
LIONS DRAG STRIP
223RD & ALAMEDA, WILMINGTON
$2.00 ADMISSION
PHONE 424-0961
AHRA SANCTION
SAT. NITE DEC. 11th

*Best buddies, Doug Thorley and Hubert Platt, look like they are ready for an Apollo mission in their silver Bell fire suits. The dapper pair were regulars on C.J. "Pappy" Hart's roster of drivers. They continually match raced the* Chevy 2 Much *and the* Georgia Shaker *long-nose Mustang.*

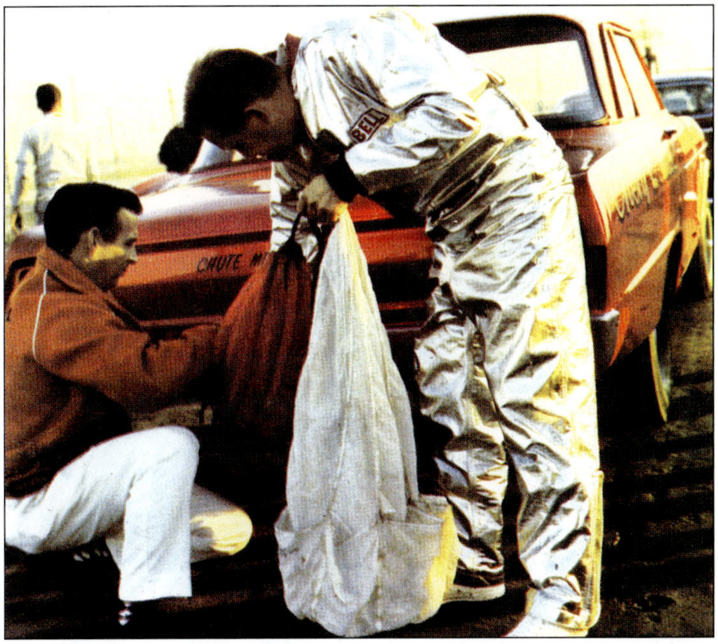

*Strong competitors on the track but great friends off, Hubert and Doug Thorley pack the chute of the* Chevy 2 Much. *The two would battle it out many times at Lions Drag Strip.*

"Hurst Floor Shift." Hubert's total investment in this car was $6,000, including the payment for the wrecked body.

After touring the AWB long-nose Mustang with great success over the winter months of 1965, Hubert decided to sell the *Georgia Shaker III* to racer Howard Pasley. Pasley renamed it the *Flying Falcon* and continued to race it around the South.

After the first few months of racing and testing the long-nose Mustang from Georgia to California and all points in between, Hubert decided to take it back to the basement and make some changes. He used lower injector stacks and set the engine back even farther. He moved it so far that the front of the engine was even with the front of the cowl. A custom but somewhat crude aluminum firewall was built in the interior to cover the engine, and the driver's seat was set back to accommodate the new engine and transmission placement.

Soon, Hubert was back on the West Coast touring the long-nose Mustang. He found even more fame, racing it as much as three times a week in match races that had four- and eight-car matchups in the newly named "Funny Car" field. The Mustang held its own with the best in the country, running low 9s at 140 mph and faster.

On Saturday, December 18, 1965, Pappy Hart staged a best two-out-of-three match race between Hubert in the long-nose Mustang and Doug Thorley in his *Chevy 2 Much*. It wasn't Hubert's day when best-buddy Doug won two straight in the little Chevy, screaming to a final-round victory with a 9.72 at 149.50 mph.

## National Recognition

In November 1965, the *Georgia Shaker III* Falcon graced the cover of *Drag Racing* magazine. Inside, there was a four-page article with nine photographs of the wheelstanding Falcon in action, photos of Hubert posing with the car, and some of Larry Yates working on it as well. Two months later in January 1966, the *Georgia Shaker* long-nose Mustang was featured on the cover of *Tach Magazine*. In just seven months, Hubert's last three cars had graced the covers of car-enthusiast magazines.

Then in the April 1966 issue of *Modern Rod Magazine,* Hubert was featured in a four-page spread with an interview and 12 pictures of the *Georgia Shaker* Mustang and the *Georgia Shaker III* Falcon, which Hubert had already sold. In the days before social media, this was a huge deal that obtained Hubert national recognition and kept him and his fast cars in the spotlight.

*The January 1966 issue of* Tach *magazine featured Hubert's home-built long-nose Mustang at Beeline Dragway in Phoenix, Arizona, on its cover. This type of coverage kept Hubert's name in the limelight.*

*Over the years, many fans believed that this photo was taken of an exhibition run. On the contrary, it was taken during a match race at Lions Drag Strip at the AHRA Grand American meet, where Hubert won the final round over Dickie Harrell. Hubert had just installed new fiberglass doors that hadn't yet been painted.*

*By the time this magazine hit the newsstands in May 1966, Hubert had already sold the* Georgia Shaker III *Falcon, but he enjoyed the publicity nonetheless.*

### Drag Strip Antics

Hubert (known to his loyal fans as "Hu-Baby") loved to put on a show and be the center of attention. He was a joker at heart and loved to get a laugh. In the early 1960s, when the announcer would interview drivers on the starting line, Hubert loved to taunt the other drivers. He was always willing to mix it up with his quick wit and a joke. An announcer might ask "Do you plan on beating your opponent?" to which Hubert would reply "I'm going to beat him like a drum." He would say or do anything to get a rise out of the fans, even running over and kissing the prettiest girl on the fence and saying, "I'm gonna win this one for you!"

Hubert and Dickie Harrell were match race rivals who put on Ford versus Chevy races all across the country. The two loved to cut up and joke with one another. They would switch cars on the starting line. Hubert would give Dickie his cigar and jump into the stands, grabbing a front row seat. When asked by the announcer what he was doing, he'd reply, "It's going to be such a good race I want to watch it."

Once during qualifying at the Indy Nationals, Hubert stalled his car at half track, got out, and looked under the hood. All of the fans were on the edge of their seats, waiting to see what the problem was. Hubert emerged from under the hood holding a rubber chicken by the neck, shaking it over his head. The fans went crazy and laughter rose up from the stands.

Even though he was dubbed the "Clown Prince of Drag Racing," Hubert's antics thrilled the fans much more than they would make them laugh. At a meet in south Texas, Hubert was doing his burnout when he noticed the guardrail next to the starting line was loose, vibrating, and about to fall off. He pulled right next to it, pushed in the clutch, and revved the engine as loud as it would go until the engine's vibration blew the guardrail off its wooden post. The fans went wild, and the story spread like wildfire. It became instant folklore that Hubert Platt's Ford was powerful enough to blow a guardrail off its post.

Hubert's bag of tricks was deep, but the one he became known for was doing huge wheelstands while

## The *Georgia Shaker* in Drag

In a match race in Houston, Texas, Hubert was scheduled to race friend and rival Shirley Shahan, the *Drag-On-Lady*. Before time trials started, Hubert put on his silver fire suit and a blonde wig and drove Shirley's Mopar to the starting line, impersonating the "Drag-On-Lady." When he stepped out onto the track and waved to the fans, he got a huge laugh and standing ovation.

When the jokes were over, the two got down to business. Shirley showed the fans she was all business, winning the first two rounds. Hubert then poured it on strong to win rounds three and four. However, this match ended in a draw when the transmission of Shirley's Mopar broke before the last run.

*Hubert, whom the press often referred to as the "Clown Prince of Drag Racing," was quite possibly the first drag racer in drag. He played it up when he put on a blonde wig and drove the Drag-On-Lady's Mopar up to the starting line in Houston, Texas.*

The Iowa Shaker *was a 1964 Falcon, but Hubert removed the 1964 trim when he got it. He painted it blue and raced it as a 1965. This is how the car looked when Hubert first saw it.*

*These custom fender well headers by Doug all collect on the outside of the frame rail, unlike the set on the* Georgia Shaker III, *which were braided over both sides of the frame. (Photo Courtesy Gary Weyrick)*

holding the driver's door open. To drop the clutch on a 750-hp nitro-burning drag car is one thing, but to do it while holding the door open is another. Most men don't have the nerve to do the first.

Reporters nationwide wrote of Hubert's showmanship and his ability to mix "a little nonsense" with hard racing, which went a long way toward giving the fans more than their money's worth. In piece after piece, Hubert was praised for bringing his Southern charm, hospitality, and big personality to ensure fans coast to coast were treated to an entertaining show and not just a race.

## The *Iowa Shaker*

Hubert was often on the road and far from home, and from time to time he found himself in need of somewhere to work on the car. He would sometimes stop at local race shops. He made one such stop in Southern California at Performance Associates, famed Ford racer Les Ritchey's shop. While he was working on regular maintenance of the long-nose Mustang, he was approached by Dick Walters, a Ford man whose dealership was in Des Moines, Iowa.

The Iowa Shaker *had a distinctive Mustang front gravel pan and bumper. The rear end has been altered more and had different wheel openings than the* Georgia Shaker III, *making it easy to tell the two Falcons apart. (Photo Courtesy Michael Goyda)*

Walters showed Hubert a Holman & Moody–built AWB Falcon that he owned. Les had been working on it and having problems. Walters knew of Hubert's success with the *Georgia Shaker III* and asked if Hubert would be interested in helping get the Falcon running properly. He told Hubert he would make it worth his while. Hubert agreed and worked on the Falcon late into the night, adjusting the injection and the suspension.

The next day, they took the newly tuned up Falcon to Lions Drag Strip for testing. The car ran great, better than it ever had. Dick Walters recognized that with Hubert under the hood and behind the wheel, this one was sure to be a huge success. He offered Hubert a sponsorship deal on the spot, giving him the Falcon and a truck that would haul two race cars.

Walters had one stipulation. Hubert was to name the car the *Iowa Shaker* to represent his dealership back home. Hubert agreed, and soon after had the Falcon

*The "Dick Walters" two-car team was a real eye catcher going down the road, especially with the* Georgia Shaker *Mustang perched over the cab. Hubert had a reserved parking space at Lions Drag Strip, as you can see by his nameplate on the fence. (Photo Courtesy Gary Weyrick)*

*The* Iowa Shaker *was looking fresh and new at Lions Drag Strip. Watertight injector covers are a must on a car being transported on an open truck.*

***Race cars in the driveway were the norm at the Platt house. Growing up going to the drag races was definitely a unique and fun way for a little boy to grow up. Not long after this picture was taken, Hubert's youngest son, Allen, made his first cross-country trip with Hubert to California.***

painted blue to match the Mustang, but he gave the *Iowa Shaker* gold leaf lettering for an ultra-flashy look. The *Iowa Shaker* was lettered by a teenage Chuck Carman, who is now a well-known hot rod artist. He recalls how particular Hubert was about the lettering on this new ride, right down to the curves in the letters of his name.

After the first of the year, the *Georgia Shaker* Mustang also received a lettering upgrade, now sporting "Dick Walters Ford" sponsorship on the doors. The two-car team was a great-looking pair on the big red Ford F-600 hauler. The custom ramps allowed the Mustang to park over the cab of the truck while the Falcon perched on the back, as it would on a regular ramp truck. This was one impressive-looking rig. Across the front of the hood, Hubert had painted "Here Comes Trouble." The doors of the truck had white squares with "Dick Walters Ford Racing Team" painted in black lettering.

**The Iowa Shaker *had a more radical altered wheelbase than the* Georgia Shaker III *and was the fastest of Hubert's Falcons.***

***It looks as if one of the injector covers is about to blow off. Maybe that's what this pit stop is about. (Photo Courtesy Michael Goyda)***

Hubert and family made several trips cross country in this rig in the early part of 1966, racing at all the tracks along the way. The *Iowa Shaker* recorded a pass of 9.21 at 160 mph at Irwindale Raceway in California, making it Hubert's fastest race car to date.

## Wheelstand Mishap

The long-nose Mustang was a beautiful car, and it seemed to jump off the starting line with even bigger wheelstands than the *Georgia Shaker III* Falcon. It regularly put the back bumper on the track when it would leave the line. A lot of the altered-wheelbase cars were doing big wheelstands now, much to the joy of the spectators. Pappy Hart at Lions Drag Strip was inspired to make wheelstands into a contest, offering a free case of oil or another similar prize for whoever could do the highest wheelstand.

Fellow competitor Dickie Harrell would do a huge wheelstand off the starting line and then stop just before

*Given the volatile nature of exotic fuels such as alcohol (methanol) and nitromethane, the fire suit was mandatory. Hubert looks right at home in this silver edition from Bell. You can tell this was after a run because of the parachute cords in the passenger window.*

***The Hilborn-injected 427 FE powerplant on nitromethane blasted the* Iowa Shaker *to speeds of more than 160 mph. (Photo Courtesy Michael Goyda)***

the finish line and pop it up again to excite the fans at the end of the track. Not to be outdone, Hubert would sometimes put a toolbox in the trunk to help him win the contest (extra weight in the back equals a higher wheelstand).

On one such occasion, Hubert hit the gas and the Mustang stood up, forcing the back bumper down onto the track so hard that the car was damaged. The trunk flew open and the toolbox fell out, scattering tools all the way down the track and shutting the race down for more than an hour while they picked the tools up!

When the track was cleared, Hubert returned to the starting line in the *Iowa Shaker* Falcon, determined to put on a show for the inconvenienced fans. Hubert launched off the line, pulling a series of huge wheelstands in first, second, and third gear. He turned around at the halfway point and did the same stunt back, stopping just before the starting line with both front wheels bent in at 45-degree angles with broken spindles. Hubert climbed out with a huge Southern grin on his face and told the fans, "I've broken two cars for y'all, and if I had a third, I'd break that one for you as well."

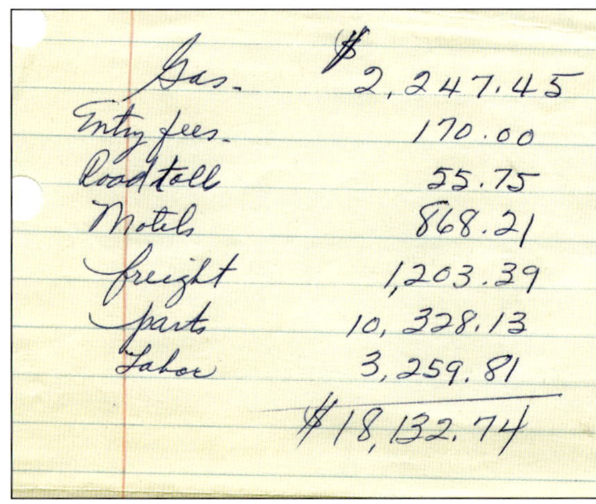

| | |
|---|---|
| Gas. | $ 2,247.45 |
| Entry fees. | 170.00 |
| Road toll | 55.75 |
| Motels | 868.21 |
| freight | 1,203.39 |
| parts | 10,328.13 |
| Labor | 3,259.81 |
| | $18,132.74 |

***This note in Hubert's wife Bee's handwriting details the cost of drag racing in 1965. The freight was for having parts shipped from California to Atlanta throughout the year.***

## Falcon Road Racer

Late in 1965, Hubert was in Detroit at one of Ford's test facilities when he noticed a 1965 Falcon Road Race car was parked out back. It had been used as a test vehicle then stripped and discarded. The car had no drivetrain, but it did have a fiberglass hood, fenders, doors, decklid, and dashboard. Hubert knew this would make a great drag car, so he asked the powers that be if he could have the used racer.

At first, he got the runaround. He just kept on asking, and finally they gave him the car. He took the little Falcon home to his basement garage and built a replica of the *Georgia Shaker III*. When he completed the build, he sold the car to Tommy McNeely, who raced the car at first but then made an exhibition wheelstander out of it. This car was the third of Hubert's three Falcons.

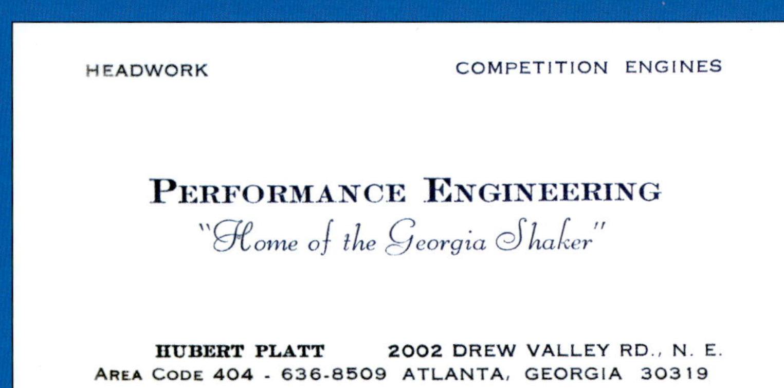

HEADWORK — COMPETITION ENGINES

PERFORMANCE ENGINEERING

"Home of the Georgia Shaker"

HUBERT PLATT — 2002 DREW VALLEY RD., N. E.

AREA CODE 404 - 636-8509 ATLANTA, GEORGIA 30319

***The speed shop that Hubert ran out of the single-car basement garage at his home was called Performance Engineering. He specialized in building racing engines and doing custom head work for competitors all around the South. This is also where he built his two famous home-built drag cars: the* Georgia Shaker III *Falcon and the blue long-nose Mustang.***

# CHAPTER 6

# THE ONE-PIECE BODY MUSTANG

In 1965, drag racing saw its biggest developments to date. The A/FX class went from stock-bodied cars with full interiors to extended tube chassis covered in aluminum and fiberglass in a short 12-month period. In the second half of 1965, it was rumored that Fran Hernandez and his assistant, Al Turner, at Lincoln/Mercury Racing Division had commissioned four custom 1966 Comets from Logghe Stamping Company in Fraser, Michigan. The Comets were to be rail dragsters that had a dragster chassis with a one-piece fiberglass body. Logghe built the chassis, and the bodies were built two hours away in Jackson, Michigan, by Plastigauge Corporation. The cars were to be powered by a 427 SOHC on nitro.

## The First Real Funny Cars

Word spread that the first two cars would be ready for the 1966 Winternationals and piloted by "Dyno" Don Nicholson and "Fast Eddie" Schartman. Feeling under the gun once again to maintain a public image of equality, Hubert told his partner and sponsor, Dick Walters, that to keep up in the 1966 season they needed to have a "sho-nuff" race car.

While the Comets were being built up north, Hubert felt his best professional race car connections were in Southern California. The day after Thanksgiving 1965, Dick Walters picked Hubert up in Atlanta in his twin-engine Beechcraft airplane, and they flew west. The two made a stop in Las Vegas, where Hubert played craps for two days straight, winning a grand total of $30,000. The next day, he spent more than half of the winnings. When asked years later what he had spent the money on, he said, "You name it." After three days in Sin City, the high rollers boarded the Beechcraft and continued the journey into So-Cal, Hubert with more than $10,000 in his pocket.

There were many shops building race cars as well as customs in Los Angeles. The area was on the cutting edge of the high-performance automotive industry. Hubert enlisted the help of future drag racing legend Pat Foster from Van Nuys, California. At the time, Pat worked for Frank Huszar at Race Car Specialties in Tarzana. The shop had been building and selling dragster chassis for years to successful racers including Connie Kalitta. Hubert knew this was the kind of shop it would take to design and build this new type of Funny Car.

Although the Comet Funny Cars were to almost exactly mimic the size and shape of the production car, Hubert decided to have his new Funny Car built off of the already successful long-nose Mustang platform. Hubert ordered and paid cash for the car with the understanding that it wouldn't be ready for several months.

## Tragedy on the Highway

Throughout the beginning of the 1966 season, Hubert waited for the completion of his one-piece body Mustang Funny Car, but he wasn't sitting idle. The drag racing scene was exploding with the A/FX cars morphing into what had become a full-blown Funny Car class. Hubert was right in the middle of the action, booking match races every weekend coast to coast. He was still enjoying much success match racing the blue, home-built, long-nose Mustang and the *Iowa Shaker* Falcon.

While on a West Coast swing in California, Hubert hired a man to drive the racing rig to meet him in Detroit. Hubert had a match race scheduled for Saturday, May 14, at Motor City Dragway against Kelly Chadwick's fastback Chevy II that had been advertised as a Nitro Showdown. On Friday, May 13, the unthinkable happened.

The man Hubert had hired to drive the rig lost control, running into a ditch. The truck tipped over, destroying the long-nose Mustang race car strapped on top. The damage was so bad that the wild wheelstanding Mustang that had gained Hubert so much popularity was sent to the scrapyard.

Knowing the new Funny Car would be ready within the next couple weeks, Hubert sold the *Iowa Shaker* Falcon to Gene Loflin. Gene was sponsored by Salinas California Ford, and he continued to race the car on the West Coast.

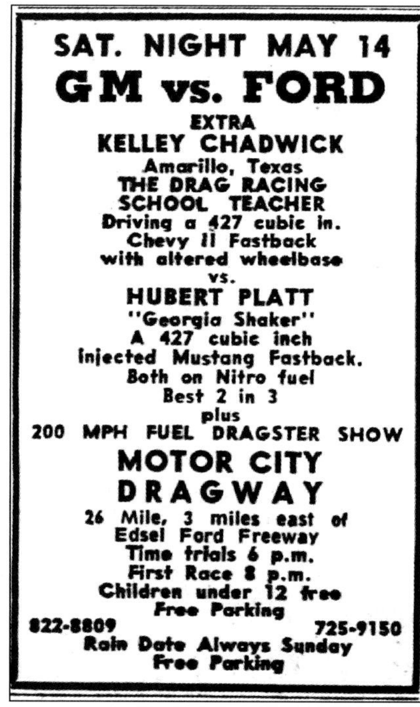
SAT. NIGHT MAY 14
GM vs. FORD
EXTRA
KELLEY CHADWICK
Amarillo, Texas
THE DRAG RACING
SCHOOL TEACHER
Driving a 427 cubic in.
Chevy II Fastback
with altered wheelbase
vs.
HUBERT PLATT
"Georgia Shaker"
A 427 cubic inch
Injected Mustang Fastback.
Both on Nitro fuel
Best 2 in 3
plus
200 MPH FUEL DRAGSTER SHOW
MOTOR CITY
DRAGWAY
26 Mile, 3 miles east of
Edsel Ford Freeway
Time trials 6 p.m.
First Race 8 p.m.
Children under 12 free
Free Parking
822-8809 725-9150
Rain Date Always Sunday
Free Parking

*The blue home-built long-nose Mustang was destroyed in a towing accident when the truck tipped over. The car was put in the scrap-yard and never rebuilt.*

### Race Car Specialties Comes Through

The Funny Car produced by Race Car Specialties per Hubert's request was nothing short of automotive artistry. It had a beautifully constructed chrome-moly tube chassis made from 1¾ inch-0.145 and 1½ inch-0.058 tubing and a custom-made tube-axle front end with no leaf springs. It had a forward-extending torsion bar assembly. The up and down travel of the front axle was limited by the upper and lower frame rails. It used drag-link steering with the cross-drag link bar located in front of the front frame vertical member.

The car was powered by 427 SOHC that had a CSC 3/8 stroker crank, Mickey Thompson rods and pistons, high-performance Crane cams, Jocko's ported and polished heads with stock valves, Hilborn injectors, a Vertex Magneto, and a set of Doug's Headers. The power was transferred through a modified Fordomatic C-6 Art Carr racing transmission with a 5,000-stall torque converter. The Ford rear end had 4.11:1 gears that used Watts linkage with coilover springs.

On the rear only there were Airheart/Cragar disc brakes pressured by a 1-inch Girling master cylinder, which would attempt to slow down the 10.5-inch Goodyear slicks. It sported Cragar S/S mags all the way around. The front tires were Pirelli Cinturatos. A good bit longer than the Holman & Moody long-nose Mustangs or Hubert's home-built long-nose Mustang, the new car had a wheelbase of 143 inches.

At the time, Pat Foster was drag racing a Corvette owned and sponsored by Corvette Auto Parts owner Don Kirby. These two worked together to modify a multipiece fiberglass body purchased from Cal Automotive in North Hollywood to create the first one-piece body Mustang. The body was not hinged like the Comets, but it could be lifted off by two men (one in the front and one at the back bumper) and easily set to one side for full access to the race car.

This body had no side windows, only a front and back windshield. The rear windshield had 1-inch holes drilled into it spelling out the word "Ford." The body was two-tone metallic blue and silver painted by Don Kirby. Doug Kruse of Kruse Engineering in Long Beach, California, did all the custom interior aluminum work, which had a Zeus buttoned-down transmission cover for easy access.

*The Ford 427 single overhead cam (SOHC) race engine was never made available in a production vehicle. This was Hubert's first of three Mustangs that would have SOHC power. This was also Hubert's first race car with an automatic transmission.*

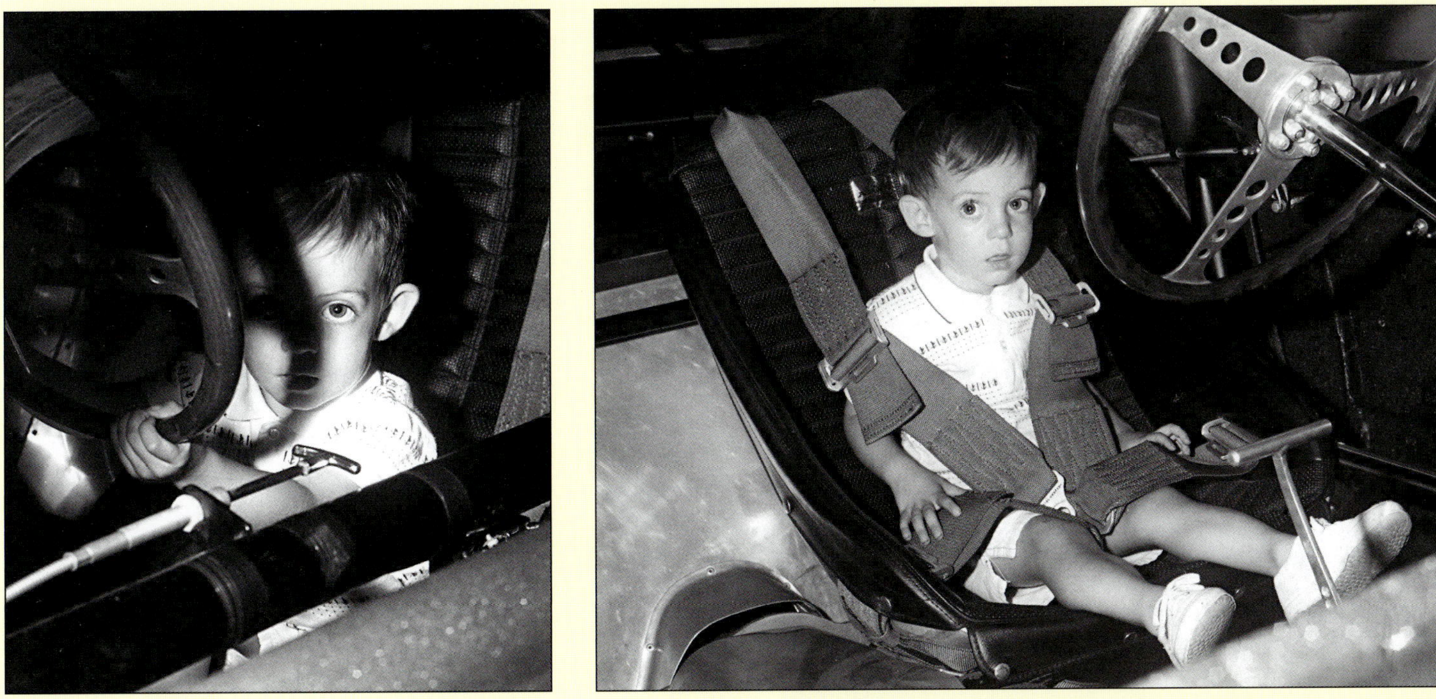

***Hubert's youngest son, Allen, prepares himself for another run down the make-believe drag strip in the one-piece body Mustang. This was obviously way more fun than playing in imaginary race cars.***

The ultra-safe roll cage was covered in a new padding material called Armaflex by the Armstrong Company. Other safety equipment included a parachute and Novel transmission blast shield made of a nylon material as well as the seat belt harness, all products of Chute Metal Company. The car had a race-ready weight of 1,740 pounds.

### *Summer of 1966*

Hubert was very excited when he debuted the new Mustang Funny Car at Lions Drag Strip in Long Beach on June 25, 1966, for the 5,736 fans on hand. Although the car was not ready and did not compete, he took time before the first round to tow the car up to the starting line without the body on. He was proud of its ultra-safe roll cage and let the fans get a close look.

This car would record a few firsts for Hubert. It was the first time he got behind a 427 SOHC engine (the Falcons and the home-built long-nose Mustang had 427 Wedge powerplants). The one-piece body Mustang was Hubert's first race car with an automatic transmission. It was also the beginning of a relationship between himself and painter Max Thompson of Alpharetta, Georgia.

Max lettered the one-piece body Mustang quite simply, similar to its predecessors. It wore the moniker *Georgia Shaker*. Below the driver's window in large letters was painted "Hubert Platt" and beneath that all the way down the side it read "Dick Walters Ford." On the

***After picking up the one-piece body Mustang in Southern California and unveiling it at Lions, its official racing debut was on the way back to Georgia at Houston Drag Raceway in Dickinson, Texas. Hubert lost the match race to Kelly Chadwick's stretched Chevy II Funny Car when the Mustang broke the rear end in the final round.***

front fender it boasted "Crane Cams" and "Cragar," and on the rocker panel it read "Headers by Doug." On the quarter panel behind the rear tire, it gave props to "Race Car Specialties," "C-T Automotive," "Art Carr Transmissions," "A & A Engineering," and "Lettered by Thompson's Body Shop Alpharetta, Georgia." The car was completely hand lettered with no contingency stickers or decals.

*Super Stock News* advertised the East Coast debut of the one-piece body Mustang on July 3 and 4 at Suffolk International Raceway, in Portsmouth, Virginia. The ad billed the first East Coast appearance of Hubert's new 1966 SOHC Mustang as the main attraction.

The following month, Hubert lined up against brother Huston on Saturday, August 13, in Biloxi, Mississippi.

This was the first one-piece body Mustang ever built. It would mark the beginning of a long-standing relationship between Hubert and painter Max Thompson, who lettered the car. Max would be Hubert's go-to painter for the rest of his career.

*Loaded for travel, the one-piece body Mustang's long wheelbase barely fits on the ramp truck. Notice that the rear window has "Ford" spelled out in vent holes.*

*In another of their legendary brother-versus-brother grudge matches, Hubert lined up the one-piece body Mustang against brother Huston's 1966 Chevy II Funny Car. The* Dixie Twister *was billed as the world's fastest unblown Chevy.*

Hubert tuned the SOHC for its next run as a flock of interested young men looked on.

Hubert was an excellent mechanic. He was always making things right between rounds.

Hubert heated the tires in preparation for his next run at Biloxi Drag Strip.

Huston was in his 1966 AWB Chevy II for another episode of their brother-versus-brother grudge matches. This time it was a nitro Funny Car Ford versus Chevy battle.

Rather than hinge the body, two men could completely remove and set aside the one-piece body of the Mustang, giving full access to everything and making it easy to complete maintenance between rounds.

### Still in the Spotlight

In October 1966, *Hotrod Parts Illustrated* ran a cover story on the one-piece body Mustang. The cover of the magazine featured a full-color shot of the car without the body on it. Inside, the two-page, 10-picture spread detailed the inner workings of the technical racer.

Articles continued to keep Hubert in the nationwide drag racing spotlight. The fans could always keep up with what he was doing.

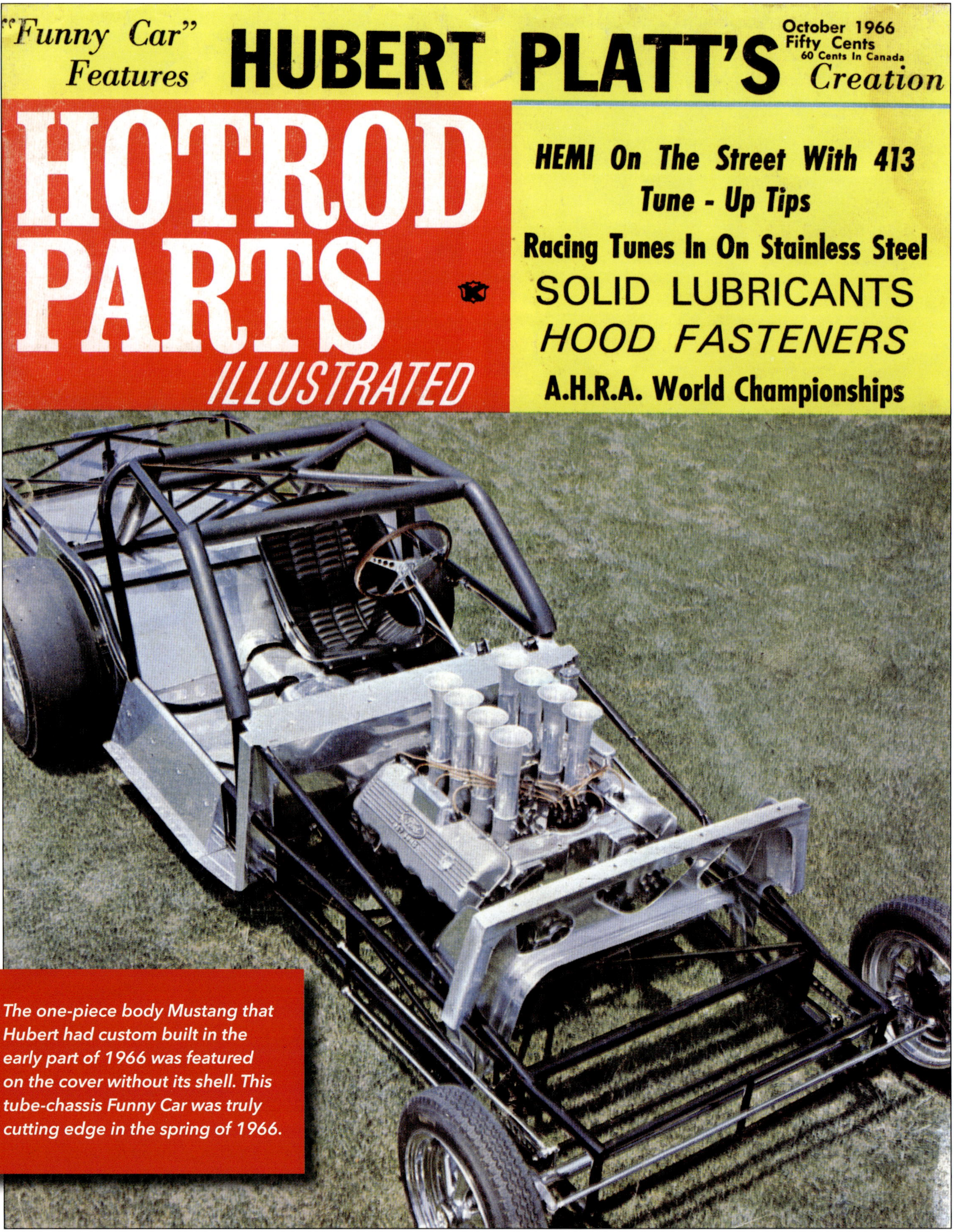


*The one-piece body Mustang that Hubert had custom built in the early part of 1966 was featured on the cover without its shell. This tube-chassis Funny Car was truly cutting edge in the spring of 1966.*

# CHAPTER 7

# THE FACTORY COMES KNOCKING

In the beginning of 1966, Ford was doing a lot of testing on its two versions of the altered-wheelbase 427 SOHC drag Mustangs under the supervision of Dick Brannan, who was now head of Ford Drag Racing Operations. Early in the year, Brannan won the NASCAR Drag Racing Championship at Daytona Beach, Florida, in an altered-wheelbase 427 SOHC Mustang. He shared driving duties with NASCAR wheelmen Fred Lorenzen and Curtis Turner.

In March, Brannan went on to win a match race against the *Seaton's Shaker* Chevelle Funny Car at Detroit Dragway. Things seemed like they were going well for Ford and its efforts testing and racing the Mustangs. Brannan was enjoying success, until the unthinkable happened. In April 1966, Brannan lost control of the fast Ultra Stock Mustang at speed. He was badly injured in a crash that destroyed the race car.

Three weeks later, Brannan was still injured when he got behind the wheel again and returned to competition. Some confused fans believed the wrecked Mustang had been repaired, but that race car had been rendered a total loss in the crash. Brannan was driving another Holman & Moody–built AWB, A/FX Mustang that he had been testing on alcohol and nitro. This Mustang was wilder than the first, resulting in yet another crash for Brannan.

***This is the aftermath of Dick Brannan's second crash in an SOHC altered-wheelbase Mustang. This car was totaled, and Brannan was badly injured. (Photo Courtesy Thomas Speight)***

## "One Hell of a Driver"

For more than two years, Hubert had been waiting for his chance with the factory. It was a chance he knew would eventually come, but he just didn't know when. Just six weeks into enjoying the most advanced race car he had owned to date (the one-piece body Mustang), he got the chance that he had been waiting for.

On Friday, August 5, 1966, Hubert was doing some testing at Old Dominion Speedway when he got his chance with Ford Motor Company. His friend and racing rival, Dick Brannan, offered Hubert the chance to drive for the factory.

Brannan told Hubert about his two recent drag racing accidents that left him badly injured and reluctant to continue driving the radical cars. Dick explained that the ever-increasing speeds of the nitro-fueled Funny Cars and their unpredictable handling traits combined with the huge workload Ford was putting on him had made him want to take a break. He was ready to give someone else a turn at these wild Mustangs.

Dick had his newest Holman & Moody–built, AWB SOHC long-nose Mustang at the track preparing to match race with Ronnie Sox in his Plymouth Barracuda. It was to be a Factory Funny Car showdown. Brannan's choice for a new driver was Hubert because of his reputation at the wheel. When Ford asked Dick why he picked Hubert, he told them, "He shows up on time, neat and clean, he does what I ask him to do, and he does it well. He's one hell of a driver." Hubert jumped at the chance to drive for the factory and agreed to race Sox.

The Mustang's wheelbase had been lengthened to improve the handling on these wild rides. The first race in the factory Mustang didn't go so well. Ronnie was on a roll, winning the first round while breaking his old track record at the eighth-mile facility of 5.84 with a 5.77 at 130 mph. As if that wasn't enough, Sox won the second round and the match with another record-breaking run 5.72 at 131 mph!

*Hubert had his game face on in the staging lanes between rounds, enjoying a cigar and checking everything out before his next run in the funny Mustang.*

Even though he didn't win, Dick thought Hubert handled the Funny Car beautifully. He asked Hubert to be the full-time driver, offering him a rate of $50 per day plus hotel and meals. Hubert accepted.

Although the one-piece body Mustang he had was technologically advanced, so was this Holman & Moody ride. It had a full tubular frame with a complete fiberglass body that did not come off. Instead, it had opening doors, a removable hood, and a decklid, but Hubert felt this wouldn't prevent it from being just as competitive as the one-piece body cars. At 2,400 pounds, the fuel-injected 427-ci SOHC engine with automatic racing transmission would eventually push Hubert to the fastest MPH and quickest ETs of his career.

### A Close Call

The following weekend, Brannan and Hubert took the gold long-nose Mustang out to Detroit Dragway for

*The quarter panels are still primered in gray after Hubert's slight brush with the wall in a test session at Detroit Dragway. Brannan's name stayed on the door the entire time he owned the car. Shortly after this photo was taken, the quarter panels were repainted gold and Hubert's name was put on the roof above the door.*

testing. The lengthened wheelbase of the Mustang was supposed to help the handling, but during the several tests they made, the car was all over the track.

It got so out of shape on the last run that the quarter panel scraped the guardrail, resulting in a trip to the body shop for a little fiberglass repair. With the team under the gun, there was no time for paint. They went to the next few races with the rear end of the Mustang primered in gray.

## Summer Championships

Hubert was very happy to have signed on as a Ford factory driver. What happened on the weekend of August 19–21, 1966, at West Salem Dragway 42 was the stuff that dreams are made of.

Brannan had the 427 SOHC Mustang ready to run at the highest level. He knew this car could have huge success with its new driver. The NASCAR Sanctioned Summer Championships was a who's who of the nation's 50 top Ultra Stock Funny Cars in an East-meets-West showdown.

On Thursday night before qualifying began, Brannan, Hubert, and the crew were fine-tuning the Mustang's setup for the weekend's competition. Hubert was concerned about the ill handling from the previous weekend. He was looking for anything that could be contributing to the problem. After an extensive inspection of the front suspension, Hubert noticed the tow-in on the front alignment was out 3/4 inch. This was corrected and believed to have helped the car go much straighter down the track.

***Hubert looks happy as can be after showing off his driving prowess in front of more than 11,000 fans. He had just set the national fuel record and won the Heads Up Eliminator title at the NASCAR Sanctioned Summer Championships in West Salem, Ohio. This was an East-meets-West showdown with 50 of the nation's top Funny Cars.***

Thursday and Friday's qualifying rounds saw the cars competing to stay within the top eight quickest ETs to hold a spot in Saturday night's running for the National Head's Up Eliminator Title. Hubert did very well smoking the competition, never losing a round in qualifying.

When Saturday night's first round came, Hubert was the number-one qualifier of the event. With Brannan's help in the pits and on the starting line, the Mustang got a big first-round win versus Billy McDull's *She Devil* (which had been Tommy Grove's *Charley Horse*). Hubert blasted to a record-setting 9.18 at 158.45 to put Billy on the trailer.

Bud Faubel beat the Ramchargers in the first round but wouldn't have enough for Hubert in the second round when Hu-Baby backed up his record-setting first round time with an almost exact ET of 9.18 at 159.73. Consistency is king in winning drag races. Having someone replace him wasn't easy, but Brannan knew he'd made the right choice in Hubert.

While Hubert was setting records in rounds one and two, Pete Gates in his flip-top Comet racked up a couple of wins with a 9.85 and 9.45 in his first and second rounds. A crowd of more than 11,000 fans had packed the grandstands on Saturday night. They were on their feet for the final round with Hubert in the gold long-nose Mustang squaring off against Gates in the red flip-top Comet.

Brannan admitted later that he held his breath on the starting line when Hubert got a little "out of shape" at half track. Hubert never lifted, keeping the accelerator to the floor. When the parachutes popped and the dust cleared, Hubert's win light was on. He beat Pete's best ET of the day (9.37 at 149.25 mph) when he passed through the traps with a 9.25 at 157.61 mph.

Winning this race solidified Hubert's spot in the driver's seat in the factory ride. He immediately sold the one-piece body Mustang he had at home to Dick Loehr, who painted the car red with a Max Curtis Ford Sponsor. This marked the end of Hubert's Dick Walters Ford sponsorship.

## Sibling Competition

Hubert raced the gold long-nose Mustang through the rest of the 1966 season under Brannan's ownership and supervision. In October, they set the A/XS NHRA national record with an 8.85 at 164.83.

That winter, Hubert faced off against his brother Huston at Aquasco Speedway in Maryland. Huston drove his 1966 Chevy II *Dixie Twister* Funny Car in another of the Platt brothers' legendary grudge matches. There

*Hubert and Huston go at it again in another of their famed brother-versus-brother/Ford-versus-Chevy grudge matches.*

was always a large crowd to see the brothers go at it in Ford-versus-Chevy action. People were so loyal to their brands in the 1960s, and the promoters really loved how this rivalry packed the stands.

Dick and Hubert worked well together. Brannan took care of the starting line prep, spreading the rosin and traction compounds, and Hubert easily won the first round with 8.68 at 162.16 mph versus Huston's 9.58 at 144 mph. In the second round, Hubert went 8.63 at 164.83 mph, but Huston broke a crankshaft, ending the Chevy II's day.

With Huston unable to continue, the track promoter found another opponent for Hubert. CC/FD dragster driver Dick Dickson would help Hubert put on a show for the fans. As the dragster and the long-nose Mustang staged, fans wondered if the full-bodied car could hold off the challenge of the rail. Hubert was a little eager and red lighted, but he stayed on the gas and clocked an 8.92 at 163.74 mph to Dickson's 10.43 at 157 mph.

### Color Me Gold

Next, Hubert took on Roger Lindamood's *Color Me Gone* Dodge in a race billed as a Mopar-versus-Ford Funny Car Showdown at Detroit Dragway. In a best-of-three match race, Lindamood suffered an upsetting lost in the first round when he red lighted and ran a 9.13 at 155 mph. Hubert passed him and ran an 8.95 at 165 mph.

The Mustang took the easy win the second round with an 8.92 at 161 mph to the Charger's 9.11 at 155 mph. Even though this was already in the bag for Hubert and Brannan, they lined up for a third round to the pleasure of the Ford fans. Roger tried to beat the Mustang off the line but red lighted again, running a 9.13 at 154. Hubert passed him at half-track for the undisputed win with an 8.97 at 163. The Mustang was definitely gold in Detroit!

### Track Record in Richmond

Brannan and Hubert took the gold long-nose Mustang to Richmond, Virginia, for a best-two-out-of-three match race against Joe Weis in his AWB Chevy II The *Swinger*. The rival Ford and Chevy fans lined the fence for round one to witness the Chevy II jumping off the line out in front of Hubert. The gold Mustang then stormed past Weis in high gear and took the win with an 8.87 at 161.29 mph to Weis's 9.80 at 134 mph.

The Chevy fans had their fingers crossed for round two to no avail. Hubert won again with an even faster 8.81 at 162 mph to Weis's 9.20 at 148 mph. With two straight wins, the match was Hubert's, but much to the pleasure of the enthusiastic crowd, Hubert and Weis lined up for round three. The Mustang stole the show, setting a new track record with an 8.59 at 166.05 mph.

### No Brakes, No Problem

Brannan scheduled a match race with the *Ramchargers* at Atco Dragway in New Jersey. Hubert took the first round of the best of five. During the second round, the bolt holding the parachute onto the car broke as soon as the chute was released. The chute dropped to the ground while the car was going 170 mph.

*These rare photos were taken presumably in January 1967, when new owner, Larry Coleman, first took possession of the gold Mustang. Although the ownership changed, Hubert remained the driver. (Photo Courtesy Marvin Smith)*

The Funny Car Mustang only had back brakes, and Hubert stood on the pedal with both feet so hard that the backing plates broke and spun off of the axle housing. With the car speeding out of control toward the end of the shut-off area, Hubert had no choice but to throw the automatic transmission into reverse to get it to stop. He did, and the car skidded to a halt and won.

When most racers would have packed it up and called it a day, Hubert borrowed a welder and fixed the brakes and the parachute before the next round. Hubert lined up for the third round and took the win along with the match, as this made three straight. It was this dedication and perseverance that promoters and fans alike loved and respected about Hubert.

## New Ownership

In early January 1967, Memphis native and transmission shop owner Larry Coleman worked out a deal with Ford to purchase the gold long-nose Mustang from Dick Brannan. Coleman purchased the complete car, including the ramp truck hauler, for $8,000. This was a hefty price; it was more than the average salary in 1967.

The first thing Larry did was return to Memphis and have the car repainted. It was still the familiar gold and blue paint scheme but now with large red block letters with black shadow beneath on the door boasting the driver as "Hubert Platt." All the way down the fender and door in gold leaf appeared the new sponsor "Paul Harvey

*The wrinkled back slicks show that Hubert is heavy on the throttle at Bee Line Dragway in Arizona. It appears that they were using an early version of a pro tree with only one yellow light.*

*The gold long-nose Mustang was a beautiful race car. Hubert always considered this Mustang his favorite.*

*Always racing before a packed house at Lions Drag Strip, Hubert donned a gas mask to help with the nitromethane fumes. This technique was created by Tom "the Mongoose" McEwen a year earlier.*

Ford Indianapolis, Indiana." Like Hubert's past four race cars, it had "Crane Cams" out front on the nose of the fender and "Headers by Doug" on the fender behind the front wheel. On the rear quarter panels, the large black and red logo "LCE" was featured for the new owner Larry Coleman Enterprises. Front to back down the center of the hood, roof, and decklid ran the blue GT-style racing stripe. The car looked beautiful with its new paint gleaming in the sun.

The car was stunning to look at on and off the track. Although Larry took over ownership, it was still a factory-backed, experimental drag car. Part of the deal with Ford was that Larry was to record the performance of every run and every round of competition and report back to Ford via Dick Brannan, who was still head of Ford Drag Racing. He was to report on engine and transmission performance.

At first, there was a transitional period when Hubert took the truck and car home with him to Atlanta, but Larry soon began taking the car back to his shop in Memphis for its regular maintenance. Larry served as the chief mechanic for the car, working on and tuning the engine while always rebuilding the high-performance custom C-6 Ford transmission with secret, experimental parts that he received from Ford.

This new partnership got off to a great start. On January 22 in Ringgold, Georgia, they won the Funny Car Meet and set a new record for the 1,000-foot mark at 7.84.

### 1967 Winternationals

Larry and Hubert's next race at the AHRA Winternationals in Phoenix, Arizona, on January 29, was

*Now sporting Cragar S/S mags on the rear, Hubert made another hit at an AHRA-sanctioned event at Bee Line Dragway in Arizona. (Photo Courtesy Michael Goyda)*

*It was a bit ironic that Hubert lost the final round of the 1967 AHRA Winternationals to Dick Loehr in his former ride, the one-piece body Mustang. (Photo Courtesy Michael Goyda)*

## Paul Harvey

In October 1963, Paul Harvey was the general manager of Bob Ford when the dealership received one of the first Thunderbolts, and Paul drove it. After being the general manager at a couple of other Ford dealerships, Paul Harvey opened his own in 1966. His performance-based dealership in Indianapolis went on to sponsor many drag racing endeavors, including that of his son Jerry Harvey and racers Randy Payne and Dick Brannan. Hubert and Paul's racing relationship began in 1967 with the Larry Coleman Mustang. Paul would go on to sponsor four more of Hubert's cars, including his final race car.

***This 8x10 Ford publicity photo was handed out at the drag races. It was used in many magazines and newspapers.***

***The gold Mustang was displayed at a Southern California dealership. Promoters would sometimes do this to generate interest and get new fans out to the drag races on the weekends. (Photo Courtesy Michael Goyda)***

bittersweet. Hubert set a new ET record for the A/XS class of 8.84, but he ended up losing the final round to Dick Loehr in his former ride: the one-piece body Mustang.

Revenge would come a week later on February 5 at the NHRA Winternationals. In a repeat final in the A/XS Class, Hubert took the head's-up title over Loehr while setting the low ET and top speed of the class with an 8.49 at 171.42 mph. This was one of the fastest runs of Hubert's career to date.

***Unlike Hubert's one-piece body Mustang, the gold Mustang had opening doors and a removable front end, hood, and decklid. The roll cage covered in padding and electrical tape was super safe in 1966, but not by today's standards. Notice the rear Halibrand wheels were mounted and installed backward to give the correct offset. (Photo Courtesy Michael Goyda)***

*With Hubert's 1967 NHRA Winternationals victory, he set the national record of 8.49 at 171 mph. The gold long-nose Mustang was Hubert's fastest race car and one of the only ones he didn't personally own.*

*Hubert smiled big after a win in Florida over an eight-car field.*

## Winning Record Back East

Hubert would continue his winning ways back East on February 12 in a match race versus Malcolm Durham's *Strip Blazer* at Southeastern Dragway in Dallas, Georgia. Then on February 19, at the third annual Eastern Winternationals at Palm Beach International Dragway in Florida, he won the Funny Car Finals in a 16-car field and set low ET at 8.49 at 172 mph.

On Wednesday, February 22, in Jacksonville, Florida, Hubert won the Funny Car Bash with an 8.51 and 169 mph pass in the Funny Car final round over a field of 17. On the following Sunday, February 26, in Panama City, Florida, Hubert took the win from younger brother, Huston, in another of their infamous grudge matches while setting a new track record of 8.61.

The streak came to an end on March 5 in Memphis, Tennessee, when an overeager Hubert lost in the final round to "Fast Eddie" Schartman's Comet on a red light. Next, they headed north to Detroit Dragway. On March 12, Hubert won the best-of-five match race in three straight against Roger Lindamood. Back down south on March 19 in Kinston, North Carolina, Hubert won the final round against Larry Reye's *King Fish* Barracuda while setting a new track record with another 8.56 at 169 mph. The following Sunday, March 26, in Chattanooga, Tennessee, Hubert won the Funny Car Meet over 11 cars.

Then on April 1 in Phenix City, Alabama, Hubert took the A/XS class with a spectacular 8.61 ET at 171.10 mph at Phenix City Dragway, setting the NHRA national record. Later that day, he returned to the line in another Paul Harvey Ford–sponsored Mustang in the C/XS class, where he won the final with a 10.57 ET at 132.93 mph. Little is known about this second Mustang, but it is believed to be one of the short-wheelbase experimental versions Brannan was working on at the time.

On April 8 in Birmingham, Alabama, Hubert was to meet Bobby Wood in the first Funny Car match race of the season at Mount Lassiter Dragway. In the first round, Hubert beat Wood with an 8.84 ET. Wood did a huge wheelstand, resulting in a bent axle that sidelined him for the rest of the day.

To keep the action going for the fans, Hubert finished the best-two-out-of-three match race against Charles Portera's blown Chevy-powered BB/A Roadster. The blown Chevy Roadster ran times in the 9s and was given a full second handicap start over Hubert. As the two cars blasted down the track, the injected Mustang flew past the Roadster in high gear, clocking an 8.92. Hubert took the win, two straight.

On Sunday, April 9, back at Ringgold, Georgia, Hubert won a four-way match race with a 7.96 final round ET at the 1,000-foot drag strip.

*A fan's view from the start line at Lions Drag Strip shows Hubert lined up against the Barracuda of Ronnie Sox. (Photo Courtesy Paul Hutchins)*

*Hubert had very close relationships with Doug Thorley, Crane Cams, Pennzoil, and Cragar Wheels. He was very loyal to these manufacturers throughout the years, rarely using their competitors. (Photo Courtesy Paul Hutchins)*

On April 16, more than 2,500 fans were on hand in Bristol, Tennessee, for the opening race of the year at Bristol International Dragway. The race was arranged by promoters Larry Carrier and Randy Bowman and featured Hubert versus the *Ramchargers'* John Livingston in his 426 Hemi Dodge Dart. Hubert took the best two out of three with two consecutive wins.

On April 22, Hubert once again was victorious in another of the famed Ford-versus-Chevy grudge matches against his brother Huston. With a final-round ET of 8.10, this was Hubert's quickest quarter-mile ET in this car. Then on April 30 at Aquasco, Maryland, Hubert took the match race over Lew Arrington in the supercharged GTO *Brutus* with a final round ET of 8.39.

Even with this hectic schedule, Hubert and Larry kept running consistent ETs. They were dipping below 8.50 and exceeding 170 mph and winning races every weekend. The gold Mustang was one of Hubert's fastest and most successful cars. Years later, fans would ask Hubert which was his favorite race car and he would always give the same answer, "The gold long-nose Mustang."

### Unbreakable

Ford asked two things of Hubert. First, to not mix the nitro any higher than 88 percent out of fear that too high of a percentage of the volatile mixture would result in an engine explosion. Second, to not start off in second gear because this car was testing secret experimental performance automatic transmission parts, and they wanted Hubert to put it through the paces in all three gears.

Hubert assured Ford he would follow its rules, but these were two of his favorite tricks. He did not refrain from doing either. Ford cared about data gathered from rounds of racing. Hubert, on the other hand, cared about nothing other than winning rounds, which led to winning races.

He threw caution to the wind and would generally mix the nitro at 92 percent, and even as high as 94 percent in the final round. Hubert said this was worth two-tenths of a second. Hubert's secret in keeping the engines from coming apart was to not over-rev. He said, "If you over-rev an SOHC, it will fall on its face and not recover. So, you have to watch the tach and not over-rev."

*The gold Mustang marked the first of several Paul Harvey Ford-sponsored cars for Hubert. Paul Harvey Ford was the premier performance dealership in Indianapolis, Indiana.*

***In 1967, Lions Drag Strip in Long Beach, California, was a hotbed of Funny Car activity. Hubert prepared for another run with Dyno Don's flip-top Comet in the staging lane right behind him.***

He would always start off in second gear because he said the car had so much torque it would fly off the line in second gear. He would only have to shift once just past half track into high gear. When Ford asked Hubert not to do these things, he consulted with Dick Brannan, who told him, "Drive it how you want to." So Hubert did, and it worked. He never blew the engine or broke the transmission.

## Almost Perfect

Hubert bragged, "I drove the gold long-nose Mustang almost a whole year, and we never tore the motor down and I never lost a round." At least one of these could be true. There are only six accounts of the car losing a round in the nine months Hubert was at the wheel; an amazing feat considering they raced almost every weekend!

The losses reported included the first two passes he ever made in the car versus Ronnie Sox; then once at the 1967 AHRA Winternationals to Dick Loehr in the one-piece body Mustang Hubert sold him; once to the Barracuda of Ronnie Sox at the NASCAR Drag Racing Winter Championships; and on March 5 in Memphis, Tennessee, when he red lighted to "Fast Eddie" Schartman's Comet.

### *The Sixth Loss*

The sixth and final loss came on May 7, 1967, in Detroit, Michigan, at Motor City Dragway to brother Huston in a big four-car match race. Hubert raced Huston in his brand-new, unlettered Logghe 1967 *Dixie Twister* Camaro; Maynard Rupp in his new STP Cougar; and John Dallafior in his *Golden Commando* Barracuda.

In round one, which would be his last run in a Funny Car, Hubert got off the line first in the gold Mustang but blew a head gasket and could not hold off his younger brother in his new Camaro. Huston won with an 8.82 ET to Hubert's fading 9.16, paying him back for the victories Hubert took from him earlier in the season. Rupp bested Dallafior's 'Cuda, running an 8.66 ET at 166 mph.

In the second round, the Camaro and the Cougar lined up. When the lights turned green, Huston did a huge wheelstand, dragging the back bumper of the new Camaro that had no wheelie bars. At about 100 feet off the starting line, the Camaro slammed down onto the guardrail, flipping over onto its roof. Huston was unharmed. The car was sent back to the Logghe shop to be rebuilt.

## Cover Gold

Like Hubert's previous few rides, the gold long-nose Mustang graced the cover of a magazine. *Hi-Performance Cars* featured the gold Mustang on its cover, but by the time it hit the newsstands in September 1967, Hubert was onto his next car. The gold Mustang was now being piloted by fellow Funny Car pioneer Sidney Foster.

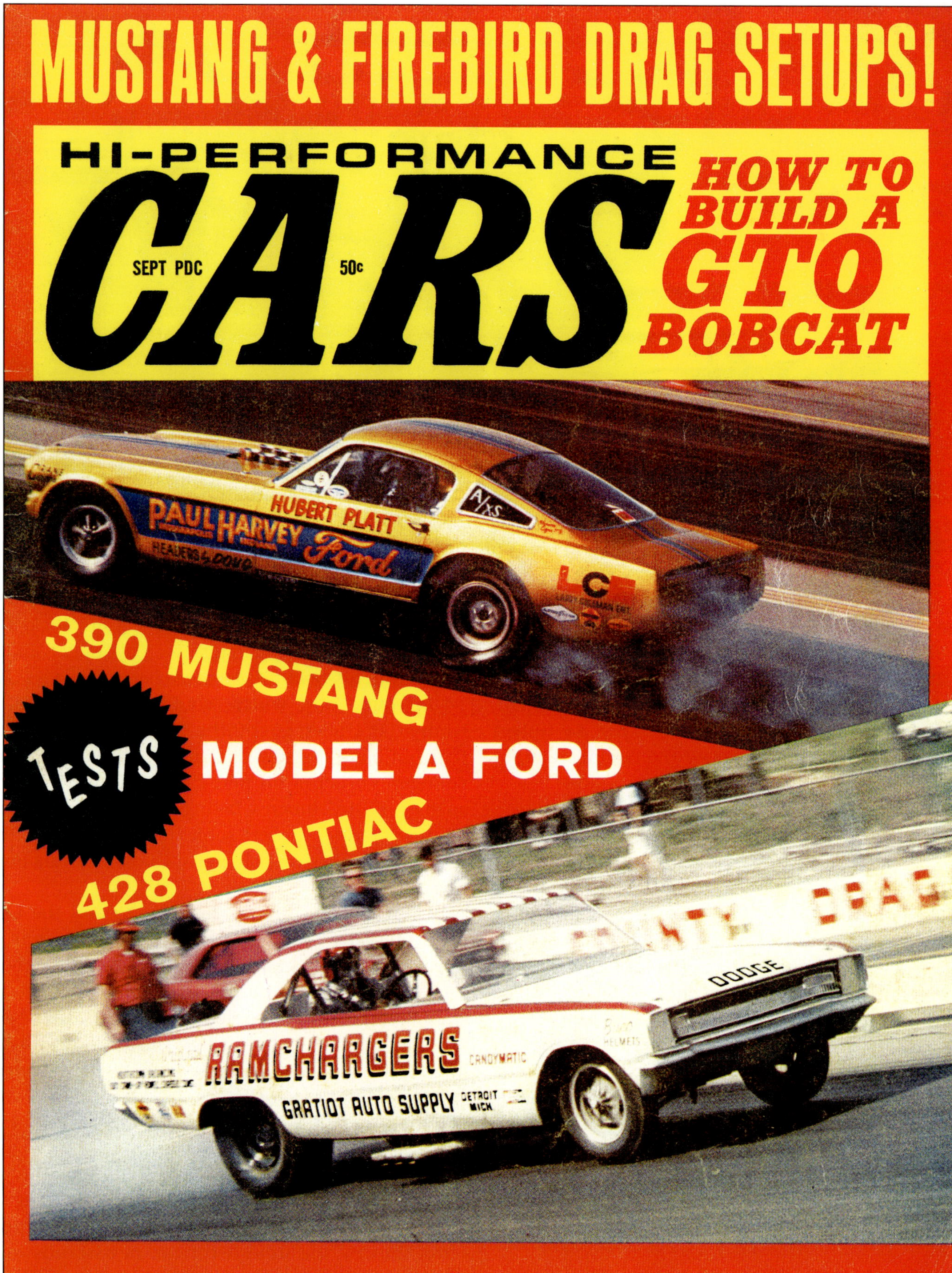


*Hubert's success with the gold Mustang Funny Car was unparalleled. In the winter of 1966–1967, this Mustang was a record setter and truly one of the fastest Funny Cars in the country.*

# CHAPTER 8

# THE SWITCH TO SUPER STOCK

As always, in the 1960s things were changing fast. Chrysler started the factory experimental altered-wheelbase craze in the early 1960s. By the end of the 1966 season, it realized the "Win on Sunday, Sell on Monday" model wasn't working with the highly modified A/FX cars that had quickly morphed into Funny Cars. It pulled two of its top drivers, Dick Landy for Dodge and Ronnie Sox for Plymouth, from the fuel ranks to have them compete in the newly reformed class of Super Stock.

Super Stock was now to be a stand-alone Eliminator in the NHRA with 10 subclasses consisting of 5 categories based on weight to estimated horsepower with 5 manual and 5 automatic transmission classes, all new for 1967. The two factory-backed Chrysler drivers competed in production-based cars targeted at the booming muscle car market. In an effort to educate the public away from the race track, they both also conducted performance clinics at dealerships and auto shows for each of their respective brands.

## Test Session

In an effort to keep up, Ford dipped into its bullpen of fuel Funny Car drivers. In the beginning of May 1967, Hubert was once again contacted by the head of Ford Racing Division, Dick Brannan. Brannan requested his services as a test driver for the sum of $100 per day (five times the national earnings average in 1967).

Ford was now playing catch up to Chrysler, who was leading the Super Stock wars with its Hemi powerplants and two top drivers. Ford's plan to combat this was to put Hubert into a Fairlane 500 with a 427 FE side-oiler.

The first test sessions took place from May 8 through 12, 1967. The first two days were spent on preparation. Hubert came in from Detroit fresh out of the gold Larry Coleman Mustang and arrived at Bristol International Dragway in Tennessee on May 10. He tested the new Fairlane for the next three days. He made 18 passes testing 4 different sizes of rear slicks from Goodyear and M&H Tires.

**Test Session Times and Speeds**

| *Run* | *Tire* | *Eighth-Mile Time* | *Eighth-Mile Speed* | *Quarter-Mile Time* | *Quarter-Mile Speed* |
|---|---|---|---|---|---|
| 1. | 10.50x15 Goodyear (30.3 diameter) | 8.82 | 67.77 | – | – |
| 2. | 10.50x15 Goodyear | 7.65 | 96.77 | 11.76 | 120.64 |
| 3. | 10.50x15 Goodyear | 7.65 | 97.08 | 11.75 | 120.80 |
| 4. | 10.50x15 M&H (29.74 diameter) | 7.47 | 98.46 | 11.45 | 122.11 |
| 5. | 10.50x15 M&H | 7.40 | 98.46 | 11.45 | 121.78 |
| 6. | 10.50x15 M&H | 7.42 | 97.82 | – | – |
| 7. | 10.00x15 M&H | 7.42 | 96.77 | 11.63 | 120.80 |
| 8. | 10.00x15 M&H (30.2 diameter) | 7.41 | 99.22 | 11.42 | 123.79 |
| 9. | 10.00x15 M&H | 7.50 | 97.19 | 11.59 | 120.96 |
| 10. | 10.00x15 M&H | 7.47 | 97.26 | – | – |
| 11. | 10.00x15 M&H | 7.40 | 98.14 | – | – |
| 12. | 10.00x15 M&H | 7.44 | 97.82 | – | – |
| 13. | 8.20x15 M&H (29.1 diameter) | 7.45 | 94.29 | 11.54 | 121.13 |
| 14. | 8.20x15 M&H | 7.49 | 95.30 | – | – |
| 15. | 8.90x15 Goodyear (29 diameter) | 7.53 | 96.87 | – | – |
| 16. | 8.90x15 Goodyear | 7.43 | 97.40 | 11.52 | 120.80 |
| 17. | 8.90x15 Goodyear | 7.56 | 96.56 | – | – |
| 18. | 8.90x15 Goodyear | 7.44 | 98.51 | 11.51 | 121.45 |

With a best time of 11.42 at 123.79 mph, which was well below the national record, Hubert was ready to take on the Hemis and throw Ford's hat into the Super Stock arena. Hubert purchased this car from Ford for the grand total of $1. This would mark the end of Hubert's fuel Funny Car drag racing days.

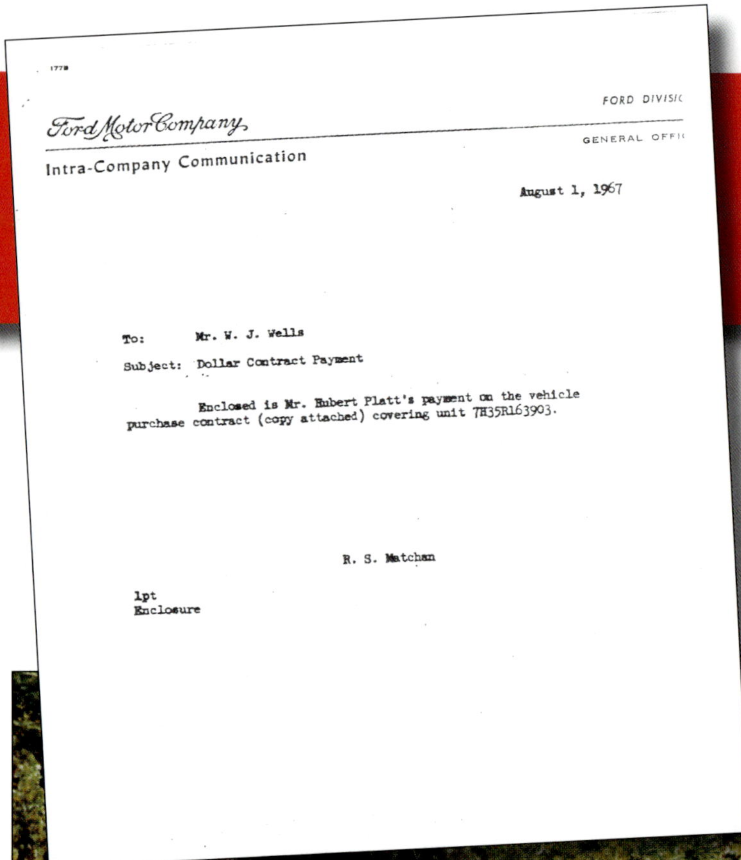

1778

Ford Motor Company

FORD DIVISI(

GENERAL OFFI(

Intra-Company Communication

August 1, 1967

To: Mr. W. J. Wells

Subject: Dollar Contract Payment

Enclosed is Mr. Hubert Platt's payment on the vehicle purchase contract (copy attached) covering unit 7H35R163903.

R. S. Matchan

lpt
Enclosure

*Switching from Funny Car to Super/Stock was a big move for Hubert, but he was happy to be driving for the factory as well as being a car owner again. To free themselves from liability, Ford sold the factory drag cars to its contracted drivers for $1 each. This is the $1 contract for the purchase of Hubert's 1967 427 Fairlane.*

## Luxury Test Car

The test car chosen by Ford was unique in that it was a fully loaded 500 model of the popular Fairlane two-door hardtop. It even had electric windows. It was unusual that a fully loaded car was picked as a test vehicle.

*Hubert only raced this one 1967 Fairlane but in four different configurations, which confused fans. Pictured here is how the car looked in May 1967 when Hubert first received it. Configuration 1.*

*By June 1967, Hubert had the Fairlane relettered in all chrome lettering. The Fairlane is still sporting its factory vinyl top. Configuration 2. (Photo Courtesy Joel Naprstek)*

*This packed house at Bluegrass Raceway Park in Owingsville, Kentucky, shows the popularity of Super Stock in 1967.*

The Fairlane was triple black (black paint, black vinyl top, with black interior). The steel hood, hinges, and springs had been replaced with a one-piece fiberglass hood held down by four hood pins. It had a functional fresh-air vent that fed through a scoop that ran the entire length of the hood. The engine was a 427 FE side-oiler with medium-riser cylinder heads. It also had an aluminum medium-riser intake with twin Holley 4-barrel carburetors.

The stock R-code engine was rated at 425 hp with 480 ft-lbs of torque. Hubert's Super Stock race version of the 427 had 13.2:1 compression pistons and an L1 P1 solid-lift camshaft along with 2-inch inside-dimension exhaust headers by Doug Thorley. The battery was mounted in the trunk and all of the sealing material was removed. The drag car also received a five-point roll bar and 10.5-inch racing slicks on black stamped steel wheels with chrome rims. It had a 4-speed transmission delivering the power to a Ford 9-inch rear end with welded traction bars and 4.86:1 gears.

#### *Changing Paint Schemes*

When Hubert received the Fairlane, it had huge block letters all the way down the side saying "Paul Harvey Ford." The "Paul Harvey" was a tannish gold with a red three-dimensional shadow. The "Ford" was silver outlined in blue. In small white block letters below the window on the doors it read "Hubert Platt." After the test session, Hubert raced the car once in this configuration before changing the lettering.

The new block lettering was all done in chrome. It read "Georgia Shaker" on the rear quarter panel, "Hubert Platt" on the door, "Doug's Headers" on the front fender, and "Paul Harvey Ford Indianapolis, Indiana" all the way down the side. Just like Hubert's six previous rides since 1964, it said "Crane Cams" out on the tip of the front fender.

### A Fast Summer

On June 3 and 4 at Myrtle Beach Dragway at an NHRA-sanctioned event, Hubert was forced to withdraw early from competition with mechanical problems but not before turning in the low ET and top speed of the meet for his class with an 11.45 at 122 mph. Harold Dutton won the event in his 427 Fairlane with an ET of 11.57, which gave him the NHRA Division 2 points lead.

The next weekend in Bristol, Tennessee, Hubert made a showing at the NHRA Springnationals, but it wasn't enough. The winner of Super Stock Eliminator was Dick Arons with an 11.63 victory over Ronnie Sox.

That summer, Hubert and the Fairlane gave the Chevys and Hemi-powered Chryslers more than their fair share of competition. On July 2 at Warner Robins Dragway in Houston County, Georgia, he set the NHRA national record at 11.38 seconds in the quarter mile. This was a huge success for Ford as well as for Hubert. Ford proved it could keep up with and even outdo the other two major automakers, and Hubert once again proved himself to the factory as a driver who could consistently produce record-setting results.

Ford was so impressed with Hubert's performance that it showed its gratitude by giving him a new personal

Certificate of Performance

NATIONAL

CLASS RECORD

authorized by

NATIONAL HOT ROD ASSOCIATION

This certifies that HUBERT PLATT - PAUL HARVEY FORD, a contestant in a National Record Run Event, did establish an official National quarter-mile acceleration record in Super Stock B class during the period of official record runs, having been electronically timed by the CHRONDEK TIMING SYSTEM at a speed of ---- MPH, with an ELAPSED TIME of 11.38 seconds. This National record shall remain in effect until such time as it is officially exceeded at an NHRA Record Run Event, or until it is otherwise declared invalid by the NHRA.

Established at Houston County Date July 2, 1967

NATIONAL HOT ROD ASSOCIATION — DEDICATED TO SAFETY

NATIONAL HOT ROD ASSOCIATION

Certified by: Jack Hart

***On July 2, 1967, Hubert, in his Paul Harvey Ford-sponsored 1967 Ford Fairlane, set the NHRA National record for Super Stock B with an elapsed time of 11.38 seconds in the quarter mile.***

car for the street: a red Ford 1967 Shelby GT500 Mustang. It was a 428 Police Interceptor with two 4-barrel carburetors. The following February, Hubert's 16-year-old daughter, Lynette, used this car for her driver's test.

## Paul Harvey Ford Two-Car Team

Paul Harvey sponsored Hubert's Fairlane and the 427 Fairlane of Harold Dutton. The two black cars were almost exactly the same, except Hubert's had a vinyl top

***This Ford press photo was taken at the 1967 US Nationals in Indianapolis, where Hubert made the first 10-second pass ever in a Factory Super Stock. By this time, the vinyl top had been removed from Hubert's Fairlane so that it would match teammate Harold Dutton's. Configuration 3.***

and side chrome. To make the two-car team match and make a good showing at the Nationals in Indianapolis, they removed the vinyl top from Hubert's car and added side chrome to Harold's. The Fairlanes now had identical chrome lettering and the only noticeable difference was the names: Hubert Platt had *Georgia Shaker* and Harold Dutton had *Drag Hag*.

### *Indy Nationals*

Over Labor Day weekend, Hubert looked like the man to beat, turning out an 11.10 at 125.17 mph in qualifying to lead the field. In eliminations on Monday, Hubert did what many said couldn't be done in a NHRA legal Super Stock: he hammered out a below 11-second pass of 10.96, which would stand as low ET of the class for the event.

This proved the Fairlane was faster than the Hemi-powered Mopars of Sox & Martin and Dick Landy, as well as the 396 big-block Camaro of Bill "Grumpy" Jenkins. But in Super Stock, handicap racing the fastest car doesn't always win. In this case, Jenkins's Camaro took home the trophy with an 11.55 at 115 mph.

***The Paul Harvey Ford two-car team of Hubert Platt and Harold Dutton was a sharp-looking duo all in black. At this point, the only difference in the two cars was Hubert's had a vinyl roof, which by the times on the windows didn't slow it down. As you can see, Hubert's dial-in is 11.38 and Harold's is 11.51. (Photo Courtesy Marvin Smith)***

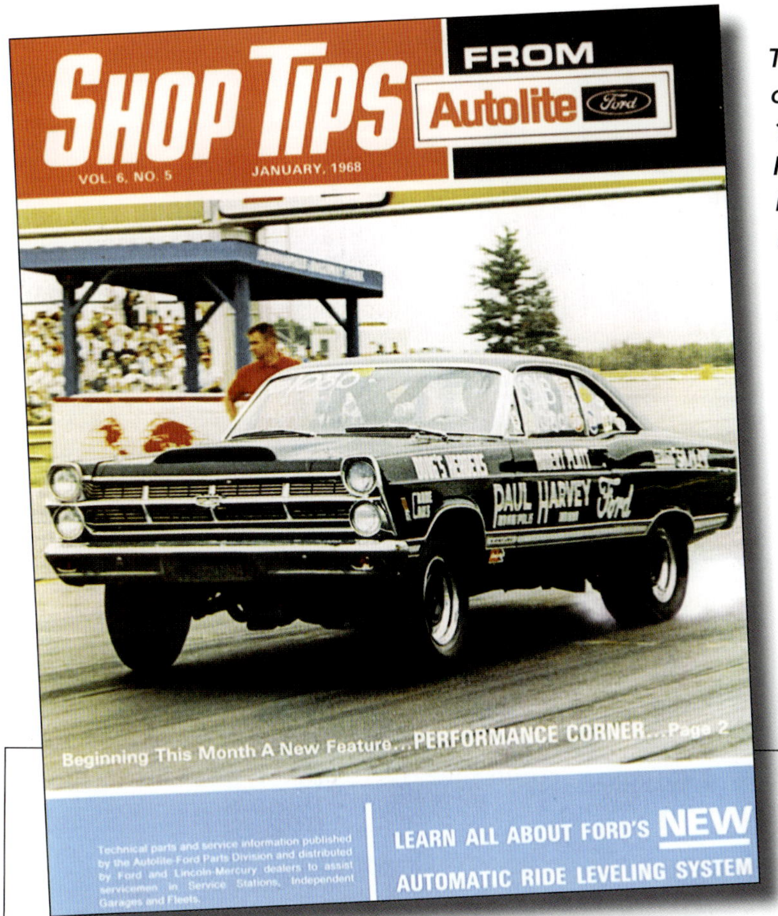


*This photo taken at the 1967 US Nationals was featured on the cover of* Shop Tips from Autolite *in January 1968. This magazine was published by Autolite-Ford Parts Division and was filled with mechanical tips and helpful advice for the servicemen working at auto repair shops, service stations, and the like. The handout was available at Ford and Lincoln-Mercury car dealerships in the parts department.*

*Hubert in the big-block 427 Fairlane gave the Hemis plenty of trouble. Arlen Vanke said Mopar would have had a big year in 1967 if it wasn't for that "pesky Fairlane."*

After the Nationals at Indianapolis, Hubert had the Fairlane repainted once again. It was painted a two-tone black with silver. Just after this photo was taken, the car was lettered in yellow.

When the Fairlane was first lettered in yellow, Hubert did not like the font where it read "Georgia Shaker" and had it removed. The car was raced one weekend before having the "Georgia Shaker" moniker repainted.

## Drag Racing with Style

In the late 1960s, there was a lot of colorful flare in pop culture. After the Nationals, Hubert felt that the plain black Fairlane with simple chrome lettering wasn't quite as flashy as his personality. To better represent himself, he took the car to Alpharetta, Georgia, to Thompson's Body Shop. He knew his friend, Max Thompson, could give the car the dynamic look he was searching for.

This two-page centerfold in Car Craft shows Hubert putting the Fairlane through its paces and enjoying a fender-length lead on the Hemi in red. Configuration 4.

Max started by changing it from all black to a black and metal flake silver two-tone paint scheme with a red pinstripe separating the two. There was also a red pinstripe across the nose of the hood scoop. The new lettering would be bigger, bolder, and bright yellow. Once again on the full length of the wheelbase it had its sponsor, "Paul Harvey Ford." Above that, block lettering on the door let everyone know who the driver was with "Hubert Platt." Down the length of the front fender it had Hubert's friend and sponsor "Doug's Headers." Different from Hubert's previous cars, the "Crane Cams" logo switched places and was now on the rocker panel behind the front wheel. Across the decklid in huge block letters was a message for all opponents who wound up behind him on the track: "Schools Out."

Hubert did not like the font on the "Georgia Shaker" lettering on the quarter panel when it was originally done, and he had the painter remove it. It was removed on a Friday, and Hubert raced that weekend at Cumming Dragway in Georgia. The car was photographed with its new paint scheme but not wearing its "Georgia Shaker" moniker. The following week, Hubert had the painter return to his home shop and apply the new "Georgia Shaker" lettering in yellow to match the rest. The changes led some fans to believe that Hubert was testing a new car and did not want to put his "Georgia Shaker" name on it until it met with success and gained his approval. It was also rumored that Hubert had more than one Fairlane, due to it showing up to the races in a seven-month period with three different paint schemes and with and without a vinyl top. All this was very confusing to fans, but the truth is Hubert only had one 1967 Ford Fairlane race car, just in four different configurations.

## The End of an Era

In late 1967, Huston Platt's Funny Car career was back on track after his accident on May 7 in Detroit. He was now driving a new 1967 Camaro Logghe flip-top Funny Car sponsored by Brooks Chevrolet out of Millen, Georgia. The owner, Mr. Brooks, also sponsored his son Johnny in a 1967 Camaro Super Stock that was painted white but lettered like the *Dixie Twister* Funny Car and named the *Dixie Twister Jr.*

*Farewell to the grudge matches. Hubert and Huston had the last of their famed grudge matches in late 1967. Huston then stepped out of his nitro Funny Car to take over driving for Johnny Brooks's* Dixie Twister Jr. *in Super Stock. Huston's 1967 Camaro was sponsored by Brooks Chevrolet. Johnny Brooks was the son of the dealership owner.*

*Hubert, with a cigar in his mouth, makes some adjustments to the 427 between rounds in the pits.*

***Being the lone Ford in a sea of Hemi-powered Chryslers would be worrisome for most, but for Hubert with the National record and sub-11-second passes under his belt, the Mopars were more worried about him. (Photo Courtesy Chuck Conway)***

## Vietnam Story

Larry Jenkins (born in 1946) was a regular Atlanta-area kid growing up in the suburbs. He graduated from Clarkston High School with the Class of 1964. Like a lot of young boys coming up in the 1960s, Larry had an interest in cars. He had a 1957 Chevy that he and his friends piled into on the weekends to go to Southeastern Dragway or Yellow River Dragstrip, two Atlanta-area racetracks where you could see the early match racers of the true "Run Whatcha Brung" crowd. Any given weekend in those days you could see the likes of Don Nicholson, Phil Bonner, Shirl Greer, Bogan Renfroe, and the Platt Brothers going head-to-head in fierce competition.

Larry readily admits that when he first saw the *Georgia Shaker III* wheelstanding at Southeastern Dragway in Dallas, Georgia, he fell in love with the exciting little car, and Hubert instantly became his hero! In fact, he was so impressed that he decided to go drag racing himself. He started with a 1964 Falcon Sprint and then moved on to a 1965 Falcon, both of which he raced in J/Stock. The Atlanta youth was having the time of his life.

Sadly, the fun came to an end when in May 1966 when Uncle Sam came calling and the 19-year-old hot rodder was drafted to serve in the Vietnam War. First, he was off to basic training at Fort Benning in Georgia. Next, he was sent to Advanced Infantry training at Fort Knox in Kentucky.

While on weekend leave for the Labor Day weekend holiday, Larry and a couple of the other GIs attended the 1966 Indy Nationals in nearby Indianapolis. After growing

***Soldier Larry Jenkins, took the* Georgia Shaker *name halfway around the world to Vietnam when he placed it on this military tow truck. This gave the GIs a memory from home and a temporary escape from their current situation. (Photo Courtesy Larry Jenkins)***

***The Georgia Shaker** wrecker truck was used various tasks, including removing engines from the Huey helicopters. (Photo Courtesy Larry Jenkins)*

up going to the small, grassroots tracks in Georgia, Larry thought he had died and gone to drag racing heaven with the spectacle of the huge national event. Seeing the fastest drag cars from all over the nation spiked his enthusiasm for the sport.

Next, he was on to Fort Eustis in Virginia, where he studied aircraft engine repair. After graduation, he was stationed at Fort Carson in Colorado, where he became part of the 195th Assault Helicopter Company. The 195th had 500 soldiers and 60 helicopters. Each helicopter had one crew chief (who stayed with his same chopper) and a pilot, copilot, and door gunner, who all rotated to other choppers. The 500 men and 60 helicopters, tow trucks, and tools boarded a World War II troop ship out of Oakland, California, in October 1967 and headed for the other side of the world.

Upon arriving in Vung Tau, Vietnam, the crew cleared land and built the Plantation Airfield Army base from the ground up. It was located near Bien Hoa Air Force Base. Once settled on the new base, the crewmembers began to feel homesick. Larry found himself in a large group of gearheads from all over the US, many of whom were drag racing fans. The group would talk for hours about times gone by and the fun they had at the drag races. Bench Racing was king, and Larry made it clear early on that he was a Ford man and Hubert Platt the *Georgia Shaker* was his favorite drag racer. These talks gave the GIs an escape to home for a moment and helped these men through the most difficult times they had ever faced in their young lives.

When the 195th got down to work, Larry was rebuilding and repairing engines and transmissions on Hueys riddled with bullet holes. He was also in charge of driving a massive 5-ton 6x6 wrecker truck that had a large crane on the back for lifting helicopters, removing engines and transmissions, towing trailers, etc.

Larry said, "When I would come driving up to a job, everyone would say: 'Here comes that Georgia Shaker' and it really picked my spirits up, so I got some paint and a paintbrush and I named the wrecker the *Georgia Shaker*. It gave my friends and I a connection with home, and it also honored my favorite drag racer, Hubert Platt."

In December 1968, Larry returned home to Georgia, where he had a wife and young daughter waiting for him. Years later, Larry gathered with Vietnam vets who had been to Plantation Airfield Army base, and he was happy to find that they all remembered the *Georgia Shaker* wrecker truck.

When Hubert was a boy growing up in South Carolina, he never imagined that someday soldiers in a war halfway around the world would be discussing him. This is another example of how the showmanship and charisma that Hubert displayed at the drag strip had a lasting effect on people.

On November 19, Huston stepped out of the Funny Car and into this Super Stock to do battle on the drag strip for the last time against his older brother. Although we don't know the outcome of the match race that day, we do know it was the end of an era for the Platt brothers. The grudge match days of brother versus brother, Ford versus Chevy, which the fans loved and had brought so much fame and fortune to the brothers, had come to an end.

With Huston pursuing a nitro Funny Car career and Hubert in factory-backed Super Stock, the fun and fleeting spirit of the grudge matches and the Run Whatcha Brung days were quickly becoming a thing of the past. Drag racing was becoming much more commercial and was now considered a professional sport with national events being covered on *ABC's Wide World of Sports*. With progress came stricter rules and more structured sanctioning bodies.

## Catching Up

In the seven months that Hubert campaigned the 1967 Fairlane, he won many Super Stock events and match races nationwide. Although he didn't rack up any national event victories, he did run the low ET at many of those events while holding the national record. Hubert's success with the 1967 Fairlane definitely made Ford a contender in the Super Stock arena for 1967.

*This ad for the NHRA 1968 US Nationals at Indianapolis offered fans for the first time ever a chance to have reserved seating at the Nationals. Hubert's photo was included because one of the high points of the 1967 event was when he was the first to put a factory Super Stock into the 10-second bracket.*

# CHAPTER 9

# COBRA JETS

In 1967, Bob Tasca Sr. was the owner of Tasca Ford, the premier performance dealership based in Rhode Island, and he recognized that Mustang sales were waning due to lack of performance. The 390-ci GT Mustang didn't quite have what it took to outrun the big-block Plymouth GTX. That didn't sit well with Tasca, and he set out to remedy this for Ford.

Tasca enlisted the help of drag racer Bill Gilbert, who helped him come up with a solution. Knowing that horsepower is made in the cylinder heads and there were no high-flow heads that would fit the 390, they used the Police Fleet 428-ci short-block combined with high-flow C8AE-6049-K 406 cylinder heads. This took a little creativity to make work.

The 428 pistons had to be notched to compensate for the larger valves in the 406 heads. Gilbert was quoted as saying, "I flycut the pistons right in the block." The heads had 427 rocker arms for more lift, lightweight valves, and 427-type valve springs. It had a Police Interceptor intake with a single Holley 4-barrel carburetor fed by a higher-flow fuel pump. They used a 390 GTA hydraulic camshaft and installed a set of 427 Fairlane headers that ran through stock exhaust.

When Tasca and Gilbert dropped their engine into Bob's daily driver, a Lime Gold 1967 GT hardtop Mustang with a C-6 automatic transmission, the car was named the *KR-8*. With technician Billy Loomis riding shotgun and sons Bob Jr. (15) and Carl (14) in the back seat, Tasca drove *KR-8* from Rhode Island to Dearborn, Michigan, for testing in the summer of 1967.

On street tires with a somewhat-stock exhaust, Tasca ripped off a 13.46 at 104 mph on *KR-8*'s first run. It then raced against some of Ford's 427 Mustangs and other cars at the test facility. Bob Jr. was quoted as saying, "We beat everything they had." The *KR-8*'s low ET and top speed of the test session was 13.39 at 105 mph.

Ford engineers in Detroit insisted on keeping the engine for further inspection. Ultimately, the brass at Ford Performance was so impressed they put the engine into production in the 1968½ Mustang. The 428 engine was named Cobra Jet and made available to the public in April 1968.

In October 1967, six weeks after receiving his driver's license, Bob Jr. hit a telephone pole and the *KR-8* was totaled.

### The Winternationals Cobra Jets

Before the 428 Cobra Jet production vehicles for 1968 were built, Ford created 50 lightweight, high-performance 428 Cobra Jet Mustangs specifically for drag racing. These original 50 have been dubbed the 135 Mustangs because of the matching first three digits of their serial numbers. Of this 50, 6 were sent to Holman-Moody-Stroppe in Long Beach, California, to undergo further modifications for Ford factory drivers. These drivers were to debut the new Mustangs at the NHRA Winternationals in Pomona.

Three received a wide-ratio 4-speed manual transmission with a high-performance Schiefer clutch and pressure plate and Hurst 4-speed shifters. The other three were automatics that had the blocker rings cut so they would shift better at high RPM, and they received high-stall torque converters.

The Detroit Locker rear ends were set up with a 4.71:1 gear for the 4-speed cars and a 4.44:1 gear for the automatics, as well as a set of Logghe traction ladder bars with forward mounts that had three adjustment holes. The ladder bars were incredibly strong "Super Bite" units.

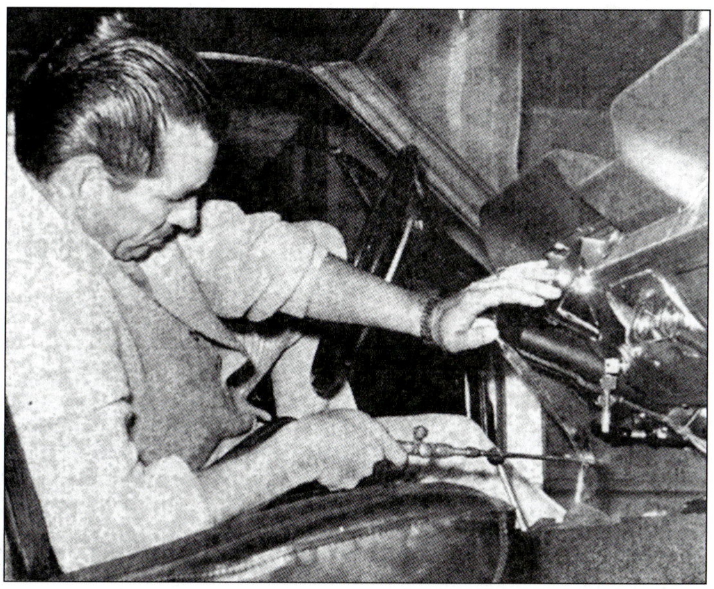

***Not many people would take a blowtorch to a brand-new Hurst shifter, but Hubert felt that if he heated the standard stick up and bent it forward he could get extra leverage and shift more aggressively into second and fourth.***

A set of stiffer shocks was added to the rear end as well. The brakes were stock except that the self-adjusters were removed from the rear units.

To get the power to the pavement, a set of 10.5x15 Goodyear Blue Streak racing slicks were installed on a pair of 6x15 black stamped steel wheels. The front tires were 7.75x15 with between 40 and 50 pounds of air pressure. This larger front tire setup allowed a driver to start sooner without fouling because the taller tire and wheel combination stayed in the stage light longer as the car began its forward roll. Shorter tires won't allow you to have as quick of a reaction time.

Under the hood, the engines' stock pistons were exchanged for high-performance, lightweight 11.6:1 compression racing pistons made by Venolia and used with 427 connecting rods. A performance C8AX-D solid-lift camshaft was installed using Crane valvetrain components that had high-performance lightweight valves and heavy-duty valve springs, retainers, and pushrods. A trick part of the race engines was the custom oil pan with a 4-inch enlarged sump that gave them a 9-quart capacity, although 7 quarts were used during actual competition. The larger oil pan reduced windage on the crank and rod ends and also helped to keep the oil at a cooler temperature.

The Cobra Jet Mustangs received a functional fiberglass hood scoop that fed fresh air into an open-topped breather mounted on the single Holley 735 CFI 4-barrel carburetor, which was atop an Offset 427 aluminum intake. High-performance, dual-point distributors were also added. Per competition regulation, the race cars received a roll bar and a driveshaft safety hoop. The sealant was removed from the bodies for a weight savings of 80 pounds and the batteries were mounted in the trunk for better weight distribution.

The six Winternationals Cobra Jets were set up for these five drivers:

| | | | |
|---|---|---|---|
| 983 | SS/E | Jerry Harvey | Paul Harvey Ford |
| 984 | C/SA | Hubert Platt | Tasca Ford |
| 985 | SS/E | Hubert Platt | Paul Harvey Ford |
| 986 | SS/E | Al Joniec | Rice-Holman Ford |
| 987 | SS/EA | Don Nicholson | Dick Brannan Ford |
| 992 | SS/EA | Gas Ronda | Russ Davis Ford |

C/SA = Stock automatic transmission
SS/E = Super Stock 4-speed manual transmission
SS/EA = Super Stock automatic transmission

To aid in the flow of exhaust, Jerry and Hubert's cars received a set of crossover-style Doug's Headers. The other three cars received a set of Jardine Headers. Hubert's 984 car that raced in Stock had fewer modifications than the Super Stocks. It had 11.0:1 compression-forged pistons instead of 11.5:1, a hydraulic camshaft C8AX-C instead of the solid-lift "D" camshaft, stock valves, 427-type valve springs, a stock intake, and smaller 7x14 drag slicks.

### *Test Session*

On January 15, 1968, Hubert got his first shot behind the wheel of a Cobra Jet Mustang at Los Angeles County Fairgrounds in Pomona. The test subject was a 4-speed

***In a private test session at Los Angeles County Fairgrounds, Hubert put the first Cobra Jet through its paces. This car went on to become Hubert's 985 Cobra Jet.***

## Cobra Jets Debut

Ford's plan was to debut the new Cobra Jet Mustangs at the NHRA 1968 Winternationals on February 2–4 in Pomona, but one week earlier, Hubert felt the need to put some test passes on the 984 car. He entered it in C/Stock at the AHRA Winternationals held at Lions Drag Strip in Long Beach, California. In the first-round eliminations, he turned in an ET of 12.62, but was disqualified from competition with a red light.

*Hubert was happy with the start of a new year in 1968, when he was campaigning not one but two new Cobra Jet Mustangs for Ford. This was the Tasca-sponsored C/SA (automatic transmission) 984 car.*

manual transmission car in Wimbledon White simply lettered with "Cobra Jet" on the door and small block letters on the fender that read "Ford" with a lightbulb in the place of the "O" in Ford.

Although we don't know the results from the test session that day, we do know that Hubert bragged that the test car performed faster than the current national record. This original test car went on to become the 985 car Hubert campaigned.

### The Cobra Jets Get Lettered

In final preparation for the Winternationals, the Mustangs were numbered and lettered. All six of the Cobra Jets came wearing Wimbledon White. All of the Mustangs had "Cobra Jet" painted on the quarter panel and their sponsor on the fender and door as well as the driver's name. The 983 car of Jerry Harvey and the 985 car of Hubert Platt were both sponsored by Paul Harvey Ford and lettered identically except for the number and the driver's name. The large lettering was black with a red outline, and each driver's name appeared under the side windows in black.

Hubert's 984 car was sponsored by Tasca Ford and was lettered in red with a blue outline with his name in red beneath the side windows. The 986 car driven by Al Joniec was lettered by a different person than the other five. It read "Cobra Jet" on the quarter panel in large blue letters of a different font from the others. "Rice-Holman Ford" appeared down the fender and door in gold as well as his name. The 987 of Don Nicholson had "Cobra Jet" painted on the quarter panel in big red letters with a blue outline. "Dick Brannan Ford" appeared on the fender and door in black with a red outline and his name was lettered in red. The 992 car driven by Gas Ronda read "Cobra Jet" on the quarter panel and "Russ Davis Ford" down the fender and door all in red with a black outline. His name was also lettered in red.

*Even though this wasn't the final round, everyone was on their feet for what would be the biggest race of the day to see if the new Cobra Jet Mustang could hold its own with the Hemi-powered Plymouth GTX of Sox & Martin. Hubert gave the brass at Ford something to cheer about when he won with an 11.09 to Ronnie Sox's 11.74.*

***This factory publicity photo was used in press info kits in 1968. Tasca Ford was the dealership sponsor for the 984 Cobra Jet at the 1968 NHRA Winternationals, but soon after, the sponsor was changed to Paul Harvey Ford.***

The cars all received a new set of wheels. On all six cars, the rear 6x15 black steel stamped wheels were replaced with a set of 7x15 chrome-reverse units. The front wheels of Jerry and Hubert's cars were replaced chrome-reverse units as well. The other three received a set of Cragar S/S mags on the front.

The official debut of the Cobra Jet Mustangs took place at the NHRA 1968 Winternationals. Although Hubert had two of the fastest Cobra Jets on hand, late in the day he was cursed with a bit of bad luck.

Things started off well when Hubert in his 985 4-speed had a first-round victory over Arlen Vanke in his Plymouth Hemi 'Cuda. It was a good start, but the big race of the event for the Super Stock fans came when Hubert in the 985 Cobra Jet Mustang lined up against Ronnie Sox in his Sox & Martin Plymouth Hemi GTX. This was brand loyalty war at its best. These two factories and drivers had been going after each other for more than five years in professional competition. Bragging rights were on the line for both the drivers and the brands in one of drag racing's biggest events.

The fans at the Los Angeles County Fairgrounds were on their feet when the lights turned green and the Mustang jumped out to an early lead. The GTX was never able to recover. When the win light came on, it was in the Mustang's lane with an ET of 11.09 to the GTX's 11.74. This victory was good for Hubert, but great for Ford.

Because of Bob Tasca's ingenuity in creating the Cobra Jet powerplant, the Mustang was back to being a winner. In the months to come, winning would make it a strong seller and true contender in the muscle car market.

When it came time for the all–Cobra Jet final round of SS/E, Ford was very pleased. Hubert felt as though he was a shoo-in for the win. He had run in the low 11s all day, and his opponent, Al Joniec, had been making passes in the 12s with a quickest run of 11.80. This is when Hubert's bad luck began.

Ford Performance executive Chuck Foulger, who was very involved in Ford's racing program, came to Hubert and Al in the pits prior to the final round to explain Ford's position. The way Ford saw things, it had already won the race with an all-Mustang final, so there was no need for the two drivers to race all out and possibly set the national record any lower. The drivers would flip a coin to see who the final round victory would go to. That way Ford didn't have to show its hand and let its competitors see the full potential of the Cobra Jets.

Chuck flipped the coin, and it fell in Al's favor. This upset Hubert, who was a gambler and highly competitive; he hated to lose. When the cars came to the starting line and staged, Hubert left on the first yellow, forcing the red light and giving the victory to Al. Hubert lost with an 11.59 at 113.06 mph to Al's 12.12 at 109.48 mph.

Meanwhile, Hubert made it to the C/SA class final with the 984 car. Due to some confusion in the pits, he was unable to hear the staging lanes call for the final round. When he did not make it to the starting line on

*For the second time in three months, Hubert made the cover of* Shop Tips *magazine. This photo is from the final round of the 1968 NHRA Winternationals.*

time, he was disqualified, giving the victory to Dave Kempton in his 1963 383 Plymouth.

Hubert wasn't the only one who had bad luck that day. Don Nicholson in the 987 car was out in the first round of SS/EA with a spun bearing. Gas Ronda in the 992 car lost the SS/EA final round with a 12.02 at 116.27 mph to Dick Landy's victorious 12.01 at 118.73.

Ed Terry, piloting Hubert's 1967 Fairlane, lost the SS/C final round to Bill Jenkins's 1967 Camaro. Ed's 11.26 at 124.03 mph wasn't enough for Bill's 11.18 at 125.87 mph. After the Winternationals, Hubert purchased both of the Mustangs (984 and 985) from the factory for the grand sum of $1 each.

## A Speedy Spring

In March, Hubert had some mechanical difficulties at Montgomery Dragstrip in Alabama. He had to make a rare for Super Stock engine swap in the pits. Many of the fans were amazed with the ease at which Hubert and his helper changed the engine in such a short time with the limited resources at the track. They were even more amazed when he came back to win the Super Stock Eliminator.

Ford and the Cobra Jet Mustang were enjoying their success in the spring of 1968. On April 7, Hubert sweetened the pot by setting both ends of the NHRA national SS/E record with an 11.67 ET at 120.96 mph. The April issue of *Hot Rod* magazine hit the shelves with a three-page article called "Hubie and His Horse." This article detailed the modifications made to the Cobra Jet Mustangs for drag racing and included 10 photographs depicting the various performance upgrades. Hubert reached into his bag of tricks and shared his own personal secrets with the editors about how to make a Cobra Jet Mustang a winner on the drag strip.

### Oh Canada

Hubert was winning match races and setting track records coast to coast. On May 12, he took the SS/E Mustang north of the border to Ontario, Canada, to Cayuga's 1320 Dragway for the All Star Super Stock Battle with a purse of $350 for Super Stock Eliminator.

A poor attempt at cleaning up after a rain delay caused some traction problems in the first round. Hubert in the 985 Cobra Jet still edged out a holeshot win over Canadian Jerry Vanek in his Dodge *Quarter Mile Hustler* with an 11.92 to Vanek's quicker 11.56.

Bill Jenkins's Camaro advanced to the second round with a red-light win courtesy of Bruce Gowland. Canadian Don Henderson bested Barrie Poole with an 11.98. The Coyote Ford entry outran Ed Miller with an 11.85. Wally Booth was outed by partner Dick Arons.

In round two, Hubert beat fellow Ford driver and the only remaining Canadian in the field, Don Henderson, with an 11.88 to an 11.93. In the first round, the Firebird

*This was the scene of the final round on a cold day in May on Canadian soil, possibly a little too cold for Hubert when Bill "Grumpy" Jenkins took the win with an 11.37 to Hubert's 11.84. (Photo Courtesy Doug Boyce)*

of Tony Knieper easily beat Jerry Dunbar, but in round two he was no match for the Camaro of Bill Jenkins, who shut him down with an 11.49. The Coyote Ford entry took out the Dick Arons car in round two.

In round three, Hubert drew a bye run and ran an 11.87. His final-round competition would either be Bill Allie in the Coyote Ford or Bill Jenkins in the *Grumpy's Toy* Camaro.

The tension was high as the fans waited under the threat of rain to see who would meet Hubert in the final. The Coyote Ford leaped out to an early lead but was no match for the big-block Camaro, which turned in a time of 11.42 to the Ford's 11.71. When it came time for the final round, Hubert's Mustang, like the other Ford, was off to an early lead but was overtaken by the Camaro. Jenkins won with the low ET of the day: an 11.37 at 122.95 mph. Although Hubert was consistent and picked up a little each run, he would have to settle for runner-up honors with his low ET of the day: an 11.84 at 120.32 mph.

### *Back Down South*

On May 31, Hubert got back to his winning ways at the Blue-Gray Drag Classic in Montgomery, Alabama, at the Montgomery International Terminal Dragstrip. He took the Super Stock Eliminator title with an 11.77 over George Warren's Chevy II that ran a 12.12.

At the Daytona Drags in Daytona Beach, Florida, the officials experienced some trouble with the timing equipment and several rounds had to be rerun. In the semifinal round, Hubert in the 985 SS/E Cobra Jet downed the Wargo's Citgo entry with an 11.86 to the Chevy II's 12.69. In the final round, Hubert faced off against Tom Crutchfield in his 1965 Dodge *Satisfaction*. The cars charged off the line with the Mustang leading the way. When they raced across the finish line, Hubert was first with an 11.18 at 108.82 mph, a little too good running way outside the bracket.

All day Hubert had been dialed in and running in the high 11s. Coming back down the return road in a hurry, Hubert jumped out of the Mustang and headed for the tower. He shouted to the officials on the starting line, "There ain't no way in the world this car will go 11.18, not even if you dropped it off of Stone Mountain!" Crutchfield ran close behind, following him into the tower. The Chrondek equipment still read 11.18 at 108.82. Hubert protested, but a rerun could not be worked out and he had to settle for losing electronically. The officials chalked it up to bad timing equipment, flaky generators, and a host of other what-ifs.

## *Georgia Shaker* Style

Hubert was eager to personalize the 985 Cobra Jet to set it apart from the pack. When he got back to Georgia, Hubert took both Mustangs to Thompson's Body Shop in Alpharetta for a makeover. He really liked the style and flash of the paint job Max Thompson put on the 1967 Fairlane. Hubert felt that the two-tone black and silver metal flake with bright yellow lettering really popped. The Fairlane had been painted in mid-October and he'd only been able to enjoy that paint scheme for a little over two months before getting the Mustang. The 985 car was Hubert's primary race car, so he decided to recreate the black, silver, and yellow paint scheme.

Like the Fairlane, Max started with a two-tone black and silver. He used a heavy metal flake silver that would sparkle every color. The Mustang had "Georgia Shaker"

***The 985 SS/E Cobra Jet Mustang was a strong contender, consistently turning in times in the low 11s. By the summer, this CJ would be sporting a custom paint job and carrying the Georgia Shaker moniker.***

***Hubert loved a flashy paint job. This silver had so much metal flake in it that it was blinding in the sunlight. It would sparkle every different color. (Photo Courtesy Doug Boyce)***

Hubert posed proudly with his newly painted Cobra Jet. This was originally the Paul Harvey Ford 985 Cobra Jet, seen here with its new Foulger Ford sponsor and more of a Georgia Shaker flare.

Hubert received fan mail from across the country. Many times, it was artwork depicting his Georgia Shaker race cars. This drawing from an unknown artist is one such piece.

The Georgia Shaker pulls away from friend and Atlanta neighbor Bob Coble. Hubert's wife, Bee, designed the Ford Cobra Jet logo on the door of Coble's car.

The Georgia Shaker is hooking up hard as Jerry Harvey began to spin, leaving no doubt who crossed the stripe first on this pass. Back at the Winternationals, these cars were twins, Hubert's 985 and Jerry Harvey's 983 were the only two painted exactly the same. They were lettered in black with red outline and were the only two that carried the same sponsor: Paul Harvey Ford.

Hubert stands hard on the go pedal before a packed house. There was no shortage of drag racing fans in 1968.

*Hubert Platt was not camera shy. He seemed to always have a moment or two to stop and smile for a photographer, and the camera was generally good to him.*

*The lines on the 1968 Ford Fastback Mustang made it one of the best-looking muscle cars of all time. It was a car that looked fast while sitting still, and few compare. (Photo Courtesy Michael Goyda)*

*This is the calm before the storm. Moments after this photo was taken in the staging lanes, the Georgia Shaker suffered a violent end-over-end crash. (Photo Courtesy Marvin Smith)*

running the full length of the quarter panel in bright yellow lettering. The sponsorship for both cars also changed. Hubert and Chuck Foulger had formed a relationship, and the 985 car was now going to be sponsored by Foulger Ford out of Monrovia, California. The new sponsor was lettered on the doors in bright yellow as well as Hubert's name. The only change made to the 984 car would be a new sponsor. It was switched from "Tasca Ford" to "Paul Harvey Ford" all in bright red lettering outlined in blue.

## "Platt Totals Pony"

Hubert was set to go head-to-head in a match race against his ex-teammate Harold Dutton. Harold had switched brands for the 1968 season and was now driving a red Hemi 'Cuda for Bob Maddox Plymouth out of Forest Park, Georgia. The Fourth of July showdown drew a big crowd at the Southeastern International Dragway in Dallas, Georgia, and there was excitement in the air when the two came to the line for time trials. Harold's SS/B 'Cuda beat the SS/E Mustang with an 11.06 to an 11.60.

*Hubert lines up against former teammate Harold Dutton's* Drag Hag. *Little does he know, this will be his last time down the strip in this car. The Mustang will crash, and the wreck will be rebuilt and raced by Randy Payne, Hubert's friend and fellow Georgia racer.*

In the next round, Hubert was given a handicap of 0.54. The Mustang launched off the starting line a few lengths ahead of the Plymouth due to the handicap. Just past half track in high gear, the rear end of the Mustang

*After the accident, Hubert kicked out the busted windshield and climbed out because the door was jammed shut. The Mustang was damaged much worse than Hubert, who escaped with only a small cut on his left arm. (Photo Courtesy Marvin Smith)*

*After the black and silver Cobra Jet was repaired, it was repainted and renamed* Bullet Proof. *Randy Payne campaigned it for a few months before Hubert sold it to Super Stock racer Rusty Gillis. (Photo Courtesy Marvin Smith)*

## Limelight

Hubert continued to be in the spotlight when the August 1968 issue of the *Speed and Supercar* magazine featured the 984 Cobra Jet on its cover. The photo was from the Bakersfield, California, summer drags. Constant magazine and newspaper coverage of Hubert's cars kept his name in the forefront of drag racing among fans and peers. Anytime Ford or Mustangs were mentioned in a drag racing conversation, the name Hubert "Hu-Baby" Platt was sure to come up. His charismatic personality and larger-than-life persona garnered him a lot of press. Whether he won or lost, he was often the fan favorite.

***After the Winternationals, Hubert had the sponsor on the 984 C/SA Cobra Jet Mustang changed to Paul Harvey Ford from Tasca.***

came unlocked, causing the car to dart into the opposite lane in a cloud of smoke.

Harold had luckily missed a gear. Before catching up to the Mustang, he saw that Hubert was in trouble. He stood hard on the brakes to avoid an accident. Hubert, trying to regain control, swerved back into the right lane and off of the track, narrowly missing the guardrail before flipping end-over-end in the air and landing on its wheels in a shallow ditch. He kicked out the busted windshield and climbed out, waving to the fans that he was okay. He was checked out by a local physician and declared uninjured. He escaped with just a small cut on his left arm.

### *New Two-Car Team*

Although Ford felt as though it had caught up with Chrysler on the drag strip, there was still progress to be made in the public arena away from the track. The Dodge program with Dick Landy and the Plymouth clinics with Sox & Martin that had started 18 months earlier were a huge hit with fans. Ford knew it needed to develop its own clinic program. The second half of 1968 was spent preparing for its scheduled debut in January 1969.

The cars campaigned by the Chrysler factory teams of Sox & Martin as well as Dick Landy consisted of sometimes as many as six different models: Plymouth's GTX, Road Runner, and Barracuda and Dodge's Charger, Dart, and Coronet R/T. Ford needed to promote more than just the Mustang and Fairlane, so Hubert received a 1968 Torino Cobra factory drag car with a 428 Cobra Jet and a 4-speed transmission prepared by Holman-Moody-Stroppe in Long Beach, California, to race in SS/F. Hubert also got a newly prepared Cobra Jet Mustang to race in SS/EA. It

*The custom look of Hubert's* Georgia Shaker *race cars is one of the many things that made him a stand out at the drags. Hubert would come up with these paint schemes and Max Thompson would bring them to life. Both sides of the Torino are shown here in front of Chesser's American service station at the corner of Clairmont and Dresden in Atlanta. Just 1 mile from Hubert's home, Chesser's was a haven for hot rodders and drag racers. Hubert's younger brothers Huston and Ray each worked there at different times. (Photos Courtesy Tim Thompson)*

Foulger Ford in Monrovia, California, was one of the West Coast's premier performance Ford dealerships. Hubert campaigned three different Cobra Jets under the Foulger Ford banner in 1968: two Mustangs and a Torino.

In 1968, Hubert had two different business cards while working for Foulger Ford. This one had his personal information on it, including his home address and home phone number.

*This tri-color Cobra Jet Mustang is the replacement car Hubert got from Chuck Foulger after the accident in the 985 black-and-silver Mustang.*

*Ford factory performance specialist Chuck Foulger's Ford dealership was in Monrovia, California. Chuck and Hubert had a great relationship and Foulger Ford sponsored three of Hubert's four race cars in 1968.*

*This tri-colored 1968 Torino Cobra got Hubert his closest to a NHRA world championship. He finished second in the NHRA Division 2 points race in 1968. (Photo Courtesy Martyn L. Schorr)*

has been speculated that this car was actually the 984 C/SA car beefed up to race in SS/EA.

The Mustang was personalized on the West Coast with a tri-color paint scheme that Hubert came up with. The driver's side was painted black and the passenger's side in white with a 16-inch gold stripe down the center. The Mustang was lettered like many of Hubert's previous rides with "Georgia Shaker" down the length of the quarter panel and a large "Foulger Ford" logo on the doors both in gold leaf with black shadow, and "Hubert Platt" beneath the side windows in black. As always, prominently displayed on the fender was Hubert's close friend and sponsor "Doug's Headers." The familiar contingency stickers of Crane Cams were placed on the tip of the fender and Pennzoil and Cragar behind the front wheel.

Hubert liked the West Coast paint job of the Mustang and the gold leaf lettering, but he still really preferred the flash of the black with yellow. Having only been able to enjoy it for a short period of time, first on the Fairlane for two and half months and then on the 985 Cobra Jet for less than six weeks before the crash, Hubert took the Torino Cobra to Thompson's Body Shop back in Georgia to get a somewhat-matching paint job. The Torino received the same tri-colored treatment as the new Mustang with black on the driver's side and white on the passenger's side with the gold stripe down the middle, but Hubert had the Torino's black side lettered in yellow to resemble his two previous cars and had the white side lettered in black outlined in bright red. Like the Mustang, it had "Georgia Shaker" down the length of the quarter panel and "Foulger Ford" across the door.

***In late 1968, Hubert raced the Foulger Ford Torino Cobra, which was a strong contender nationwide. It didn't seem to have much trouble with the big-block Camaros and Mopars of the day.***

## Alabama Showdown

On August 17, 1968, at Courtland Dragway in Courtland, Alabama, Hubert was scheduled to square off in a fan favorite Ford-versus-Chevy match race against Anthony Butler's SS/E 396 Camaro *Scrappy*. For this challenge, Hubert brought out the Torino Cobra, which he raced in SS/F. Both of the big-block 4-speed Super Stocks made their way to the starting line under overcast skies threatening rain.

In the solo time trials, the *Scrappy* Camaro went first with a strong ET of 11.64. Hubert followed with a slower 11.90 but broke a clutch on the run. Hubert, flexing his mechanic skills, had the Torino Cobra on the back straightaway banging gears with a new clutch in 45 minutes.

When it came time for round one, Bobby Boyd (strip manager at Courtland) asked the racers how they would like to run the race: with a 0.26 handicap or heads up. Hubert said with a 0.26 spot for the first run. Boyd agreed, but only if Hubert would go heads up after that if he won. Hubert said okay but insisted he should get a bigger spot if *Scrappy* won.

When the two cars pulled to the line for round one, Hubert was out first with the 0.26 handicap, winning with an 11.87. Since Hubert won the round, the match race would be two-out-of-three heads up as agreed. In the first of the two out of three, the Camaro was off to a strong start ahead of the Cobra in three gears, but Hubert pulled a strong fourth gear and passed *Scrappy* in the traps for the win.

In round two, the Camaro pulled out strong again, having a fender on the Torino. This time, Hubert was not able to overcome, and the big-block 396 Chevy took the win. For the third and final round, there was high tension and the fans were ready. *Scrappy* launched from the starting line first, but he left a red light behind to the dismay of the Chevy fans. A red-light win wasn't good enough for Hubert, and he stood on it hard, passing the Camaro to the thrill of the Ford fans! In a record time of one hour, the officials were able to complete this match race with rain closing in. It turned out to be a good idea to run the main event first, as Street and Stock Eliminator were rained out shortly after the final round of the match race.

## Ford Takes Drag Racing to Forgotten Youths

In the beginning of 1967, the expectation was that Ford would aggressively engage in a competitive promotion against Chrysler's clinic program. However, Ford took time to consider how best to proceed. Instead of starting at the dealerships with a sales-based seminars, Ford decided to take a less commercial approach.

Headed up by Ford's longtime racing director Jacque Passino along with Chuck Foulger, Ford devised a more civically minded pilot program for its upcoming seminars to begin in 1969. With the help of promoter John Durbin, the first event was held on September 25, 1968,

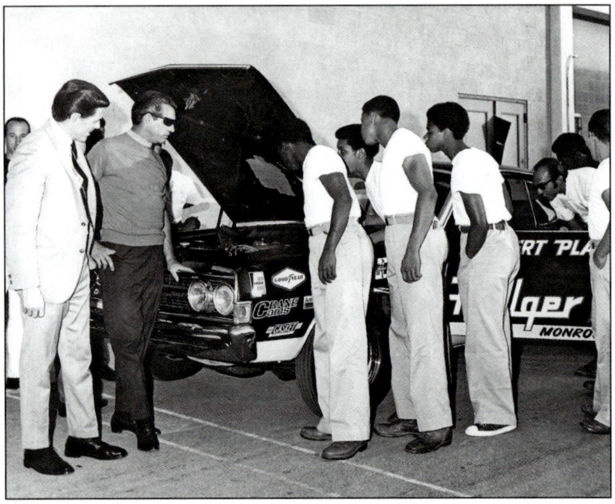

Hubert and Chuck Foulger took drag racing to the Los Padrinos Juvenile Detention Home in Los Angeles, California. This was a test run for the seminar program Ford was planning for the coming year.

at Los Padrinos Juvenile Detention Home in Los Angeles, California.

The Los Padrinos facility housed youths between the ages of 8 and 18 who were wards of the court. Three hundred youngsters were assembled in the courtyard of the detention center for a presentation by Chuck and Hubert with the star of the program being Hubert's Super Stock Torino Cobra. After giving the youths a description and understanding of the sport of drag racing and the many employment opportunities in the automotive industry, Hubert entertained the group with an exhibition burnout in the brightly colored drag car.

The enthusiastic wards of the court bombarded Hubert with questions for more than an hour, which he patiently answered. The questions on this day were less technical than Hubert was often asked at the track. Most of the boys just wanted to know basic things such as how fast the car would go, why the battery was mounted in the truck, and why the rear tires were screwed to the rims.

Ford had set out to provide a meaningful and memorable experience for those less fortunate. John Durbin pointed out that youths in adverse situations had fewer exciting moments in life, so when something special was done for them it was long remembered. Ford's wish was that in the future when these young men were in the position to buy a car it would be a Ford.

### Another Record Run

Jacque Passino and the heads of Ford Racing were very pleased with the success of the Los Padrinos seminar. Hubert had proven he could speak well in front of a large crowd and command the attention of his audience with his Southern accent and charm. His larger-than-life personality had already made him a fan favorite, and it had now made him the number-one contender to be the face of Ford's clinic program. What happened next just helped seal the deal.

On October 12, 1968, Hubert was the man to beat at Orange County International Raceway in Irvine, California. Fans rooting against Platt thought the man who could get the job done against him was Bob Lambeck. Lambeck was driving the Dick Landy factory-sponsored Dodge Dart and had been running quicker than Hubert all day.

In the second round, as the two lined up, the fans held their breath as the green light fell and both cars left with an exact reaction time of 0.06. The Dodge enjoyed a slight lead through first and second gear, but the Mustang crossed the finish line first. Both racers recorded an exact ET of 11.80. Platt's 118.26 mph was the difference, the Dodge coming up short at 117.03 mph. The 118.26 mph Hubert recorded on this run would stand as the NHRA national record in SS/EA.

Certificate of Record

This is to certify that Hubert Platt

established a new track record for

SS/EA class on October 12, 1968

118.26 mph elapsed time

ORANGE COUNTY INTERNATIONAL RACEWAY

Officials

Hubert broke several records during his career. This one is for the track record he set on October 12, 1968

# CHAPTER 10

# FORD DRAG TEAM

In the winter of 1968, it was all systems go for Ford Division's performance promotion program. Chrysler called its program "clinics," so Ford decided to call its "seminars." The dealership seminars provided a lecture on subjects such as "preparation of a drag car" and "Ford performance parts for your street vehicle," basically an education for the public on how to make a stock Ford go fast with over-the-counter parts. Then, it promoted safety and performance through an interactive Q & A with top drag racing drivers. The program was aimed at increasing Ford's foothold in the booming muscle car market. The seminars were a way to influence the youth to come out to the drag strip and take racing off the streets.

So far, the preparation for the upcoming 1969 race season was being spearheaded by the head of Ford Drag Racing, Chuck Foulger. But Ford corporate and Ford Division seemed to always put a buffer between themselves and programs of this nature, so Ford hired a

***When it was time for formal attire, Hubert suggested the drivers wear matching suits. Car Corporation agreed, and matching suits were purchased for both the East and West Coast teams. Hubert and Randy Payne pose in front of the Q-code Mustang and Torino Cobra.***

subcontractor to run the Ford Drag Teams. The contract was given to Car Corporation out of Livonia, Michigan, which was already having success running the Ford Total Performance Show and was heavily involved in the National Council of Mustang Clubs.

The seminar program consisted of two touring, two-car teams, one based on the West Coast and one on the East Coast. The teams shared the same three objectives: to put their cars in the winner's circle every weekend, to travel to Ford dealerships during the week and put on drag racing safety and performance seminars, and to start up Ford Drag Clubs at each dealership.

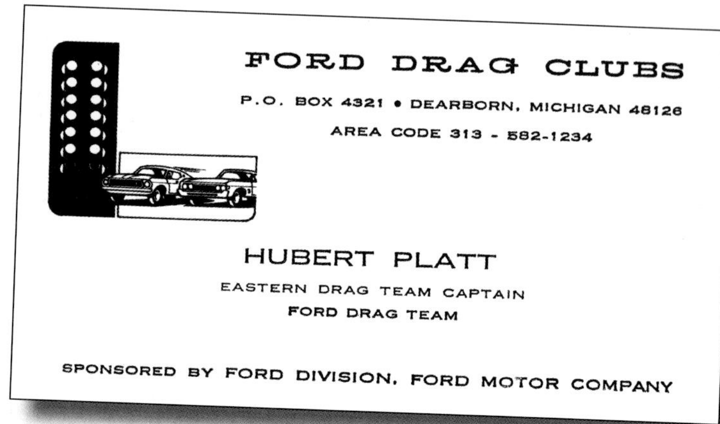
FORD DRAG CLUBS
P.O. BOX 4321 • DEARBORN, MICHIGAN 48126
AREA CODE 313 - 582-1234

HUBERT PLATT
EASTERN DRAG TEAM CAPTAIN
FORD DRAG TEAM

SPONSORED BY FORD DIVISION, FORD MOTOR COMPANY

***Hubert handed out his Ford Drag Team business card to fans, encouraging them to join their local Ford Drag Club. The information on the top was for Car Corporation in Dearborn, Michigan, where you could call to find out where your nearest local chapter of the Ford Drag Club was located.***

## The Drivers

Hubert (now 38 years old) was chosen to be the captain of the East Coast Ford Drag Team. He received a salary of $15,000 per year plus expenses. In 1969, the average salary was around $6,000 per year.

Hubert picked fellow Georgia racer, Randy Payne, a 245-pound former high school football tackle as his partner. Like Hubert, Randy had been drag racing since the late 1950s, and he was considered a veteran of the sport who held both ends of the NHRA SS/E national record in 1967. Randy received a salary of $12,000 per year plus expenses. The Drag Team drivers were paid by Car Corporation.

***What Ford saw in Hubert Platt was the total package: confident good looks, an outgoing personality with the ability to speak to large crowds, and a winning reputation behind the wheel. Add this to his Southern accent and charm and it's obvious why he was the face of the Ford Drag Team.***

The West Coast drag team was headed up by team captain Ed Terry from Hayward, California. Ed was also a veteran drag racer who won titles at the NHRA 1963 and 1965 Winternationals as well as the Eliminator honors at the 1964 *Hot Rod* Magazine Meet. Ed's partner was Dick Wood of Fremont, California, a skilled racer who won class honors at both the 1967 and 1968 Winternationals.

These four men now represented Ford Motor Company in the public eye at the drag races and dealership seminars. The drivers' attire was very dapper; at the drags they had matching racing suits. The East Coast team wore navy blue pants and jackets with white stripes down the sleeve and leg, while the West Coast team sported light blue with white stripes. On the left chest of all of the jackets was a Cobra racing patch and the driver's name was embroidered either on the opposite chest or down the sleeve. Both teams received zip-up coveralls to wear when working on the cars that also had the racing stripes and Cobra branding.

For the dealership seminars, the teams were dressed in gray dress slacks, white knit crew neck dress shirts, and dark gray sport jackets. This type of dress furthered what career drag racers had been doing for years, giving drag racing a more professional and corporate aesthetic. The teams also received heavy winter coats that were blue with gold trim and had their names on front and "Ford Drag Team" on back, all embroidered.

This Q-code 428 Cobra Jet Mustang Mach 1, with an automatic transmission brought Hubert much success in the form of national records and national event wins.

### The Cars

Each team received two Super Stocks to accomplish their racing goals: an Q-code 1969 Mustang Mach I and an R-code 1969 Torino Cobra. All four were powered by Ford's 428 Cobra Jet engine.

On the West Coast, Ed Terry's R-Code Mach I (manual transmission) raced SS/I and Dick Wood's Torino Cobra (automatic transmission) ran in SS/JA. On the East Coast, Hubert Platt's Q-Code Mach I (automatic transmission) raced SS/IA and Randy Payne's Torino Cobra (manual transmission) ran in SS/J. Each team had two Super Stocks in different classes (automatic and manual), ensuring that the two would not meet in class eliminations but could race in the final of Super Stock Eliminator. Both teams were to race at Super Stock bashes every weekend in their respective geographic areas and then meet up to compete together at all of the major AHRA and NHRA national events.

The first 1969 Cobra Jet SportsRoof Mustang pulled from inventory at Foulger Ford in Monrovia, California, was a Q-code with a C-6 automatic. This car was for Hubert. A second SportsRoof Mustang with a 4-speed and an R-Code Shaker-style hood scoop was pulled for Ed, and a Torino Cobra for Dick.

All three cars were sent to Holman-Moody-Stroppe (H-M-S) in Long Beach to undergo upgrades for drag racing. The cars basically got the same treatment as the 1968 Cobra Jet Mustangs: beefed-up rear suspensions with the addition of Logghe traction ladder bars, 10.5 racing slicks, roll bars, blueprinted Cobra Jet engines, modified racing transmissions, etc. The tri-colored 1968 Torino Cobra that Hubert raced at the end of the 1968 season was already a successful competitor, finishing the season as the NHRA

Hubert piloted this Super Stock for around 18 months, longer than most of his rides to date.

Division 2 runner-up. So, they removed the five chrome fins on the side of the roof characteristic to the 1968 and rebranded the car as a 1969. It became the Torino Cobra for the East Coast team that Randy would drive.

## The Rigs

The heavy-duty Ford C-750 truck was chosen as the base for the Ford Drag Team rigs. Custom C-shaped parts lockers with tire racks on top made from special high-strength aluminum were constructed and installed on the front of the ramp trucks behind the sleeper cabs. The trucks were sent from Dearborn, Michigan, to Chicago, Illinois, to be outfitted with California-designed, custom-made tow-behind trailers with a large box on front. Most people thought this was a toolbox, but it actually served as basic storage for the crew's personal belongings.

*The Ford Drag Team rigs were impressive to say the least. They demanded attention at any track they pulled into.*

*Immaculate from end to end, the Ford Drag Team rigs had everything team members could need at the races, including a spare 428 Cobra Jet engine. (Photo Courtesy Doug Boyce)*

*Platt and Payne made a pit stop at Ford headquarters in Detroit to have a meet and greet with Ford executives and show off the new race team.*

*The beauty of the Ford Drag Team hauler was only matched by Miss Cobra and Miss Mach 1 perched high on top for this press photo.*

On the return trip to Dearborn, one of the trucks broke an axle. The trailers had to then be outfitted with dolly wheels located at the union of truck and trailer. Next, the rigs made the trip west to H-M-S in Long Beach, where construction was finished. H-M-S set up the rigs with a spare 428 Cobra Jet engine (stored below the car on the ramp truck), spare parts for racing, as well as four showcases each filled with Ford performance parts to be used at the seminars as a visual aid. The four 6-foot-tall showcases were heavy, so a small hoist was installed on top of the rig to take the cases in and out and could also be used for the spare engine.

The rigs carried the Torino Cobras on the ramp truck and towed the Mustang Mach I's on the trailer behind. By the time they were complete, Ford had invested $50,000 on each of the custom rigs.

## Paint Scheme

The colors chosen for the Ford Drag Team were Ford Division Metallic Blue and Pearlescent White. The West Coast team cars were painted white with blue stripes, and the East Coast team cars were the opposite: blue with white stripes. The cars were lettered by a famous Southern California artist named "The Brush."

On the doors of the West Coast cars it read "Terry & Wood" and on the East Coast cars "Platt & Payne" in gold leaf. Under the names on the door of the Mustangs and on the quarter panels of the Torinos appeared Ford's new slogan "The Going Thing." The Mustangs had a Boss 302–style stripe, while the Torinos had a stripe similar to the stock GT Torinos, except that it stopped and turned back before the front wheel.  All four cars had a huge Ford logo covering the decklid.

*This was Hubert's favorite photo of this car, he loved to correct fans who thought the car had a 4-speed because of the way the back tire is wrinkled. Hubert would tell them, "If you got the power, an automatic will wrinkle the tire too!"*

The trailers were painted to match the trucks. The surface of the ramp truck and trailer where the race cars sat was covered in blue indoor/outdoor carpet. After picking up the new rig at H-M-S, Hubert took the East Coast truck to a Southern California upholstery shop and had the interior diamond tucked and had a black velvet curtain put between the cab and sleeper.

The fully dressed race cars and rigs were bright and beautiful. They were every bit as flashy as, if not more than, Chrysler's patriotic, red, white, and blue race cars and rigs campaigned by Sox & Martin.

The cars also had opposite color hoods with "428 Cobra Jet" on them in gold leaf lettering. Below the side windows read the drivers' names in gold as well as a small Ford logo beside it that said "Prepared by Holman & Moody-Stroppe, Inc. Long Beach, California" all of which was hand painted.

The rigs were painted to match the race cars with huge C-stripes on the side of the ramp trucks with a large Ford logo inset. On the doors of the C-750 cabs were Ford logos followed by the words "DRAG TEAM" in all capital letters painted gold. Under the Ford logo on the door it read "Platt & Payne" on the blue East Coast truck and "Terry & Wood" on the white West Coast truck.

## Performance on the Line

When the West Coast rig and cars were complete, they were taken to Orange County International Raceway in Irvine, California. There, they filmed the final scenes of a short movie Ford Division had been working on for the Ford Drag Teams. The completed 14-minute film was titled Performance on the Line.

*Hubert Platt and Randy Payne were what you would call characters: clever, witty, and quick with a joke. They had a presence when they would enter a room, and the two of them together was nothing short of a comedy routine.*

*Linda "Miss Hurst" Vaughn is an icon and treasure to the sport of drag racing. Linda's friendship with the Platt family goes way back. In the late 1960s, Linda's apartment was 1 mile from the Platt's home in Atlanta.*

**Left:** *Linda Vaughn dressed all in gold is looking more like a Bond girl than Miss Hurst! You can tell she feels right at home with these two Southern gentlemen.* **Above:** *Hubert Platt and Linda Vaughn were great friends who loved to flirt and joke around with each other. This iconic photo was taken in the interior of Hubert's 1969 Super Stock Cobra Jet Mustang, which was equipped with a Hurst Dual Gate shifter with a Hurst Line Lock.*

The film began by showing clips of some famous drag racers while giving a brief history of the sport. It went on to show a typical weekend at Orange County International Raceway. It also took the opportunity to introduce the Ford Drag Team captains Hubert Platt and Ed Terry. The film showed the two captains working together in the pits then in a drag race in their 1968 race cars before each taking a turn down the strip in Ed's new Ford Drag Team, Super Stock Mustang with an in-car camera.

The short featured top-name Funny Car drivers, including Gas Ronda, Tom Grove, Don Schumacher, Big John Mazmanian, and Sidney Foster in Larry Coleman's Super Ford, enticing the viewer to come out to the drag races. During the film, the narrator really spoke to the hot rod and drag racing enthusiast, letting them know that if they wished to pursue the sport of drag racing, Ford was there to give them all the help that was available. It was made very clear that the Ford dealerships were ready to supply them with the best parts and equipment as well as eager service and parts professionals to help them achieve total performance out of their Ford on the drag strip.

The film went on to say, "The Ford Drag Team is here because we believe your enjoyment of this great sport can be increased as a member of your own local Ford Drag Club!" This movie was shown at the dealership seminars throughout 1969.

## The First Ford Drag Team Seminar

During the first week of January 1969, formal invitations were sent out to VIPs that read: "Foulger Ford, Inc. cordially invites you to attend the premier showing of the Ford Performance Seminar and Ford Drag Club featuring Hubert Platt and Ed Terry on Tuesday, January 14, 1969 at 3:30 P.M. Foulger Ford, Inc. 147 Huntington Drive Monrovia, California 91016, Cocktails R.S.V.P."

This first seminar was held in the showroom of Foulger Ford, where the brand-new drag cars were on display. At one end of the showroom was a podium with

*Hubert Platt and Ed Terry share the stage at the first Ford Drag Team seminar. These two men can't begin to image how busy their schedules are about to get. After this seminar, they will split up to do their separate tours.*

*Having the drag cars in the showroom was a thrill for fans. They were able to see the cars close up and ask the drivers questions, which made for a personal experience and lasting impression. (Photo Courtesy Bob McClurg)*

a microphone and PA system (so the speakers could be heard by the crowd) and the four 6-foot-tall showcases that displayed Ford performance parts to be used as a visual aid during the lecture. The first case featured performance parts for 427 engines; the second had 352, 390, and 428 performance upgrades; the third contained small-block performance parts for the 260, 289, and 302; and the fourth case showed off high-performance accessories such as chrome valve covers, dual quad air cleaners, and Shelby wheels.

Hubert and Ed discussed how to set up a Ford for drag racing with over-the-counter parts that could be purchased at a local Ford dealer. They also took questions from the audience and spoke about the upcoming tour. Everyone who attended the seminar received a press kit that contained a folder with a short bio on the drivers, 8x10 glossy black-and-white photos of the race cars, as well as literature on Ford performance parts. The seminar was a success. The groundwork and format for how the seminars should go was now set in place, and the teams were ready to start the new year and national tour.

## *Hot Rod* Magazine Cover Story

The 1969 February issue of *Hot Rod* magazine featured Hubert on the cover with *Hot Rod* reporter John

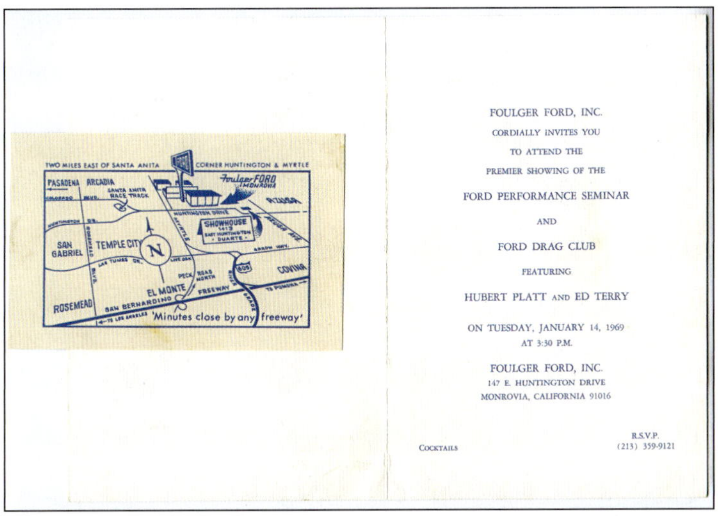

FOULGER FORD, INC.
CORDIALLY INVITES YOU
TO ATTEND THE
PREMIER SHOWING OF THE
FORD PERFORMANCE SEMINAR
AND
FORD DRAG CLUB
FEATURING
HUBERT PLATT AND ED TERRY
ON TUESDAY, JANUARY 14, 1969
AT 3:30 P.M.
FOULGER FORD, INC.
147 E. HUNTINGTON DRIVE
MONROVIA, CALIFORNIA 91016

COCKTAILS

R.S.V.P.
(213) 359-9121



*This invitation was sent to Hubert's wife Bee for the first Ford Drag Team seminar, which was held at Foulger Ford in Monrovia, California.*

*Hubert looked more like a Hollywood movie star or a New York model than a race car driver from the South.*

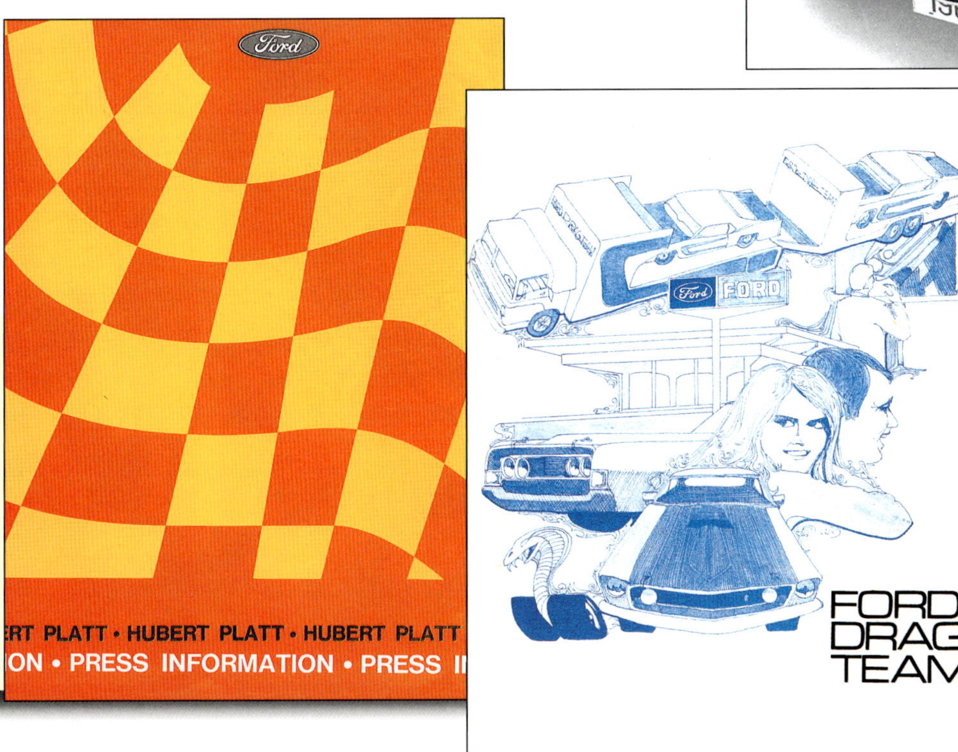



*These Ford Drag Team press kits were handed out at dealership seminars and the drag races. They included black-and-white 8x10 photos of the race cars as well as driver bios and basic Ford Drag Team and Ford Drag Club information.*

***Wanna race? Don't press your luck, these two together would be any muscle car's worst nightmare in a street race! Don't let the smile fool you.***

Thawley looking over an experimental, big-block 1969 Mustang. The caption on the cover read: "Exclusive coverage: HUBERT PLATT'S '69 "Canted Valve" 429 Mustang: Ford's answer to the Hemi Mopar Barracuda." Inside, the three-page article with nine pictures called "Mighty Tough Horse" told of Ford's plan to put the Boss 429 Hemi head engine into production so that it would be eligible to compete on the NASCAR circuit as well as in the AHRA and NHRA stock classes. The article discussed in detail the technical aspects of the engine and the modifications the Mustang received to accept it. Hubert was featured in this article as Ford's celebrity driver and spokesperson.

### NHRA Winternationals

On February 2, the executives at Ford Division and Car Corporation were given something to celebrate. By the end of the weekend, to the delight of the Ford fans on hand at the Los Angeles County Fairgrounds, the Ford

***Hubert was very proud of this 1969 Boss 429 4-speed Mustang that was given to him by Ford. He would say, "Ford will give me anything I want to drive and put a Thunderbird in the driveway for my wife."***

Drag Teams had achieved their first success. Hubert and Randy were both class winners in their respective classes at the NHRA Winternationals. Hubert also set the SS/IA national record with an ET of 12.07, and the West Coast team of Terry and Wood won "Best Appearing Crew." The newly formed Ford Drag Teams served notice to the competition that they were here to compete with performance and style!

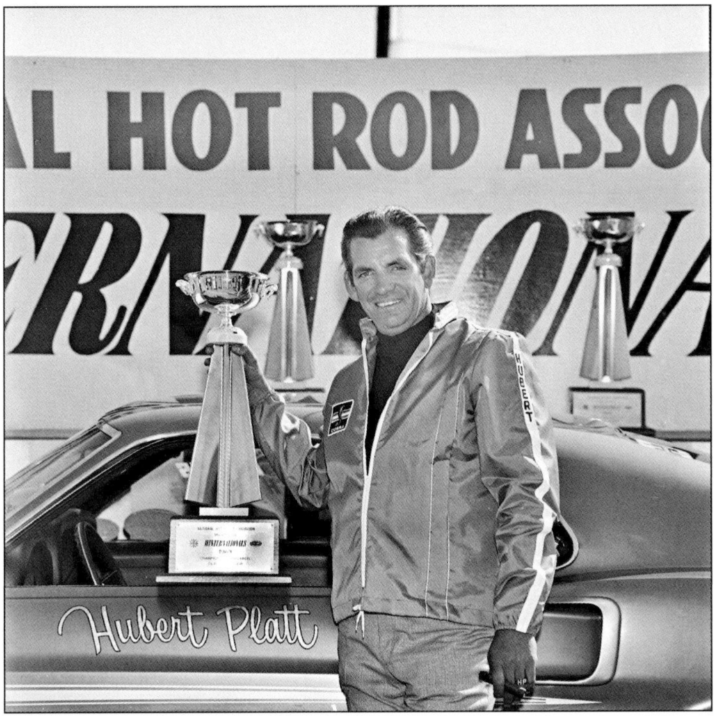


*Hubert was in the final round at the NHRA Winternationals in 1967, 1968, and 1969. He won two out of three. (Photo Courtesy Bob McClurg)*

*Hubert and the Cobra Jet Mustang put a hole shot on the Hemi Dart of Shirley "Drag-On-Lady" Shahan before a standing-room-only crowd at the Los Angeles County Fairgrounds.*

*It doesn't get any better than this! The first race in their new factory-backed race cars was the 1969 NHRA Winternationals. Hubert and Randy both won their respective classes, and Hubert set the national record in SS/IA.*

*The California sun is visible on Hubert's face as he poses with the Winternationals trophy. The Mustang now sported wheels from new sponsor Kelsey-Hayes, and the Torino Cobra would have them soon as well.*

*The tag on the rear of the Mustang reads "Ford has a better idea." This promotion photo was in press kits and seminar handouts.*

### Florida Drags

After the NHRA Winternationals, Hubert and Randy headed east to Florida to compete in two big events. The Georgia duo put on the first East Coast seminar at a Fort Lauderdale Ford dealership. On the following weekend, Hubert and the Mustang were in fine form once again at the NASCAR Drag Racing Series Winter Championships in Miami, where he successfully captured the Super Stock Eliminator title, beating Randy in the final.

Next, the pair headed north to Daytona for another seminar and competition at the Daytona Winternationals held on February 19–22. During eliminations, Hubert and Randy each won their classes the first two nights and raced each other in the Super Stock Eliminator final. Randy won both the runoffs with an 11.98 on Thursday and 11.89 on Friday.

On Saturday, Randy won his class again. Hubert lost the SS/IA final to Bill Tanner in the Lenox Dodge Dart, when he hit the brakes a little too hard trying to keep from breaking out and Tanner passed him in the traps.

## Tragedy at Yellow River

In March 1969, while Hubert was riding a wave of success, his younger brother Huston's racing career was also soaring. Huston had a brand-new Logghe chassis 1969 Camaro AA/FC nitro Funny Car and had just been sponsored by Coca-Cola, joining its "Cavalcade of Stars." Things were going well, but sometimes actions beyond our control can alter our lives forever, and that is what happened to Huston Platt.

On Sunday March 2, 1969, Huston was racing at Yellow River Dragstrip in Covington, Georgia. Near the end of a run, a fan ran onto the edge of the track and was caught up in the Camaro's fully blossomed parachute, causing the car to go out of control and crash at more than 180 mph.

Eye witness accounts say the fan who went onto the track was trying to retrieve a dropped beer can. He was killed instantly along with 10 others who were watching from behind a fence constructed of nothing more than farm wire on weathered wooden posts. Forty other fans were seriously injured and a 12th victim died later that week in an Atlanta-area hospital.

The accident made national news, and the media sensationalized the crash with graphic photographs of the bodies of the victims at the scene. The national government launched an investigation, and investigators concluded that Huston had done no wrong nor could he have prevented the crash. The tragedy was ruled an accident caused by an unsafe track that didn't have a fence in place that would protect fans or in this case prevent fans from accessing the racing surface. Nationwide law went into effect after this accident, in which all tracks would now have to be sanctioned, licensed, and insured.

Huston was uninjured physically in the crash, but he was emotionally scarred forever from this horrific incident. It was almost a year before he returned to the seat of a Funny Car and the sport he loved. To this day, the Yellow River crash of 1969 is known as the deadliest accident in American motorsports history.

## The Bob Swaim Story

Photographer Bob Swaim was on assignment at the 1966 NHRA Winternationals for Crower Cams, taking photos of all the cars the company sponsored for its upcoming catalog. Bob recalls taking pictures of almost every car that went down the track, one of which was a front-engine dragster that suffered a blower explosion just as Bob snapped his shutter.

The photo showed the cockpit of the dragster fully engulfed in flames. It was so dynamic that Bob entered it in *Hot Rod* magazine's yearlong photo contest and won segment number one. After entering two more pictures and winning segments two and three, Bob landed a job with *Car Craft* magazine in October 1966.

While working for *Car Craft,* Bob took the most iconic Ford drag racing photo ever of the *Super Snake*. The photo is a close-up overhead shot of Don "The Snake" Prudhomme's SOHC-powered front engine dragster, which was used in Ford's Shelby catalog.

In 1968, while photographing test sessions of Hubert's 1968 Cobra Jet Mustang for the magazine, Bob and Hubert met, and the two hit it off. In September at *Car Craft* magazine's annual awards banquet, Hubert and Bob crossed paths again. Hubert told Bob about the upcoming Ford Drag Team and Ford Drag Clubs and offered him a job as the East Coast director. Bob gladly accepted and was later contacted by Car Corporation and welcomed to the team.

Bob's job was to be Hubert's PR man and coordinator. His actual duties were to go ahead of Hubert, weeks in advance if possible, to cities with upcoming races. Once there, he was to approach the local Ford dealerships and see if they would be interested in having the drag team come in and put on a seminar. If a dealership was interested, he would set the date, make all the plans, and run large ads in the local newspapers to advertise the upcoming seminar. He had to do everything, right down to making sure the dealer had sufficient chairs and enough refreshments on the evening of the event.

Another of his responsibilities was to find at least two employees at the dealership with a passion for performance and hopefully drag racing who would be interested in starting and running their own local chapter of the Ford Drag Club. The Ford Drag Clubs were to be the fan clubs of the Ford Drag Teams.

Bob's last assignment for *Car Craft* magazine was to photograph the 1969 NHRA Winternationals. After the race on Monday, February 3, Bob left Pomona, California, in Hubert's personal 1968 Lincoln Continental Mark III and drove straight to Fort Lauderdale, Florida, where he began to set up seminars for Platt and Payne all up and down the eastern seaboard. Bob stayed on the road and continued to set up seminars for the next three months.

Feeling overwhelmed and overworked, Bob called his bosses at Car Corporation to tell them how things were going. He stressed the need for a national coordinator who could oversee operations from the office in Dearborn, Michigan. They replied with "Congratulations, you've got the job." So, in May 1969, Bob went into the Car Corp office to begin his new job as national director of the Ford Drag Teams. In June, he hired Jon Brantmeier to replace him in the field as East Coast coordinator.

***Bob Swaim's new bride, June, poses on their honeymoon at Lake Tahoe with Hubert's 1968 Lincoln Continental Mark III. It's hard to tell from this photo, but Hubert's Mark III had a super custom paint job, modeled after the lowriders of Southern California. It was pearl baby blue with fish scales all the way down the side. (Photo Courtesy Bob Swaim)***

***A grand opening party was held for Car Corporation's new facility in Livonia, Michigan. Attendees included (left to right): Hubert Platt, Bob Swaim, Edsel Ford II, Dick Loehr, Mac McCoy, and an unknown gentlemen. Edsel Ford II is the great-grandson of Henry Ford.***

Gainesville Sun

SPORTS

Saturday, Sept. 13, 1969 9

ATLANTA'S HUBERT PLATT (INSET) IS STRONG CONTENDER FOR HONORS
. . . in super stock category of Southwest World Championship series

# O.J., Broadway Joe Clash As AFL Begins Season

O.J will try to get it going and Broadway Joe will try to keep it going when the American Football League opens its regular season Sunday.

Attention will be focused on War Memorial Stadium in Buffalo, where the Bills will play host to the world champion New York Jets in a game nationally televised by NBC. Kickoff is 1:30 p.m., EDT.

The focal points of the game will be Buffalo rookie O.J. Simpson, launching a career as pro football's most publicized rookie since Broadway Joe Namath, and Namath, the cool and controversial quarterback out to prove the Jets' Super

Namath Simpson

In other games, Houston is at Oakland, Kansas City at San Diego, Miami at Cincinnati and Boston at Denver.

Another incentive for Namath and the Jets is the fact they have never won in

Slated to start, along with Simpson, is rookie fullback Bill "Earthquake" Enyart.

Veterans Matt Snell and Emerson Boozer will handle the running chores for the Jets while Namath will be throwing to the talented George Sauer and Don Maynard.

Daryle Lamonica, the league's second best passer in 1968, again will be at the helm for Oakland, which won its last eight regular season games last year before losing the championship clash to the Jets.

Besides the passing of Lamonica, the Raiders again will count on the running of

kicker Roy Gerela, who made good on eight of 11 field goal attempts, including one of 52 yards, in pre-season play. Gerela does his thing soccer style.

If pre-season play is an indication of things to come, San Diego, is in for a rough afternoon against Kansas City. The Chiefs, who beat San Diego twice last year, won all six exhibition games.

Len Dawson, the AFL's leading passer last season, will guide the Chiefs, who also will be counting on a defense that gave up 170 points, the fewest in the league last year.

Out to test the Kansas City

*It's pretty cool for Hubert to be pictured above O. J. Simpson and Joe Namath on the sports page. It goes to show that drag racing had a huge fan base in 1969, especially down South.*

The Dart would not have enough for Randy in the Super Stock Eliminator final, as he downed the Dodge with a 12.07 to put the Torino Cobra in the winner's circle for the third night in a row.

### Ford Drag Clubs

A big part of Ford Division's Performance Promotion Program was focused on helping Ford excel in the very competitive muscle car market. Special promotion coordinator, Frank Hurley, of Car Corporation explained it best when he was quoted saying, "The strip is where the muscle car customers are. Dragging drew more than 20 million fans last year, making it the number-two spectator sport. Most of that crowd is in the 16- to 25-year-old bracket. If you don't think those youngsters' opinions count, check out the number of cars on the highway today with racing stripes and hood scoops. Dad may be driving, but the kid with him probably picked out the car."

Ford Division and Car Corporation's marketing estimates concluded that 20 million fans went to 10,000 events at 800 drag strips in the United States in 1969 alone. Obviously, the Ford Drag Clubs would be an integral part of the program's success in reaching this young demographic.

At each seminar along with the regular program, the host had attendees who were interested in signing up and joining that dealership's local branch of the Ford Drag Club. Being a member of the Ford Drag Club came with many benefits. Upon initial sign up, members received a membership card, Ford Drag Club decals for their car, and Ford Drag Club jacket patches as well as a monthly national Ford Drag Club newsletter. The monthly newsletter reported on drag racing events and race results for the East and West Coast Drag Teams, and it also contained a segment on new performance information from Ford.

Many of the members of the Ford Drag Club were teens who had a hard time affording the hot rod hobby, so one of the biggest benefits of being a member was the 25-percent discount on parts and labor at their club Ford dealership. Some dealers even provided club members with a project car that they could prepare at club meetings and race at local events.

During the next few months, the Ford Drag Teams of Platt and Payne and Terry and Wood crisscrossed the United States, conducting seminars during the week and drag racing over the weekends. The seminar schedule was rigorous, but the teams were always met with high attendance, which made the racers' efforts worthwhile.

*Having the four performance display cases in the showroom at the seminars as visual aids helped educate the consumers in how to make their Ford fast at the drag strip with over-the-counter parts from their local Ford dealer.*

***Standing-room-only crowds were filling dealership showrooms to hear the Ford Drag Team's talk about safety and performance. The seminars were an immediate success, and club membership soared.***

*The Platt and Payne two-car team was stunning to see but also packed a punch on the drag strip, usually winning their classes and racing each other for Super Stock Eliminator. (Photos Courtesy Marvin Smith)*

| 1969 Platt and Payne East Coast Ford Drag Team Partial Schedule | | | | |
|---|---|---|---|---|
| *Date* | *Dealership* | *City, State* | *Attendance* | *Signed Up* |
| 3-4-1969 | Stark Hickey Ford | Royal Oak, Michigan | 780 | 145 |
| 4-3-1969 | Forest Cate Ford | Chattanooga, Tennessee | 629 | 53 |
| 4-7-1969 | Bob Frensley Ford | Louisville, Kentucky | 344 | 100 |
| 4-11-1969 | Sunny King Ford | Anniston, Alabama | 500+ | N/A |
| 4-22-1969 | Tasca Ford | Providence, Rhode Island | 15,000 | N/A |
| 4-23-1969 | Harr Ford | Worcester, Massachusetts | 644 | 274 |
| 4-29-1969 | Delta-Grange Ford | New Haven, Indiana | 900 | 412 |
| 4-30-1969 | Detroit Ford | Detroit, Michigan | 800 | 175 |
| 5-1-1969 | Detroit Metro Ford | Detroit, Michigan | 700 | 125 |
| 5-4-1969 | Southwest Ford | Cleveland, Ohio | 442 | 176 |
| 5-13-1969 | Pankopf Ford | Washington, Pennsylvania | 363 | 125 |
| 5-16-1969 | Foss Ford | Etna, Pennsylvania | 508 | 34 |
| 6-3-1969 | Beach Ford | Virginia Beach, Virginia | 757 | 244 |

When Hubert was asked about the overwhelming response they had to the seminar program and the incredible number of club members recruited, he said, "We help kids set up drag clubs. We teach the novices the best and safest way to drag, give engine tuning tips, share the latest engineering information, and answer questions. Man, do we answer questions. An average driver isn't likely to ask us if a 780 carb will be too big for a 260 powerplant with 289 parts, but 85 percent of the

*At Ford Drag Team seminars, fans joining the Ford Drag Club received a press kit called "Welcome to the World of Performance." Today, a complete press kit similar to the ones the gentlemen in the front row are holding is worth $1,000 to collectors.*

*Ford legend Bob Tasca, creator of the Cobra Jet engine, has a moment on the microphone at a Ford Drag Team seminar at his dealership Tasca Ford in Rhode Island. When these two would greet each other at the drag races, Hubert would yell "The Big Bopper" and Bob would yell "Hu-Baby!"*

When a dealership had a small showroom, it would hold the Ford Drag Team seminar in the garage area or outside if the weather permitted. Pennzoil sponsored the team, and the three door prizes on the table are from them. The bags contained 5 quarts of racing oil, a hat, and stickers.

Ford gave Hubert this 429 Super Cobra Jet Torino with shaker hood for his wife Bee to drive in 1970. It served as their family car.

Hubert's heavy on the gas in Riverside, California. Even though they were the East Coast team, Platt and Payne also raced all over the West Coast at major events.

kids ask questions like that all night long. We give 'em the straight answers with a heavy foot on the bit about safety. Dragging belongs on the strips and we tell 'em so."

Even with a busy schedule of seminars that included hundreds of highway miles per week, the Drag Teams were still able to make things happen at the track. On June 15, in Dallas, Texas, Hubert proved once again that the Cobra Jet Mustang Mach I was the car to beat when he took the SS/IA class honors at the NHRA Springnationals.

Hubert and the Super Stock Mustang were having a great summer, and it showed when he set the NHRA SS/I record with an 11.50 at 120 mph on July 4.

### "Go-In Thing"

The NHRA Nationals in Indianapolis, Indiana, held every year during Labor Day weekend is and always has been considered the premier drag racing event of the year. It brings competitors from all corners of the nation to compete in what is affectionately called "The Big Go."

Jon Brantmeier, East Coast Coordinator for the Ford Drag Team, planned a pilgrimage to Nationals for the Ford Drag Clubs. He used the national newsletter to bill it as the Ford Drag Club "Indy Go-In Thing."

## Lynette's Falcon

Hubert was in the middle of his busiest summer ever with almost every weekend scheduled for racing and sometimes as many as two or three seminars on weeknights, but he somehow found time to customize a car for his 17-year-old daughter, Lynette. He took a 1965 Falcon Sprint and had Max Thompson put a slick paint job on it: seven coats of Candy Apple Red with diamond dust mixed in the paint. Then, he set it on a set of Cragar S/S mags all the way around. Next, he had the interior completely reupholstered in diamond-tucked black Naugahyde; even the headliner and inside the trunk were diamond tucked! Doug Thorley sent a set of headers from California for the 289 V-8, but Lynette refused to let Hubert put them on, worried it would be too loud for a girl's car. The little Falcon was stunning; nothing short of a custom show car. Lynette drove the little Falcon to her senior year of high school and beyond, racking up well over 100,000 miles before selling it after she married.

*Now known as the US Nationals, the NHRA Nationals in Indianapolis has long been regarded as the biggest drag race in the world: "The Big-Go!"*

FORD DRAG CLUB **Newsletter**

Official Publication of Ford Drag Clubs

Volume 1, Number 2 — Headquarters: P.O. Box 501, Dearborn, Mich. 48120 — July, 1969

# Ford Drag Club "Go-In"

**COME TO THE FIRST CLUB GET TOGETHER; THE "GO-IN THING" AT THE NHRA NATIONALS IN INDY**

Photo by Leslie Lovett, Courtesy N.H.R.A.

*Indy — the magic word for race fans. In May, it is the famed "500" for oval buffs and in September it is NHRA's "Big Go."*

The site is just outside of Indianapolis in Clermont and the scene is also just slightly outside of anything else you may have seen.

There is nothing in drag racing to equal this Labor Day Weekend classic — and now, you can be a special part of this great event at the first annual Ford Drag Club "Indy Go-In Thing".

Be on hand to cheer for Hubert Platt, Ed Terry, Randy Payne, Dick Wood and a host of other stars. In fact, you name a racer and the odds are that he will be at Indy because this is the big one, this is the meet that tops them all.

What is the "Indy Go-In Thing"? It is the first annual national get together of Ford Drag Club members. You will have a special reserved section in the reserved seats — practically front row center — plus pit passes, free goodies, parties and more.

The total package will cost you $20.00 and is worth much more! If you're an early bird and send in before August 1, you save $2 as the cost is only $18 till then.

What do you get? Among other things, reserved seats, general admission entrance and pit passes for Sunday (August 31) and Monday (September 1). These are the two big final days of great racing. Also included will be T-shirts and hats with Ford Drag Club logos and a special dash plaque commemorating this first national club Go-In.

A special Ford Drag Headquarters Office will be in the pits directly behind your starting line seats. Jackets and other special Ford Drag Club goodies will be available there. On Sunday night, there will be a big gala party — for members and dates only, with food, drink and lots of door prizes.

In addition to your package of tickets and pit passes, you will receive a list of camping areas and hotel and motel rooms in the area. A word of caution — get your reservations in early. As we said, this is the crown jewel in drag racing's year and there will be over 100,000 pouring through the Indy gates by the time the four-day bash is over. So make your arrangements early. The same goes for the special "Go-In Thing" package. It will be first come, first served. Just as those who sleep (on the green), weep; those who delay, will pay (by missing out.)

A trophy to the out of town club with the best attendance at this national fun-for-all will be presented.

If you've never been to NHRA Summernationals, we urge you to make it. If you have been there, then you can skip down to the coupon and fill it out. For you veterans know what it is like to have over 1500 of the nation's top machines — of every class and type — in one place battling it out for the gold and glory that come only at the N.H.R.A. National Championships.

By itself, Indy is great; but as part of the first national meeting of Ford Drag Clubs, it will be too much. All of this at a special bargain price makes it the drag racing buy of the year. See you there!

TICKET ORDER FORM

FORD DRAG CLUBS
"GO-IN THING"

NHRA NATIONALS
INDIANAPOLIS, INDIANA

AUGUST 31 - SEPT. 1

NAME
ADDRESS
CITY ... STATE ... ZIP
SPONSORING DEALER'S NAME
SPONSORING DEALER'S CITY ... STATE
NUMBER OF TICKETS REQUESTED
AMOUNT ENCLOSED $

$18.00 PER PERSON IF MAILED BEFORE AUGUST 1.
$20.00 PER PERSON AFTER AUGUST 1.

MAKE CHECKS PAYABLE TO: FORD DRAG CLUBS

MAIL THIS ORDER AND CHECK TO:

Go-In Thing
Ford Drag Clubs
P.O. Box 501
Dearborn, Mich. 48120

*Ford Drag Club members were invited to the first ever multiclub gathering at the 1969 NHRA Nationals in Indianapolis. There, they had exclusive reserved seating near the starting line, a hospitality tent with food and parties, as well as driver meet and greets.*

The first national get-together offered club members a special reserve section in the reserved seats that were front and center near the starting line, pit passes, event T-shirts and hats with Ford Drag Team logos, exclusive parties, and a commemorative dash plaque of the event. A special Ford Drag Team headquarters was set up behind the starting-line seats in the pits under a hospitality tent, where Ford Drag Club jackets and other club merchandise was available.

The club organized social functions so that wives and girlfriends could be involved as well. On Sunday night under the tent, they hosted a pizza party for all 200 attending club members and their dates. Thirty different clubs were recognized from 22 states. Emceeing the event was National Ford Drag Team Director Bob Swaim, but the guests of honor were Drag Team stars Hubert and Ed, as well as team sponsor Doug Thorley. They ate pizza with the club members then fielded a Q & A session and gave away multiple door prizes, including a set of Doug's Headers. This whole package including admission for Sunday and Monday cost club members $20 bucks.

*Hubert with friend and team sponsor Doug Thorley had some pizza at the "Go-In Thing" club get-together at the Indy Nationals with more than 200 club members and their dates.*

FORD DRAG CLUB

Newsletter

Official Publication of Ford Drag Clubs

Headquarters: P.O. Box 501, Dearborn, Mich. 48120

Volume 1, Number 3

October, 1969

# "GO-IN THING" AT INDY NATIONALS, SMASH SUCCESS

Both the 15th annual NHRA Indy Nationals and the first Ford Drag Club "Go-In Thing" were smash successes.

The Nationals story is told in detail elsewhere in this issue. It's success is no surprise to any one who has followed the past Nationals at Indy. However, some doubted that the "Go-In Thing" would be a similar success. After all, this was the first time that any national drag club organization had ever tried to organize such a gathering. The odds on pulling off such a first were not helped any when the organization itself was only eight months old. Nevertheless, you—the members of the Ford Drag Clubs around the country—beat the odds and made it happen. Those of you who attended started

BEST ATTENDANCE Award went to the Delegrange Ford Drag Club. National Director Bob Swaim presents the trophy to Joe Pittenger (left) and Mike McCoy. The New Haven, Indiana club had 19 members present.

THE MAN, HIMSELF—When Jerome Lippert of the Downtown Motors Ford Drag Club won a set of Doug's Headers as a door prize, he received an unexpected bonus when Doug Thorley turned up to offer his personal con-

*The Ford Drag Club newsletter was quick to boast about the success of the "Go-In Thing," which had members of 30 Ford Drag Clubs from different dealerships in 22 states attend.*

*Hubert raced the ex-Jerry Harvey car in the summer of 1969 at Dallas Georgia's Southeastern International Dragway. This car presumably became the Indy Nationals "Platt & Payne" car Hubert set the record in. (Photo Courtesy Marvin Smith)*

A national multiclub gathering had never been attempted by any other drag club. Though it had its skeptics, the "Indy Go-In Thing" was a smash success for the newly formed Ford Drag Club.

## Double Duty

At the Indy Nationals, Hubert had to work harder than usual. Not only did he have his normal duties of running the Mustang in SS/IA competition and meeting with sponsors as well as club members, Ford also had Hubert race a gold 1965 Mustang in A-Modified/Stock.

The Mustang was painted like many of the factory 'Stangs of the past few years, gold with a blue inset separated by a white outline. It said "Platt & Payne" on the door in white and below that it had "FORD DRAG TEAM" in small capital letters in black. Just under the window in cursive it read "Hubert Platt" in black. The front wheels were gray old-style Americans and on the rear were steel stamped wheels painted silver. Under the teardrop fiberglass hood was the infamous 427 SOHC with two Holley 4-barrels.

There has been some confusion among fans as to what car this was and where it came from. It was thought to be the #290 car sponsored by Paul Harvey Ford and driven by Paul's son Jerry Harvey. Although many things look the same in the old photos of the cars (the wheels and both having a large white upholstered headrest behind the

*Hubert, wife Bee, and close friend NHRA starter Buster Couch share a laugh at a NHRA Banquet.*

*Hubert only drove this Mustang a few times. This photo was taken at the Indy Nationals in 1969, where he set the national record in A/Modified Stock.*

*It is unclear which Mustang this was before it was painted like this for the Indy Nationals. It is believed to have been the one raced by Jerry Harvey, which Hubert had driven earlier in the year.*

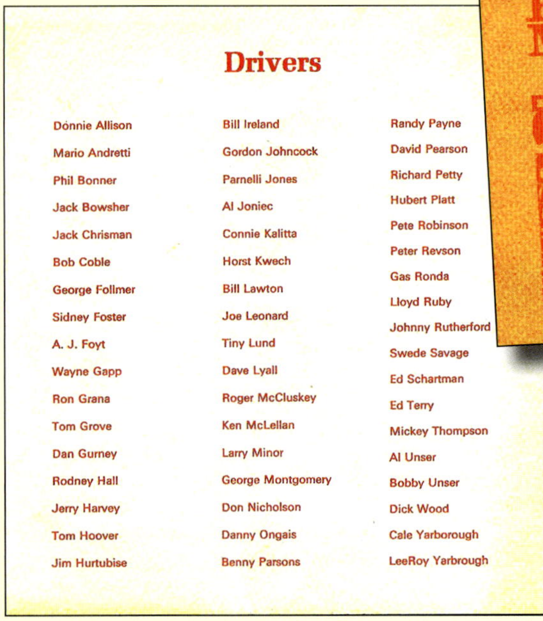

**Drivers**

Donnie Allison
Mario Andretti
Phil Bonner
Jack Bowsher
Jack Chrisman
Bob Coble
George Follmer
Sidney Foster
A. J. Foyt
Wayne Gapp
Ron Grana
Tom Grove
Dan Gurney
Rodney Hall
Jerry Harvey
Tom Hoover
Jim Hurtubise
Bill Ireland
Gordon Johncock
Parnelli Jones
Al Joniec
Connie Kalitta
Horst Kwech
Bill Lawton
Joe Leonard
Tiny Lund
Dave Lyall
Roger McCluskey
Ken McLellan
Larry Minor
George Montgomery
Don Nicholson
Danny Ongais
Benny Parsons
Randy Payne
David Pearson
Richard Petty
Hubert Platt
Pete Robinson
Peter Revson
Gas Ronda
Lloyd Ruby
Johnny Rutherford
Swede Savage
Ed Schartman
Ed Terry
Mickey Thompson
Al Unser
Bobby Unser
Dick Wood
Cale Yarborough
LeeRoy Yarbrough

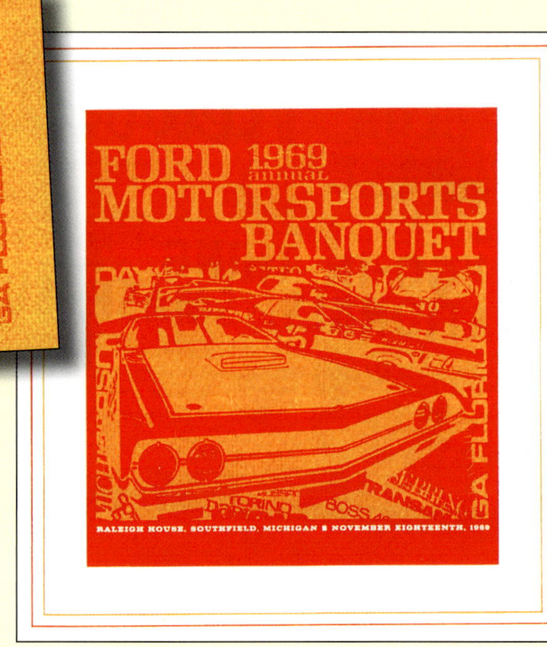


*The 1969 Ford Motorsports Banquet was a who's who of race car drivers from all forms of auto racing. The list speaks for itself. Hubert was on top of his game and proud to be on Ford's A-list of drivers.*

driver's seat), the facts are unclear as to if they were the same car or not. What we do know is Hubert raced this car at the Indy Nationals and was so tired from the huge weekend's festivities that he fell asleep in the driver's seat while in the staging lanes. He had to be woken up by crew member Rusty Gillis to make his run. Rusty remembered Hubert was so "out of it" he missed a gear, but he still won the round!

Although he didn't win the class, he did set the National Record in A-Modified/Stock at the event.

### Team Makeover

The Ford Drag Team was in full swing and enjoying the warm response from fans at the seminars and at the track. Ford, recognizing the success of the Performance Promotion Program, decided to go all in. On September 9, the day after the Indy Nationals, the East and West Coast rigs and cars were taken to Car Corporation in Michigan for a makeover.

The major recognizable change that was made was the removal of "Platt & Payne" and "Terry & Wood" from the doors of the race cars. The names were replaced with "FORD DRAG TEAM" all in capital letters painted in gold leaf. It was a bold statement, and Ford's way of taking ownership of the program.

With the success and exposure of the Ford Drag Team, clubs, and seminars, Bob Swaim realized that he could now replace the contingency stickers on the race cars with paying sponsors. The stickers would be paid for by the manufacturers biannually instead of on the contingency of winning a race. The more popular the driver, the higher the sponsors would pay. Hubert's popularity was so large that he received a $25,000 check twice a year from Car Corp for the collective sponsors on the Mustang. With these endorsements, Hubert was now making more money than he ever had.

One of the Drag Team sponsors was Kelsey-Hayes Wheels. All four of the drag team cars received a set of its 20-spoke aluminum racing wheels. The Drag Team also enjoyed the addition of a few extra crew members who drove the trucks to events and set up the cars and displays at dealership seminars, allowing the team drivers to focus on their driving duties as well as interacting with the fans. Two of the East Coast Drag Team assistants were Dan White and Rusty Gillis. Hubert often flew or drove his Lincoln to meet the team at the races or dealerships.

### Mustang Stays on Top

With some fresh paint and new wheels, the Platt and Payne Drag Team headed south to Gainesville, Florida, for the NHRA Division 2 Points Meet. By the end of the weekend on Sunday, September 14, Hubert had set the NHRA SS/HA national record with an 11.79 at 118.26 mph. Two weeks later, after several seminars in Georgia, South Carolina, and North Carolina, Hubert was back on the track, competing in the U.S. Open National Drags.

A group of the nation's fastest drag racers had gathered to compete at Rockingham, North Carolina, at the brand-new AHRA facility. The competition was fierce, and the fans were treated to some low-7-second runs by the Funny Cars on hand.

The Mustang's 428 Cobra Jet gets out first ahead of the Road Runner's 440 6-barrel. This was a big win for Ford. Don Carlton was driving for Sox & Martin.

Hubert is loving life in the winner's circle. He is shown here with Linda Vaughn at the U.S. Open National Drags.

The crew is posed together (left to right): Randy Payne, Hubert, unknown crew member, Rusty Gillis, and Dan White.

After a long day of defeating some of the nation's toughest Super Stock competitors, Hubert found himself in the final round of Super Stock Eliminator for a factory versus factory showdown. Hubert's 428 Cobra Jet Mach I Mustang was to battle the 440 6-barrel Plymouth Road Runner of Sox & Martin driven by Don Carlton. When the lights dropped, the Mustang came out of the hole strong and held the lead all the way to the win light.

When the two cars came back down the return road, the drivers were notified that they had both went a little too quick and broken out of the index bracket. The officials insisted on a rerun, so it was back to the starting line for the two big-name competitors. This time, the ET index would be discarded and the two would race heads up: first to the finish line wins. The two factory drag cars roared down the track, the Mustang held the lead by a fender the whole way and took home the trophy along with the AHRA D/SA-Formula II Class record at 118.26 mph. The AHRA D/SA-Formula II class was identical to NHRA SS/HA.

### Match Race Cammer Mustangs

In 1969, Super Stock was king in drag racing. Although there was no doubt fans loved the action of the nitro Funny Cars and nitro dragsters, it was the full-bodied Super Stock cars that were accredited for bringing in the factory and aftermarket manufacturers' sponsorship money. This made it lucrative for everyone involved, but the Super Stock cars were leaving the fans wanting a little more in the way of heads-up racing.

The NHRA had made plans for a Pro Stock class to begin in 1970 that would have a more liberal set of rules and throw the handicaps out the window. In the fall of 1969, Holman-Moody-Stroppe, in preparation for the new class, built the East and West Coast Ford Drag Teams each a 1969 Mustang match racer. They were highly modified compared to the Super Stocks they were already racing.

H-M-S started with the R-code 428 Cobra Jet Mustang. First, a cover was welded over the side scoop, making it easier to convert the cars to 1970 models at the end of the year, knowing that no 1970 model Mustang would have a side scoop. The biggest difference between the Super Stocks and the match race Mustangs was the 427 SOHC powerplant crowned with an aluminum intake and two Holley 740-cfm carburetors that fed fresh air through a custom cold-air induction system via cutouts behind the grille. The big engines had a bore of 4.234 inches and stroke of 3.875 inches with 12.5:1 compression Forged True pistons and a set of Mickey's aluminum rods as well as single-overhead-cam aluminum heads that had Crane 640-lift cams in them, all breathing through a set of Doug's Headers.

Another big difference was that the stock interiors had been removed and replaced with a single Grand National –style seat. Both cars had a 4-speed with Hurst shifter and Schiefer clutch-pressure plate-flywheel assembly. Out back, it had a 4.86:1 gear to help put it through its paces

## Behind Prison Walls

Hubert and the East Coast Drag Team did not only visit dealerships with the safety and performance seminars. They also were known for civic events, such as taking the show to prisons to share with the inmates. One such seminar took place in the fall of 1969 at the Ohio State Reformatory. The event was sponsored by Citizens Aiding Public Offenders (CAPO), a group that was devoted to the rehabilitation of juvenile offenders started by Don Brondes, owner of Brondes Motor Sales, a Ford Dealership in Toledo, Ohio.

The Ohio State Reformatory offered an Auto Mechanics course, and Brondes sometimes recruited graduates to work at his dealership. This led to the creation of the CAPO in order to assist reformed youth in securing employment of any nature. Of the 2,200 inmates, 1,000 attended the Ford Drag Team seminar, including 50 members of the Ohio State Penal Racing Association, a car club that had built its own drag car behind bars from a 1958 Ford purchased for $50 and fixed up with donated parts. The drag car named the *High Wall Special* was driven by a former guard at the reformatory and finished fifth among 60 racers at an informal local race in 1968.

Projects like this combined with the Ford Drag Team seminar had a lasting positive effect on these young men.

***Captive audience? One thousand inmates enjoyed the Ford Drag Team seminar at the Ohio State Reformatory in the fall of 1969.***

and a set of H-M-S ladder bars. The match racers looked a little tougher with their large Boss hood scoops added to accommodate the two 4s. They also had larger Goodyear 12-inch rear slicks mounted on Bottleneck mags with black centers and old-school American mags on the front that also had black centers.

Although they were painted the same as the Drag Team Super Stocks with the Boss 302 C-stripe, the gold leaf "Ford Drag Team" on the door was not in all caps. Unlike the Super Stock, Hubert's new Mustang would once again carry his Georgia Shaker moniker on the quarter panels in all caps painted in gold leaf. The cars were a stunning addition to the Drag Teams.

***Unlike the Super Stock Mustang, the new SOHC match racer carried the* Georgia Shaker *moniker. (Photo Courtesy Doug Boyce)***

*This rare photo gives you a look into the interior of the SOHC Mustang. Not too much was left stock other than the steering wheel with the addition of the Grand National–style seat, Hurst 4-speed shifter with line lock, and racing tachometer and gauges.*

*The 427 SOHC Georgia Shaker Mustang was a terror on the match race circuit late in 1969. It was only in this configuration for less than three months.*

*The 427 SOHC is massive in the engine bay of the 1969 Mustang. Hubert adjusts the linkage on the twin Holley 4-barrel setup. Notice the polished valve covers on the big overhead cam Ford.*

*Phenix Dragway (Phenix City, Alabama) owner/operator and former Chicago Cubs pitcher Jerry Coley and Hubert were great friends. Jerry served as Ford Drag Team crew chief and Hubert's PR man for 1970.*

*Hubert found much success with this 1969 SOHC match race Mustang at the end of year before it underwent its transformation for the 1970 race season and the new class of Pro Stock.*

*The* Georgia Shaker *transformed from a 1969 match racer to a 1970 Pro Stock. This photo was taken at Los Angeles County Fairground before the 1970 NHRA Winternationals.*

*The Mustang is now wearing a taller hood scoop to accommodate the larger tunnel ram intake.*

*In 1970, Fleer Baseball Card Company produced a set of drag racing cards. Hubert was picked as one of the drivers honored with a card.*

On October 12 at the NHRA World Finals in Dallas, Texas, Hubert took possession of his new match-race Mustang. It was delivered from Holman-Moody-Stroppe by new crew member Rusty Gillis on a plain white ramp truck. Hubert made a couple test passes with the car with a best of 10.50 at 135 mph. The Super Stock Mustang was the real star of the weekend when Hubert set the NHRA SS/EA record at 118.26 mph on Sunday.

Hubert had Rusty Gillis drive the white ramp truck carrying the match-race Mustang back to Atlanta after the World Finals. After spending the night in Atlanta at Hubert's home, the entire Ford Drag Team crew headed north to Epping, New Hampshire. At New England Dragway, Hubert in the Super Stock Mach I took on Lloyd Woodland in the Smothers brothers' Oldsmobile in a SS/HA best-two-out-of-three match race. The Mustang bested the Olds in the first round with an 11.62 at 118.52 mph. The match was over when Hubert shut down the Olds again with an 11.61 at 119.10 mph, proving that the Cobra Jet Mach I had a little more in it than when it had set the SS/HA record the previous month.

Hubert put his new SOHC into competition for the first time against some of the best heads-up cars in the nation. Among them was "Jungle Jim" Liberman's

*On this Saturday in January 1970, Francis Cook, National Dealer Placement Manger for Ford Heavy Truck, was invited by friend Emil Loeffler, Ford's Product Engineering Officer to tour the Car Corporation facility in Livonia, Michigan. The facility housed the Ford Drag Team while on the East Coast. Francis brought along his son, Bill, who was a senior in high school at the time. Young Bill Cook brought along his camera and captured these photos of Hubert's Super Stock Mustang being prepped and loaded to head to Pomona for the 1970 NHRA Winternationals. This is the last known photograph of the Ford Drag Team Torino Cobra. The car had been retired and Randy Payne's name had been removed from the door. As the Ford Drag Team rig and Super Stock Mustang headed west, they met up with the sister Mustang SOHC match racer that had now been converted to a 1970 Pro Stock at Holman-Moody-Stroppe in Long Beach. Francis Cook would faithfully work for Ford for 43 years. Son Bill would follow in his father's footsteps, working for the brand for 38 years before retiring in 2014. (Photos Courtesy Bill Cook)*

*In this rare photo, the Super Stock Mustang has a different hood without the Mach 1 hood scoop. (Photo Courtesy Doug Boyce)*

match-race Camaro. Hubert won three rounds with a best of 10.33 at 131.77 mph but lost in the final round. He was satisfied with the new Mustang's performance, knowing that it was barely broken in and definitely not up to its full potential yet.

During the next two months, Hubert would match race the Cammer Mustang extensively throughout the country, booking as many as two or three matches per week. This came to an end halfway through December, when the car had to be taken to Holman-Moody-Stroppe in Long Beach for its makeover for the new Pro Stock class and the 1970 race season.

The major change made to the Mustang was that it was switched from a 1969 to a 1970 by swapping the front end and replacing the 1969 C-stripe with the new 1970 hockey stick–style Boss stripe. "FORD DRAG TEAM" had been repainted on the doors in all capital letters again in gold leaf. The new fiberglass hood now sported a taller hood scoop to accommodate the larger tunnel-ram aluminum intake that the SOHC would use in the new Pro Stock class.

The remodeled Mustang was beautiful and when the NHRA released its new rule book for the 1970 season it featured a photo of the Georgia Shaker Ford Drag Team Mustang right above the section outlining the rules for its Pro Stock class. In addition, the NHRA gave Hubert the number 201, signifying him as having the first Pro Stock in NHRA Division 2 (the Southeast Division).

## Changing Seasons

There were more changes being made for the 1970 season back in Dearborn, Michigan. The Torino Cobra and Randy Payne had been retired from the team. The FDT rig was given a slight makeover. The most noticeable difference was a gold stripe that was added to the inset of the C-stripe on the side. The lettering on the cab had been changed from "Platt & Payne" to "Hubert Platt," and it also read "Safety/Performance Seminar" on the side of the sleeper now.

Jon Brantmeier was promoted to national coordinator of the Ford Drag Clubs. His job as Hubert's PR man was given to Phenix Dragway owner/operator Jerry Coley. Chrysler had added a Midwest drag team to its clinic program with veteran drag racer Don Grotheer out of Oklahoma, so Ford added a third team as well with veteran Funny Car driver Dick Loehr. Dick, out of Portage, Michigan, had a rig exactly matching the East and West Coast rigs, but painted gold with blue stripes and hauling a Maverick. This gold Maverick originally had a Boss 351 small-block with Hilborn injectors and ran in Modified Stock, but later was switched to carburetors and raced Pro Stock.

## *Super Stock* Magazine Cover Story

When the January 1970 issue of *Super Stock & Drag Illustrated* magazine hit the store shelves, it had a full-color photo of Hubert sitting on the fender of his 1969 Ford Drag Team cammer match-race Mustang. The beautiful picture was taken on a winding one-lane road in Long Island, New York. It was a different setting than most drag car photos, and Hubert was looking a little more like a refined gentleman than a race car driver in his brown dress slacks and black short sleeve knit shirt and as always not a hair out of place.

Inside, there wasn't really an article, but there was a two-page spread with seven pictures and four captions detailing the Mustang's modifications and its 427 SOHC powerplant. When this issue was released to the public, the Mustang had already undergone its transformation and now had a 1970 front end and Boss stripe. So, any fan looking to see the 1969 match racer featured in the magazine at the drags was disappointed and thought the 1970 Pro Stock Mustang was a different car when actually it was not.

## *Super Thrill*

At the beginning of the 1970 drag race season, Car Corporation produced a new film to be shown at the dealership seminars. The three Ford Drag Team captains starred in and narrated the 13-minute short movie titled Super Thrill, which featured the Ford Drag Teams in action at the drag races. Each of the three drivers talked about different aspects of drag racing, always with a heavy emphasis on safety.

One of the super thrills of the film was the in-car camera footage of all three of the Ford Drag Team drivers. Ford took some liberties with the editing in the beginning of the video when showing Hubert's 1969 SS/IA (automatic class) Mustang making a run. The in-car camera footage was taken in Hubert's 1970 Pro Stock Mustang, which had a 4-speed. It also shows a wing-tipped dress shoe hitting the clutch, a style of shoe Hubert had never worn. This scene was filmed in the pits and was the foot of West Coast Ford Drag Team Super Stock driver Dick Wood. Nevertheless, many fans were none the wiser.

The movie also featured cameos by some of the hottest drivers in Funny Car, including Ford driver Danny Ongais (who wheeled Mickey Thompson's Mach I), the Hot Wheels Racing Team of Don "the Snake" Prudhomme and Tom "the Mongoose" McEwen, as well as the very popular "Hawaiian" Dodge Charger of Roland Leong. The movie was a great tool at the seminars to encourage new fans to come out to the drag races, which would potentially take a drag racer off the street and get them into sanctioned legal competition on a controlled strip. The film was a huge hit, and the teenage fans in attendance would often beg Hubert to play it a second time, which he would always oblige.

### 1970 Ford Drag Team

For the first half of the 1970 drag racing season, Hubert carried the 1970 Pro Stock Mustang on the truck and the 1969 Super Stock Mustang on the trailer, racing both cars at major events. The two Mustangs were a sharp-looking tandem, and Hubert kept them looking fresh by changing the wheel combinations so they always matched.

At the first of the season, he changed the wheels on the Super Stock from the Kelsey-Hayes 20 spokes to Bottleneck mags on the rear and old-style American mags on the front. Both had the centers painted black to match the Pro Stock Mustang.

Hubert was busier than ever. On May 5, Hubert conducted a safety and performance seminar at Rice-Holman Ford in Pennsauken, New Jersey. Now that Randy was no longer with the team, Hubert was conducting the seminars by himself, but at the Rice-Holman seminar Hubert had fellow Ford racer Al Joniec, who was sponsored by Rice-Holman, as a guest speaker.

Before the next Nationals, the wheels on both of the Mustangs were changed again. This time they each got

*This is the actual box containing the 8-mm film* Super Thrill *shown at the Ford Drag Team dealership seminars in 1970.*

Fenton polished-aluminum slot mags on the front and the Bottleneck mags on the rear were changed to blue centers. Sometime during the summer, Hubert retired the 1969 Super Stock Mustang to focus his efforts solely on the 1970 Pro Stock Mustang, which was having mixed success. It seemed to have some problems keeping pace with the lighter Hemi 'Cuda that Ronnie Sox was dominating the new Pro Stock class with.

### Ford Drag Club's Continued Success

By the summer of 1970, the Ford Drag Teams had established Ford Drag Clubs at 143 dealerships across the US and Canada with a total of 16,500 members. At the first seminar in Canada, more than 1,200 people packed the dealership.

The average dealership seminar in 1969 exceeded 500 people per show, and the Drag Team drivers appeared before more than 2 million people at racing events and seminars to date. The Ford Drag Clubs helped build the dealerships' performance image and improved their vehicle and parts business.

### Pro Stock Mavericks

In the summer of 1970, Hubert had fellow Ford racer Ed Skelton working with him on the development of the Boss 429 for drag racing. Hubert was first seen testing a red 1970 Ford Maverick that had a small black hood scoop and no lettering being carried on the Ford Drag Team ramp truck.

Next, Hubert was seen with the same red Maverick, but now with a one-piece, black fiberglass hood that had a large Pro Stock–style hood scoop. The car was lettered in white, reading "Hubert Platt, Ford Drag Team" on the

*In the first half of the 1970 race season when Hubert was campaigning both the S/S and the P/S Mustangs, he always had them with matching wheels. He loved the aesthetic of a two-car matching team.*

| Hubert's April 1970 Appearance Schedule | |
|---|---|
| April 1–2 | Atlanta District Seminars |
| April 4–5 | Phenix City, Alabama. NHRA Div. 2 Points Meet |
| April 7–9 | Atlanta District Seminars |
| April 14–16 | Atlanta District Seminars |
| April 17–19 | Rockingham, North Carolina. AHRA Grand American Meet |
| April 21–23 | Richmond District Seminars |
| April 25–26 | Suffolk, Virginia. NHRA Div. 2 Points Meet |
| April 28–30 | Washington District Seminars |

***This is how Hubert would transport the cars in 1970. The 1970 Pro Stock SOHC Mustang rode on the ramp truck and the 1969 Super Stock Cobra Jet Mustang on the trailer. Hubert drove both classes at events through the first half of the 1970 race season.***

door and "229 Pro Stock" on the side windows. It was clear that this car was being tested.

At the same time, Car Corporation had two more Mavericks built at Holman-Moody-Stroppe in Charlotte, North Carolina. These Mavericks were similar to the one they had built at the end of the previous year for Dick Loehr's Midwest Ford Drag Team. When the two were done, Hubert's was painted blue with white Boss stripes to match the East Coast Drag Team cars. The Maverick Pro Stock had all the same lettering as Hubert's Pro Stock Mustang, "Ford Drag Team" on the doors and "Georgia Shaker" on the quarter panels all in caps painted in gold leaf.

There were two big differences between the Pro Stock Mustang and the Maverick. First was the weight; the Maverick was lighter. Second was the engine; the Maverick had a Boss 429 instead of a 427 SOHC.

***This was the cover of a pamphlet for ordering tickets to the second ever Gatornationals. In this photo, Hubert runs against Chevy legend Bill "Grumpy" Jenkins at the inaugural Gatornationals in 1970, which was also the first year of NHRA Pro Stock.***

The debut of the East and West Coast Ford Drag Team Mavericks came at the Indy Nationals Labor Day weekend. Hubert entered two Mavericks in the race under the Ford Drag Team banner. The blue #201 and the red #229 test car.

Bob Swaim took some promotional photos for Car Corporation of the three official Ford Drag Team Mavericks together. One of the photos showed all three of the Mavericks on the track together doing a wheelstand at the same time! The photos turned out great, but the new Mavericks were plagued with mechanical difficulties and didn't fare well in eliminations at the event.

After the Indy Nationals, Hubert now had two Pro Stock Mavericks that were both painted blue with white and lettered exactly the same. It is believed that the red test Maverick was painted to match the original #201, but this has never been confirmed. The only noticeable differences were the second car had a chrome piece of trim the length of the rocker panel and the wheelie bars were shorter.

## Esquire

*Esquire,* "The Magazine for Men," was an upscale men's fashion magazine. It was a large magazine, measuring 2 inches wider and taller than a regular magazine. *Esquire* cost $1 when a *Hot Rod* magazine was 60 cents. In the September 1970 issue of Esquire, there was an eight-page article called "Drag Racing Goes Legit." The author told of drag racing's rise from having a lower-class image to becoming a major league sport.

The article very thoroughly explained drag racing to the reader with detailed interviews with automaker executives such as Edsel Ford II and Carroll Shelby; aftermarket performance parts manufacturers; tire makers M&H, Goodyear, and Firestone; drag racing officials from the AHRA and NHRA; and three different car magazine

*This promotional photo taken before the NHRA Nationals at Indy was an attempt to get a shot of all three Mavericks with their front wheels in the air! (Photo Courtesy Bob Swaim)*

publishers. The article stated that drag racing was getting so popular and selling so many magazines featuring as many top drivers as possible that most any drag enthusiast worth his salt could "rattle off names of the really super drivers." The article then featured this list: Don "the Snake" Prudhomme, "Dandy" Dick Landy, "Dyno" Don Nicholson, Bill "Grumpy" Jenkins, Hubert "Georgia Shaker" Platt, Dick "Mr. Everything" Harrell, and "Big Daddy" Don Garlits.

Hubert was one of the five drivers interviewed. He was quoted as saying, "I once drove a long distance just to beat a guy because he was said to be the baddest cat around."

## The Call

In November 1970 at the World Finals in Ontario, California, all three of the Ford Drag Teams were together again at the big year-end national event. At the track, Bob Swaim got a call from Car Corporation informing him that Henry Ford had pulled the plug on the Corporate Racing Department. This department funded Car Corporation and the Ford Drag Teams.

Ford Division continued to support the drag teams because the race cars reflected what they were selling, but the end was imminent. The teams found out later that the plans to cut racing funds had been started in February 1970.

## 1971

On January 24, 1971, in Gainesville, Florida, Hubert got the Maverick running the best it had yet. He made a pass of 10.07 at 137.15 to earn himself a spot in the Big Four Manufacturers Run Off.

Hubert's Ford was to go against Melvin Yow's Dodge, while Ronnie Sox driving Reid Whisnant's Plymouth would go against Billy Denby in his Chevy. Hubert's 10.11 wasn't enough for the 10.02 of Yow's Dodge, but

*The red 1970 Pro Stock test Maverick underwent more modifications before it went into competition. These modifications included removal of the exhaust pipes and the addition of wheelie bars.*

*The red 1970 Pro Stock test Maverick is seen here on Hubert's Ford Drag Team rig. It was being tested and prepared for its debut at the Indy Nationals.*

*The Ford Drag Team Mavericks were much lighter and took the place of the heavier Mustangs. This photo was taken at the debut of the East and West Coast Mavericks at the NHRA Indy Nationals in 1970. (Photo Courtesy Bob Swaim)*

***Hubert launched the Maverick versus a Hemi Dodge Dart. The gauge on the cowl of the Maverick was for fuel pressure.***

Hubert and teammates Jerry Coley and Ed Skelton were very happy with the progress the Maverick was making.

Yow went on to beat Sox in the Manufacturers Final with a strong 9.93 ET.

## End of a Good Thing

Ford Motor Company and the Ford Drag Team had helped Hubert exceed any dreams he may have had about achieving fame and fortune from drag racing. When he first began drag racing in the late 1950s, he could never have imagined all of this success. As much as he wished this support wasn't over, there was nothing he could do.

Even though he had his Mavericks running better than ever, he knew the end was growing closer for the Ford Drag Teams. His fears were realized when he received word that the budget was cut for the teams. He was told he could now focus all his efforts on racing because the seminar program for 1971 was canceled.

The thought of Ford pulling out of racing was depressing, but Hubert had no intention of stopping, at least not anytime soon. Drag racing was his passion, and he would continue to pursue it.

Hubert kept the Holman & Moody–built Maverick, but "Ford Drag Team" was removed from the door. He kept the test car for a short time before selling it to fellow Georgia racer Buck Pike at the beginning of 1971. Buck only changed two things: the name on the door from Hubert Platt to Buck Pike and he took off "Shaker" and put "Cracker." Buck even left Ford Drag Team on the side, which was a little misleading since he was never actually on the team.

CHAPTER 11

# THE PRO STOCK YEARS

Like all bad news, the story of Ford pulling out of racing spread like wildfire. A lot of people in the drag racing community began to predict that Hubert would quit racing without Ford's support. Many wondered if he would even show up at the Winternationals.

When the gates opened at Los Angeles County Fairgrounds in Pomona for the 1971 NHRA Winternationals, Hubert was there. To the surprise of his naysayers, he had a new sponsor on the door of the *Georgia Shaker* Pro Stock Maverick: Delta Airlines! He also had the Pro Stock Maverick on the back on a flatbed truck that looked to be owned by the airline. There was a huge buzz around the pits about this new sponsor.

In actuality, Hubert and Jerry Coley were playing a big trick on everyone. The truth was, Hubert had gotten two big Delta stickers from a friend at the airline and put them on the car. The truck was a loaner. There was no sponsorship.

Hubert and his crew got a big kick out of the deal. Their laughter was soon silenced. In a qualifying pass, Hubert's longtime friend and fellow Atlanta racer Pete Robinson blew a front tire on his AA/Fuel Dragster and had a fatal crash. This loss of a close friend in a drag racing accident had a huge impact on Hubert. It bothered him for the rest of his life.

After the Winternationals, Hubert and crew headed east to Nevada for the Las Vegas Open at Stardust Dragway. The weekend started out on a bad note when Hubert blew an engine during a qualifying pass. The crew worked right up until time for the first round to replace the engine, leaving Hubert no choice but to race with an untested engine.

In the first round, he lined the Maverick up against Jim Marshall driving his Dodge Dart, which was the former national record holder of Bill Bagshaw. When the green light dropped, the two cars were neck and neck the entire race. No one could tell who won until the win light came on in Hubert's lane, showing the time 10.43 to the Dodge's losing 10.45 ET.

In the second round, Hubert and the Maverick wasted no time putting away Bob Anderson and his *Generation Gap* Chevy II, which had turned its best ET ever in the first round.

***Hubert shocked the competition when he showed up at the 1971 Winternationals with new sponsor: Delta Airlines. Little did they know he was playing tricks! (Photo Courtesy Autoimagery.com)***

***Gambling on a new motor paid off in Las Vegas, when Hubert was the first in a Ford Pro Stock to win a national event on the West Coast. Hubert popped the champagne as friend Jerome "JB" Bradford, an NHRA official, and Jerry Coley, Hubert's former Ford Drag Team PR man, look on. (Photo Courtesy Steve Reyes)***

Hubert's biggest foe of the day came in the final round with Bill Blanding's *Mimi* Camaro driven by Rich Mirarcki. The *Mimi* Camaro was definitely the quickest Pro Stock at the event. Mirarcki had already clocked a couple of 10.20 ETs earlier in eliminations, which had Chevy fans thinking this one was in the bag. All the Vegas fans were on their feet for this Ford-versus-Chevy Pro Stock showdown. It was Hubert out of the gate first, putting a fender lead on the Camaro and holding it for the full 1,320 feet!

The *Georgia Shaker* Maverick's holeshot 10.45 at 132.15 mph was enough to beat the *Mimi* Camaro's quicker 10.39 at 132.93 mph. Hubert's Las Vegas win was the first Ford Pro Stock victory on the West Coast at a major event.

## New Digs

Back in Atlanta at the beginning of March, Hubert was ordered to turn over the Ford Drag Team rig. Bob Swaim flew to the Atlanta airport to meet with Hubert, and the two had lunch. Afterward in the parking lot, Hubert returned the truck to Bob, who was to take it back to Car Corporation in Michigan.

Now that the Ford Drag Team was done, Hubert was ready to move on. He had no thought of going backward, only forward. He purchased a huge Ford box truck and had it customized to haul the Pro Stock Maverick in the back.

The box truck was a big step up. The car was protected from the elements. Hubert would never carry his primary race car on an open-ramp truck again. The cargo box of the new truck was so large that in addition to the Maverick there was room in the front for a camper area that would sleep two people in bunk beds, a small kitchen with a refrigerator and wet bar, and a closet for suitcases.

The camper area had a large door on the right side of the cargo box and also had a crawl-through from the cab of the truck where the back window would be. Hubert had his father-in-law, Reverend Martin Flegel, help him build the cabinets in the camper of the new race rig. He

***This box truck was roomy enough to accommodate the race car, a spare engine, tools, and also have a large camper/lounge area in the front. (Photo Courtesy Tim Thompson)***

***Hubert had Max Thompson paint the Pro Stock Maverick on the side of the new box truck so there would be no doubt as to what cargo was inside. (Photo Courtesy Tim Thompson)***

***Hubert's new box truck was much larger than the old Ford Drag Team ramp truck. The enclosed race car area was ahead of its time and a hint of things to come. In the future, most all race rigs would be enclosed. (Photo Courtesy Tim Thompson)***

had his painter Max Thompson paint the new rig in Ford blue and white with a full-size portrait of the *Georgia Shaker* Pro Stock Maverick painted on both sides as well as his name "Hubert Platt" in all gold block letters with a black shadow. This rig was a little before its time. Most all of the big names in drag racing still were carrying their cars on open ramp trucks and trailers.

## A New Spot

For the past five years, Hubert had factory support in one form or another and hadn't needed to have his own shop. His cars had been taken care of at Holman-Moody-Stroppe in Long Beach and Charlotte. Now that his racing operation had outgrown the single-car basement garage at his home, it was time to find a new place.

Hubert rented a double garage in Chamblee, Georgia, 3.5 miles north of his home. The garage was located in the old Lawson apartments off Chamblee-Tucker Road.

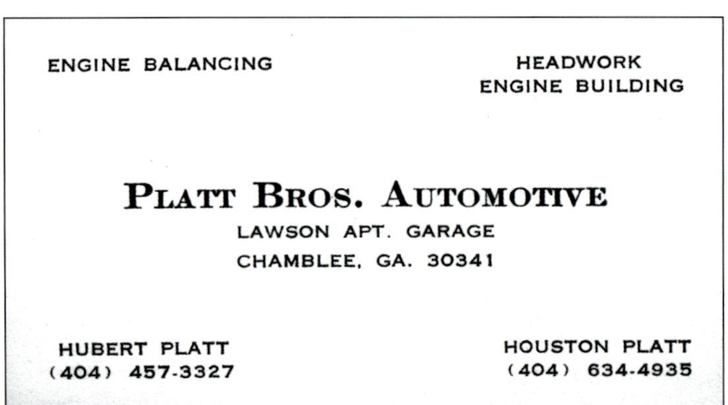
ENGINE BALANCING

HEADWORK
ENGINE BUILDING

PLATT BROS. AUTOMOTIVE
LAWSON APT. GARAGE
CHAMBLEE, GA. 30341

HUBERT PLATT
(404) 457-3327

HOUSTON PLATT
(404) 634-4935

***Platt Brothers Automotive was a speed shop just outside of Atlanta where performance-minded individuals could bring their hot rod or drag car to have it worked on by two of the best in the business.***

The Lawson apartments were old, run-down, low-income housing and in a rough part of Chamblee, which at the time was a middle-class suburb of Atlanta. Many of its residents worked at the nearby Doraville GM plant.

The two garages (both of which had a large roll-up door) were about 30 feet deep and 65 feet wide. They were separated by an office and a bathroom. There was plenty of room to work on race cars and build engines. Hubert and his brother Huston opened a business there called Platt Brothers Automotive, specializing in engine balancing and head work for performance-minded individuals.

With Hubert and Huston's fame, there was no shortage of customers from drag racers to local hot rodders and even some high-stakes professional street racers. The shop served as the base of operations for the *Georgia Shaker* drag cars.

Hubert, Huston, best friend Slick, and the crew loved to joke about the old garage in the apartments. They sarcastically nicknamed the apartments "Lawson Towers." Slick was known as "Lawson Towers Heavy," and Hubert was affectionately called "Skid Row" by his closest friends.

## New Sponsorship

Even though Ford had officially pulled out of drag racing, Hubert still had friends at Ford in Detroit. They were sending him parts, so the big Ford logo on the decklid of the Maverick stayed in place, but Hubert had to have more support.

Holman & Moody still had interest in drag racing, and the company sponsored the Maverick with Boss 429 engines and parts for the rest of the 1971 season. At

***After the Ford Drag Team was over, Holman & Moody gave Hubert some sponsorship for the beginning of 1971, and he ran this large logo on the door. H&M had built the Ford Drag Team Mavericks, so it had some stake in how the cars performed. Hubert would get parts as well as complete Boss 429 engines from them.***

*Hubert stages against Plymouth standout Don Grotheer, who covered the Midwest for Chrysler's clinic program.*

*The polished-aluminum slot mags were all the rage in the early 1970s. Hubert was sponsored by Fenton, who supplied these beauties.*

*Martini & Rossi were the first to put an alcohol ad on a racing car in 1968. Hubert wasn't too far behind in 1971, when he was one of the first to put an alcohol ad on a drag car with this Falstaff Beer sponsorship.*

first, Hubert put a large Holman & Moody Competition Proven logo on the door under his name. Soon after he landed his next sponsor, the logo was moved down to the inset of the Boss stripe.

During his career, Hubert's outgoing personality and general enthusiasm for the fun things in life along with his willingness to share in a drink with friends gained him the reputation of a partier. When his peers and fans saw him pull up at the track, they shouted "Hu-Baby!" and everyone knew things were about to get a little more fun. So it was no surprise, and seemed like a fit, when in the summer of 1971 Hubert landed his next sponsor: Falstaff Beer.

A medium-size Falstaff Beer sticker was placed in the center of the door below his name, making them the primary sponsor of the car. There were also three other smaller Falstaff logos: one on the tip of each fender and

*You can see the need for the huge hood scoop with this extra-tall Weiand Tunnel Ram intake! The towel is keeping dirt and dust from the pits out of the twin Holley carbs.*

*The* Silver Bullet *of Ed Terry is in the process of becoming a* Georgia Shaker. *Hubert bought the ex-West Coast Ford Drag Team ride from Ed when he retired from the sport. This was Maverick number three.*

one on the center of the front bumper. Hubert received travel money and an untold number of cases of beer for each event from the brewing company.

## Buying the Silver Bullet

When Hubert heard that Ed Terry was getting out of drag racing, he quickly called Ed to see if he might be able to buy the *Silver Bullet*. It was the Ford Drag Team Maverick that was just like his and built at the same time at Holman & Moody. Ed agreed, and Hubert headed out to the West Coast to pick the race car up.

When he arrived, Ed had the Maverick ready to go. All of the Ed Terry, Ford Drag Team, and "Silver Bullet" lettering was already removed. The car was white with the blue Boss stripe, blue hood, and blue decklid. Hubert brought the car back to Georgia and raced it a couple of times, testing different engines, with it still in the plain white paint scheme the way he picked it up.

## The United States Racing Team

There's an old saying that goes, "When one door closes, another one opens," and this couldn't have been truer or come at a better time for Hubert than in 1971. With the recent end to the Ford Drag Team, being selected to be one of the four Ford drivers on the newly assembled United States Racing Team (USRT) was a big boost for Hubert's career.

The USRT was the brainchild of Al Carpenter (PR man for Hurst), Buddy Martin (Sox & Martin), and Chevy racers Bill Jenkins and Dave Strickler. It was a manufacturers showdown where 16 Pro Stock cars, four from each manufacturer (Ford, Chevy, Plymouth, and Dodge), battled it out on the drag strip for supremacy on Wednesday nights nationwide. A Wednesday night show ensured there would never be a conflict with any national events the drivers may want to attend, and track owners loved putting folks in the stands on a weeknight.

The stars of the USRT were nothing short of Pro Stock royalty. The roster was as follows: Ford drivers Don Nicholson, Hubert Platt, Eddie Schartman, and Wayne Gapp; Chevy drivers Bill Jenkins, Dave Strickler, Rich Mirarcki, and Wally Booth; Plymouth drivers Ronnie Sox, Arlen Vanke, Don Grotheer, and Ronnie Lyles; and Dodge drivers Dick Landy, Mike Fons, Herb McCandless, and Don Carlton. When the team was first assembled, it went to Washington, DC, to get permission to use the name "United States Racing Team" and to take promotional photos all dressed in matching suits on the Capitol steps.

The USRT was a very professional outfit. It rolled into town on Tuesday and displayed the cars at local car dealerships and auto parts stores to promote the race as well as do a spot on the local radio station. All of the drivers were nicely dressed with embroidered shirts with their name and USRT-logo sleeve patches, no T-shirts or dirty

*Hubert is at the top of this pyramid of the best 16 Pro Stock drivers in the world: the 1971 United States Racing Team. These drivers are standing in groups of four according to their respective brands. Plymouth standing left, Ford standing right, Chevy kneeling left, and Dodge kneeling center.*

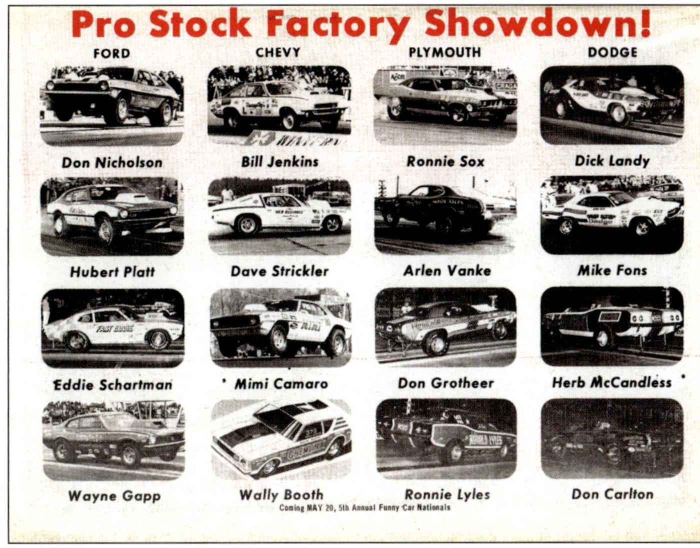


*A thick field of some legendary wheelmen was lined up to compete at the Pro Stock Factory Showdown held on May 10. USRT events were always held on Wednesday nights.*

jeans were allowed. The cars were nice too, the fastest, best-looking Pro Stocks in the country.

At this time, most weeknight drag racing shows had a match race with two or four national stars, so a 16-car show with these big names would put 5,000 to 6,000 fans in the grandstands. That was close to the same kind of numbers the NHRA was getting on a Sunday afternoon. Tracks had to pay $15,000 to host a USRT event, money easily recouped at the gate and concessions. At the track, the USRT brought its own announcer, Jon Lundberg, who knew all the drivers and their backgrounds well, which added to the professionalism of the show.

The racing format was a little different than a normal race. In the first round, everyone paired up, and it didn't matter who was racing because this was just a time run. The quickest car from each of the four manufacturers would go head-to-head for the money. Round two was 1 vs. 3, and 2 vs. 4. In the final round, the winners would race for $300. The other 12 raced in a ladder-style runoff. All drivers would receive $200 for car show participation on Tuesday and $900 for race participation on Wednesday. This was a huge paycheck in the early 1970s, more than two months wages for the average American worker.

After the races, drivers were required to keep their car out for one hour after the final run was made. This gave fans time to mill around, meet the drivers, and see the cars up close. This was a strict rule, and everyone obeyed it. There was no losing the first round and loading up and leaving.

The USRT was a success and continued throughout the 1971, 1972, and 1973 seasons. Hubert was very proud to be a part of this elite Pro Stock team. This, like so many parts of drag racing history, was never to be seen again.

*It was common for Hubert to do a spot on the local radio station in any given town to entice fans to come out to the track on race day. Hubert was always willing to give his time to help promote a race.*

The days of a 16-car pro field at your local track on a Wednesday night are truly days gone by.

### A Visiting Friend

Longtime buddies Hubert and Doug Thorley got together in the fall of 1971 when Doug was on the East Coast visiting friends. He and Hubert spent a Saturday together doing what they loved best: taking on the competition at the track. The two worked together perfectly, wrenching on the Falstaff-sponsored *Georgia Shaker* Pro Stock Maverick. Doug was on the starting line pouring the bleach for Hubert's burnouts.

The place was Drag City Dragway, a small eighth-mile drag strip in north Georgia, almost on the Tennessee border in the town of Ringgold. A lot of big name Atlanta-area

***Doug Thorley poured the bleach as Hubert smoked the tires in preparation to do battle with some of Georgia's best Pro Stock drivers in 1971.***

Pro Stock racers were on hand that night, including Reid Whisnant in his Sox & Martin–prepared Plymouth Duster, Randy Payne in his Camaro, Buck Pike with former national record holder Donnie Brewer turning the wrenches on his Boss 429 Maverick, Calvin Nabors, and Roosevelt Johnson to name a few. Whisnant's Plymouth was the low qualifier with a 6.50 in the eighth mile, and Hubert was a close second with a 6.51.

As eliminations went on, the Duster looked unbeatable when it downed the Barnett brothers' Dodge with the low ET of the night: a 6.48. Randy Payne's Camaro broke a transmission on a solid 6.65 pass and was out for the night. In the semifinals, fans got what they had hoped for when Hubert's *Georgia Shaker* Maverick came to the line to face off against the quickest car of the night: Reid Whisnant's beautifully custom painted gold Plymouth Duster.

At the first sight of green, the Maverick put a fender on the Duster. And in second gear, Hubert pulled a little more ahead. The mighty Plymouth was never able to recover from the holeshot, and at the stripe it was the *Georgia Shaker* for the win! Reid clocked a 6.50 on the run, but the tower lane clocks weren't working and Hubert's ET didn't post.

Hubert came back in the final round to beat James Lake for the first-place prize money. It was awesome that Hubert and Doug, two close friends who didn't get to spend that much time together, got to celebrate their visit with a win!

## New Help

In 1971, Hubert was just about to turn 40 years old. He was a one-man show when he had to be. He could drive the truck on long trips and wrench on the race car by himself. Like many drag racers of the 1970s, he could run the whole operation alone, but he preferred to have some help.

Slick and his other buddies had full-time jobs and Huston was running the speed shop, so they weren't always available. Hubert had Ford dealership mechanic Ronald Everett help wrench on the race car on nights and weekends, but he needed more full-time help.

Sammy Brown was a 18-year-old beginning mechanic and parts runner for Nash Chevrolet, a local dealership, who would drop parts off at Hubert's shop from time to time. One day while delivering parts, Hubert offered him

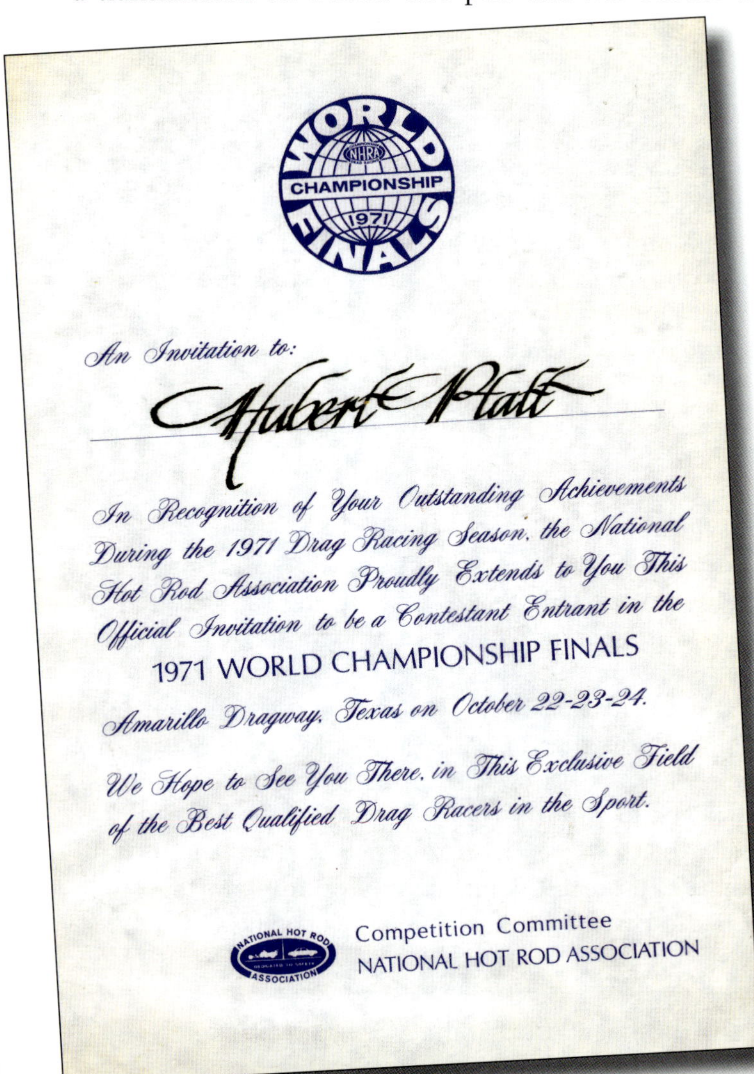
WORLD CHAMPIONSHIP 1971 FINALS

An Invitation to:

Hubert Platt

In Recognition of Your Outstanding Achievements During the 1971 Drag Racing Season, the National Hot Rod Association Proudly Extends to You This Official Invitation to be a Contestant Entrant in the

1971 WORLD CHAMPIONSHIP FINALS

Amarillo Dragway, Texas on October 22-23-24.

We Hope to See You There, in This Exclusive Field of the Best Qualified Drag Racers in the Sport.

Competition Committee
NATIONAL HOT ROD ASSOCIATION

***The NHRA sent out personal invitations for those who were eligible to compete at the 1971 World Championship Finals.***

a job. Starstruck, Sammy quit his job at the dealership and went to work for Hubert that same day. He admits his life has never been the same.

Sammy had never met anyone quite like Hubert, who he describes as a wild and funny "life of the party" type one minute and a charming Southern gentleman the next.

The only road trips young Sammy had ever been on were the times he had crossed the South Carolina border to buy fireworks, and now he found himself traveling the country with Hubert Platt, driving his racing rig. Sammy was overwhelmed on their first trip together to New York. He had never really been out of Georgia, and he remembers feeling like he was in a foreign country.

Sammy says working with Hubert was very educational. Hubert was a wealth knowledge and took Sammy's mechanic skills to the next level by teaching him the tricks of how to get every bit of performance out of a drag car. For the remainder of Hubert's racing career, Sammy worked with him. He later went on to be on the World Championship crew of Warren Johnson.

## Three Mavericks

Hubert's Mavericks have been a source of confusion for fans through the years, mainly because of matching paint jobs and the fact that he would sometimes bring two to the track and other times show up with one. For the record, Hubert had three Pro Stock Mavericks: the first was the red test car, the second was the blue Ford Drag Team car, and the third was the white Ford Drag Team car he bought from Ed Terry.

The confusion started when the red test car was painted blue to match the East Coast team in 1970 and then later sold to Buck Pike, who left the car blue and only changed the names. This was very confusing even to the announcers in the tower, who would sometimes call the wrong name when one would pull up to the line, saying, "Here comes Hubert, no-no, that's Buck."

Hubert hated this. He always wanted to stand out, so he took his two Mavericks (the original blue and Ed Terry's white, which were the two Holman & Moody–built cars) to Thompson's body shop in Alpharetta, Georgia, in the winter of 1971. His friend Max gave the cars custom matching paint jobs.

Hubert loved flashy custom paint jobs. He was inspired by the beautiful lowriders of Southern California, and a couple of years earlier he'd had his Lincoln painted baby blue with fish scales down the sides and on the Continental spare cover on the trunk. With this style in mind, the matching Mavericks were painted in a paneled-type paint job with scales, bubbles, and spider web effects. The two cars were a definite reflection of Hubert's persona. The portrait of the Maverick on the box truck was also updated to the new paint scheme.

## Platt & Yates

Having the shop in Chamblee helped Hubert reconnect with his partner from 1965: Atlanta-area friend

*The new paint for the Pro Stock Mavericks in 1972 was getting back to the more custom, less corporate style Hubert preferred. (Photo Courtesy Tim Thompson)*

*From fish scales to bubbles and spider web effects, the Platt and Yates Mavericks were beautiful on and off the track. (Photo Courtesy Michael Goyda)*

*Hubert puts on a show as he rips through the gold dust rosin. It takes nerve to drop the clutch on a Boss 429 Pro Stock Maverick, but to do it with the door open takes moxie! More than anything, Hubert was comfortable behind the wheel of a race car, and he loved to show off for the fans. (Photo Courtesy Michael Goyda)*

*Hubert's two Mavericks were hard to tell apart because the custom paint jobs only had subtle differences, one way to tell them apart is by looking at the trim around the side windows. Hubert's original blue Ford Drag Team Maverick (pictured) had chrome, and the white one didn't. (Photo Courtesy Michael Goyda)*

*Another way to tell Hubert's two Ford Drag Team Mavericks apart after they were custom painted was the doorjambs, which remained their original color. You can tell this is Maverick number three, the one Hubert got from Ed Terry, because of the white in the doorjamb.*

Larry Yates. Larry had helped build and wrench on the Falcon and the blue long-nose Mustang and had toured with Hubert throughout 1965. In January 1972, Larry was working for entrepreneur Ed Edwards, a real estate investor who owned a shopping center and a car lot in the Atlanta area. Larry was running Edwards Car Sales for Ed, and the pair decided to go in together and sponsor Hubert's two Pro Stock Mavericks as advertisement for the car lot.

Hubert welcomed the sponsorship help from his old friend and had "Platt & Yates" painted on the doors of the Mavericks. He also put a license plate from the Edwards car lot on the back of both race cars. For the next few months, Larry attended some match races and Pro Stock shows with Hubert and even drove the second Maverick on occasion. The friends were having fun, but by the summer, Larry turned his focus to other endeavors and the partnership came to an end.

*A third difference between the two custom-painted Mavericks was that the original white Maverick (pictured) had a full roll cage, while the blue one didn't.*

*Looks like Hubert was playing stage last, leave first against the Nova.*

*Hubert proved that a good smoky burnout produces a solid launch in front of a full house. Not sure what caused the damage on the quarter panel but the custom paint was fixed shortly after this photo was taken. (Photos Courtesy Bob McClurg)*

Hubert had the box truck upgraded to match the new custom paint of the race cars. (Photo Courtesy Tim Thompson)

*The forward-facing headers were really cool, but they became a thing of controversy. In 1972 Pro Stock, you could not have a front spoiler in fear that it would trip the finish line lights before the front wheel, and some of Hubert's forward-facing headers would do just that! The headers were outlawed by the NHRA.*

*Hubert always had time for his fans, Stopping to pose for a photo (as you can see here). Notice the foam rubber blocks that were glued to the bottom of the hood to keep it from scratching the roof. (Photo Courtesy Carey Woodall)*

### Double Teaming the Competition

Many times during the 1971–1972 season, Hubert took two Mavericks to local tracks around the South and entered them both in Pro Stock "match bash" races that would have a lot of regional Pro Stock drivers. Hubert would generally be the only nationally known name at the event. The two Mavericks would clean house at these events. Most of the time, Hubert would have to race himself in the final and brother Huston or another local racer would drive the second Maverick.

In April 1972, the competition at Southeastern Dragway was getting tired of this one-two punch from the national star and protested. The drivers were saying it wasn't fair to let Hubert enter and drive two cars in the show. The track owner didn't have a problem with it since Hubert was such a big name and attracted so many fans to these smaller events. After some arguing, they decided on a compromise. Hubert would drive his primary car and would let fellow Georgia racer, Roosevelt Johnson, drive his second car. Hubert would also drive Roosevelt's car.

Roosevelt Johnson was a dedicated Pro Stock racer on a budget. He had a 1970 Maverick Pro Stock that he bought used; it was a car that was said to have more than 1,000 runs on it and had been discarded by a couple of other racers. It is safe to say the car was worn out. Roosevelt often bought used parts from Hubert or other Ford racers just to keep it going. The car didn't even have shoulder harnesses, only a lap belt.

*Everyone on hand feared for Hubert's life in this terrible rollover crash that ended up only costing him a night in the hospital. The car, however, was a total loss. (Photo Courtesy Ricky Shackelford)*

*In Hubert's 20-year racing career, he had only two wrecks, and they were both at Southeastern International Dragway in Dallas, Georgia. The second of the two was in fellow Georgia racer Roosevelt Johnson's Super Maverick (shown). (Photo Courtesy Ricky Shackelford)*

The unthinkable happened when Hubert dropped the clutch on Johnson's Maverick. The car leaped off the line sideways. Hubert fought it back straight, but at half-track it got out of shape again and went into a barrel roll down the track and over the left guardrail, nearly missing the concession stand. Sammy Brown was on the starting line and said Hubert's head was hanging out of the window as the car was rolling over, and he feared for his life. Hubert was taken away to the hospital in an ambulance. Sammy said Hubert's helmet had big black marks on it where it had contacted the racing surface.

It was a close call. Hubert was treated for minor injuries and released from the hospital the next day. Roosevelt's race car was demolished, a total loss.

### Camrod

Willie "Camrod" Campbell was the owner/operator of a speed shop in Brooklyn, New York, in the Bedford-Stuyvesant district. There were actually two garages next to each other, each about 60 feet wide and 75 feet deep. Camrod's shop was at 171 Lexington Avenue, and he rented 173 Lexington next door to his friend and famed New York racer "Brooklyn Heavy." Camrod was a street and strip racer.

In the early 1970s in Brooklyn, big money was gambled on street racing. The stakes were super high, bets for over $100,000 went down in the streets of New York 40 years before *Street Outlaws* was ever thought of. Some cars out of Camrod's shop were like Pro Stocks with the weight taken out. They were basically 9-second street cars.

Camrod was also a fan of professional drag racing from way back, and he had seen Hubert race many times at Atco Dragway at Englishtown, New Jersey, and at some of the New York tracks as well. He was already a fan when he attended a US Racing Team event in the summer of 1972 at Raceway Park in Englishtown.

*This is how the Maverick was lettered when Willie "Camrod" Campbell first owned it. Hubert had sold Camrod Maverick number three, the one that was originally Ed Terry's West Coast Ford Drag Team car. (Photo Courtesy Michael Goyda)*

*The Maverick is now sporting a set of polished, front-exiting headers. This Maverick also had a rare aluminum-block Boss 429 powerplant.*

Camrod recalls seeing the Platt & Yates Pro Stock Maverick in the pits and liking everything he saw. From its custom paint job to its aluminum-block Boss 429 (bored out to 494) with forward-facing chrome headers, he was in love with this car. On the starting line, Hubert was doing long, smoky burnouts and dry-hop wheelstands while stiff-arming the door open. Camrod couldn't believe what a showman he was. When the light turned green, Hubert was hard on the wheelie bars, bringing the front wheels off the ground in first, second, and third gear then hitting fourth with the car going straight as an arrow. Camrod said to himself, "I've got to have that car!"

He approached Hubert back in the pits and asked if the car was for sale. Hubert replied, "Hell yeah, money buys anything!" Camrod was serious, so he asked Hubert, "How does 40 thousand sound for the car and truck?" Hubert said, "If you've got the cash, you've got a deal." Within 30 minutes, Camrod was back with a suitcase full of cash. Hubert thought, *I like this guy*.

For the next hour and a half, Hubert and Camrod sat in the race camper and counted money. Part of the cash was stacks of $1 bills in $100 bundles. Hubert asked "Where in the world did you get all these ones?" Camrod winked and told him a good bit of this cash was from gambling. Hubert knew then that he and Camrod were birds of a feather. The two men bonded that day and became lifelong friends.

The race car was sold with the stipulation that Hubert could borrow the car to fulfill his contract with the U.S. Racing Team for the two races he had left that season. Camrod told Hubert, "You just let me know and I will send my crew with the car anywhere you need it. You can run it like you want to run it." The following week, Camrod had the doors on the Pro Stock Maverick relettered to read "Platt & Campbell" in custom block letters where it used to say "Platt & Yates." He also had the truck repainted with huge custom block letters on the side that also said "Platt & Campbell."

Hubert with Camrod and crew raced the car at Atco Dragway to complete one of Hubert's two races left on his contract. The next month, Hubert was home in Georgia when he notified Camrod of another obligation with the Maverick, not with the US Racing Team but a different meet on Saturday, August 26, at Cumming Dragway in Forsyth County, Georgia. Camrod had a prior commitment, but he sent the car and his four crew members down from Brooklyn for the race.

Hubert and Camrod's Brooklyn crew unloaded the race car at the track the evening of the event. Before the crew could prep the car for a run, Hubert was accosted by the track management and told that he was more than welcome to stay but his all-black pit crew would have to leave! The South in 1972 was still a very racist place, and Hubert had no choice but to ask the men to leave.

He gave them his Lincoln and told them to head back to his shop in Chamblee and wait for him there. The crew was a little shocked. Being from New York, they had heard of but never actually seen anything quite like this.

Hubert was upset, but he shook it off and went up to the starting line to make his first qualifying pass. Hubert lined up against Robert Nance's *Mr. Plymouth* Barracuda. The Maverick did a big smoky burnout, and it looked like he might be letting off a little steam from being upset. Next, Hubert stiff-armed the door open and revved the big-block Ford as loud as it would go and dropped the clutch.

The Maverick's front tires launched into the air as the rear bumper slammed the track. The crew had been forced off the grounds so quickly that they hadn't had time to set the wheelie bars after unloading. In all of the confusion, Hubert hadn't noticed. When the Maverick came back to earth, Hubert jumped out and raised hell with the officials, saying this was caused by ejecting his crew.

He set the wheelie bars, got back in the car, and made his run, beating the *Mr. Plymouth* Barracuda. But, the engine was blown, and he was done for the night. Hubert told some curious fans that the wheelstand cost him $5,000 for an engine.

## Pro Stock Pinto

Since the beginning of Pro Stock in 1970, Paul Harvey Ford in Indianapolis, Indiana, owned and sponsored a Boss 429 Maverick called *The Quiet One*. It was first driven by Randy Payne and then Dick Brannan. In 1972, Ford teams were changing from the big-block Mavericks to small-block Pintos to take advantage of the new weight breaks the NHRA was giving to small-blocks. Ronnie Sox and his Hemi Plymouths were dominating the class, so the cubic inch to weight ratios were put in place to even the playing field, so to speak.

*The Pro Stock Pinto is shown here in its original paint scheme. The car was first driven by Dick Brannan for a couple of races before being relettered and given to Hubert in December 1972.*

*The little Pinto looked tough from all angles, but Hubert soon grew tired of this paint job and changed it up to something more flashy.*

Not to be left behind, in the fall of 1972 Paul Harvey ordered a Pro Stock Pinto from M&S Welding, a race car shop in Azusa, California. Like the Mavericks, the bodies of the Pintos were stripped down and acid dipped to lighten the body considerably. The little car was equipped with a full roll cage and a heavy-duty rear suspension. A 5.57:1 gear in a Dana 60–series rear end was used with Monroe adjustable coilover shocks and adjustable ladder-style traction bars. To build the power for this little monster was a Boss 351 Cleveland.

Sitting on top were two Holleys and a Weiand intake dumping fuel to the TRW 12.75:1-compression pistons with Perfect Circle rings and "Mr. Rod" aluminum connecting rods with Clevite 77 bearings. The heads had custom aluminum blocks to raise the exhaust ports, which aided in the smooth flow of exit exhaust. The fire was lit by an Accel Eliminator ignition and Autolite performance spark plugs. The Pennzoil racing oil was pumped by a Milodon wet-sump oil pump.

The big-block Mopars were using dry-sump systems, but Hubert didn't believe that this would work efficiently on the small-block Fords. In an effort to keep the car looking as real as possible, the gutted interior's sheet metal was covered in black carpet that snapped in and out over the transmission tunnel. A black fiberglass dashboard with tach, oil pressure, and water temperature gauges was sleek and simple. A Hurst Super Shifter with reverse lockout was used to control the Doug Nash 4-speed racing transmission with Schiefer clutch and flywheel. On the ground was a set of Cragar lightweight spun aluminum wheels with Firestone meat all the way around. When the car was complete, it was custom painted Ford blue with gold panels.

Originally, Paul had Dick Brannan driving the car and Bill Rider working on the engine, and that was how the car was lettered: "Driver Dick Brannan, Mechanic Bill Rider" and "Paul Harvey Ford" on the lower part of the door. Brannan only drove the car a couple of times before hanging up his helmet for good.

Paul offered Hubert the car, and he accepted. The lettering was redone in a Western-style font done in gold leaf with a black shadow that read "Hubert Platt" on the door with "Paul Harvey Ford" below that and "Georgia Shaker" on the quarter panels. Hubert debuted this car at the Super Nationals in Ontario, California, in November 1972. The hot little Pro Stock Pinto was featured in *Rodder and Super Stock* magazine in a three-page article with nine pictures called "Hey Hubie Baby."

### Red Hot!

By spring of the 1973 race season, Hubert was growing tired of the blue with gold panels paint scheme on the Pro Stock Pinto. He decided to step it up to something a little more flashy. Once again, he returned to Thompson's body shop in Georgia, where he had Max's son Tim put a super custom paint job on the little Pinto. For the previous four years, Hubert's race cars had been Ford blue, so for a big change he had the Pinto painted bright red, almost Candy Apple.

There were many custom elements to this paint job. It had large gold and red "hot rod" flames coming out of the wheel wells with a black shadow. All across the roof and hood were multicolor stripes, spider web effects, and fish scales. Coming out of the back side windows was an airbrushed painted cartoon of a woman's foot with toes shooting a peace sign, leading you to believe there was a naked lady in the back seat with her feet hanging out of the windows! This type of custom paint was mostly seen on nationally touring custom show cars.

On the cover of *Playboy* magazine's 1973 March issue appeared a series of 32 photos of a Playmate in various stages of undress. She was fully dressed in the first photo and totally nude in the last. Hubert had this cover laminated under the clear coat between the taillights. This was a show stopper and Kodak moment for fans in the pits. Everyone wanted to see and get a picture of the risqué photos on the back of the drag car. This just added to Hubert's showman, playboy persona.

The car was lettered once again with gold leaf in a Western-style font, but for the first time the "Georgia Shaker" was painted on the doors and "Paul Harvey Ford" was on the quarter panels. A full-page photo of the Pinto's new paint scheme was featured in *Popular Hot Rodding* magazine. Hubert was especially proud of the Pinto and the way it looked, and in September at the 1973 NHRA U.S. Nationals in Indianapolis, he was proud of its performance when he qualified in the quickest Pro Stock field to date and beat Bill "Grumpy" Jenkins's Vega in the first round. This was one of the biggest victories for Hubert's Pinto, if not the biggest.

Although Bob Glidden would go on to win this event (his first national event win as a pro), it was fun for Hubert to take out one of the top drivers to ever race a Pro Stock in Jenkins. The majority of Hubert's success with the Pro Stock Pinto came at match races and regional events.

Hubert continued to tour the country and race the Pinto for the next four years while running the Platt Brothers Automotive speed shop with his brother Huston in Chamblee, Georgia. At the beginning of the 1975 race season, Hubert upgraded the Pinto with the newest technology: the Lenco transmission.

Lenco transmissions revolutionized Pro Stock. It could be shifted without using the clutch after you left the line, and shifted into second, third, and fourth gear with individual levers. After this, the 1970–1974 Pro Stock seasons would be considered the 4-speed years because the conventional H-pattern 4-speed would no longer be competitive or used.

***The Lenco 4-speed transmission was a real game changer in Pro Stock. The far-right lever was for reverse. The other three when put all forward are first gear, once you drop the clutch for first gear you just pull back the tallest lever for second, the next for third, and the next for fourth, clutch free.***

*Hubert does a dry hop, preparing to make Bill Jenkins a little Grumpier when he put him on the trailer with this first-round win at the 1973 NHRA U.S. Nationals in Indianapolis. (Photo Courtesy Bob McClurg)*

*Hard on the wheelie bars in first gear, the Pro Stock Pinto ran a best of 9.08 at 148.76 at NHRA legal weight. Over the next couple of years, it would dip into the 8s at over 150 mph. This photo was featured in* Popular Hot Rodding *magazine.*

*After Hubert had the Pro Stock Pinto painted to his liking, it was definitely a show stopper. Fans in the pits would take photo after photo of the little racer that looked more like a show car.*

*The Pinto hooked up and was working right as it came off the starting line at the NHRA Summer Nationals.*

With the Lenco, the Pinto was running in the 8s at over 150 mph. Hubert was keeping up with the times, but now in his 40s, he was finding it harder to keep up with the young guns of the sport such as Bob Glidden, who was 13 years his junior.

Throughout the 1960s and early 1970s, Hubert had achieved fame and fortune along with superstar status in the drag racing world, but in these last years of his racing career, going to the races was just as much a social event as it was a competition. He was paid appearance money to show up, and there was never a shortage of his peers or fans who wanted to party with the legend.

This was all well and good, and he indulged himself and had a lot of fun, but Hubert was a racer at heart. If he could no longer be competitive, winning national events and setting national records, then he knew the time had come for him to hang up his helmet. In the fall of 1977, after drag racing for 20 years, Hubert Platt officially retired and walked away from the sport he so dearly loved.

*This was the back license plate on Hubert's Pro Stock Pinto. He was very proud of this name, which was now well known in the world of drag racing.*

*Hubert finishes packing the parachute after another run. His hair is beginning to show a touch of gray, and there is no telling how many miles he has put on drag strips from coast to coast.*

*Hubert's son Allen poses for a photo with family friend Linda "Miss Hurst" Vaughn at the 1976 NHRA Gatornationals.*

*The 1970s were a wild time. Hubert's T-shirt says "Save a tree, eat a beaver." The man on the right is Jerome "JB" Bradford, Hubert's longtime friend and drag racer who would go on to be a Pro Stock team owner. His driver, Warren Johnson, would win two IHRA Pro Stock World Championships for him in 1979 and 1980. (Photo Courtesy Carey Woodall)*

*Hubert won many trophies and was a crowd favorite at South Georgia's Warner Robins Dragway.*

*At Warner Robins Dragway in the 1970s, they would still spread the gold dust rosin to put on a show. Hubert loved to dry hop through with the door open and wheels up to impress the fans!*

## Hubie's Shelby

Around 1973, a customer brought two Shelby Mustangs to the Platt Brothers Automotive Speed Shop: a 1967 drag car and a yellow 1968 GT500KR. A deal was made for Hubert to build and install a race engine in the 1967 and help set it up to compete. The payment would be the 1968 Shelby.

Hubert did the deal and drove the yellow Shelby for almost a year. It was used as an extra family car for the Platts. Hubert decided this would be the perfect car to fix up for his son Hubie, who was about to be a senior in high school.

Hubert took the car to award-winning show car painter Kenneth Allen in Sugar Hill, Georgia. Allen proceeded to completely strip the yellow Shelby down to the bare metal and cover it with 20 coats of black, hand-rubbed lacquer. Hubert ordered new Shelby 428 Cobra Jet emblems and GT500KR stripes for the car from his friends at Ford.

For the drivetrain, Hubert left no stone unturned, starting with the 428 Cobra Jet engine. Hubert took his sons Hubie and Allen into his parts room at the shop and showed them a box of parts. Inside was a set of 427 aluminum racing rods handmade at Holman & Moody; a 600-lift 330-duration Crane Fireball, strip only; solid-lift cam; and lifters. Hubert told the boys that he had been saving these parts since 1968. They came from one of the engines that was in the black and silver Cobra Jet Mustang that had been wrecked. Now, he was going to use them in the Shelby.

There had been much conversation at the Platt home about Hubert building this car for teenage son Hubie. Bee felt that there was no need for a high-performance engine or a black paint job for a car that a teenage boy would drive to high school. Hubert paid her no mind and told the boys, "I want it to kinda fly!"

Hubert proceeded on with the build the way he wanted. The custom 428 Cobra Jet engine was a work of art with a huge Holley, dual line, double pumper with manual secondaries, custom CJ heads with bigger valves and stiffer springs, and Cobra LeMans valve covers. The Crane Fireball cam and the racing rods Hubert had showed the boys were used along with a steel-forged race crank, a high-volume oil pump, and a custom-made 8-quart oil pan nestled between a set of Doug Thorley cross-over headers. All the stock hoses and lines on the engine had been swapped out with aluminum braided lines with the red and blue aluminum fittings, including the header hoses. The radiator hose was the only rubber hose on the engine. Hubert said the engine had 750 hp and was worth $5,000, which was the price of a new car in 1974.

The Shelby Mustang was an automatic, so Hubert replaced the stock unit with a Wynn's C-6 racing transmission with a B&M 5000-stall torque converter. The rear end was a Detroit locker with a spool and a 3.73:1 gear so the car could be driven on the highway. Every time it turned a corner at slow speed, the inside tire would chirp because of the spool.

Hubert finished the build at the beginning of Hubie's senior year. The car was a stunner, to say the least, and the engine was loud and strong. Sitting in the driveway idling at 2,500 rpm, it would rattle the widows in the house. Seventeen-year-old Hubie drove the car as you would imagine a 17-year-old son of a race car driver would, and he soon became a neighborhood legend. It was the fastest car on the street. Kids would come around from all the nearby high schools in their big-block Camaros, Chevelles, and Mopars, but no one could touch Hubie's Shelby.

Having the baddest car around came with a price. It cost young Hubie his Saturdays because Hubert made him be at the shop every Saturday morning to change the oil (20W50 Pennzoil racing oil, no exceptions) and the spark plugs while Hubert adjusted the valves on the solid-lift cam; a must for the car to run right.

When Hubie stabbed the gas from a dead stop, the Shelby would smoke the tires like no street car in town had ever done before or since. The rear tires would start to boil smoke out from under the fender well toward the back of the car and drift up to the tip of the spoiler with a full white cloud trailing behind like something only seen done by the *Chi-Town Hustler*. It was truly a thing of beauty!

# CHAPTER 12

# THE REUNION YEARS

In the late 1980s, Hubert was approached by Donnie Reeves, a race car builder from North Georgia who had built a replica of a 1965 long-nose Mustang drag car similar to the ones Hubert raced in the 1960s. Donnie explained that he wanted to paint the car blue, letter it like the *Georgia Shaker*, and make it a tribute to Hubert's original home-built long-nose Mustang.

Hubert checked out the race car and found some differences. The biggest was the distance of the altered wheelbase. The rear end on the original had only been moved forward 2 inches, but on this car the rear end was much farther forward. Other noticeable differences were the aluminum sheet metal interior, the absence of Cragar S/S mags, and the addition of a parachute and wheelie bars (two things his car never had).

Even though it was not an exact replica of his Mustang, it was a nice car. Hubert was flattered that someone had taken enough interest in something he did more than 20 years before to invest their money and build a replica as a tribute to him. Hubert agreed, and the car was painted and lettered to closely match the original. It debuted at the 1989 World of Wheels car show at the Georgia World Congress Center in Atlanta, Georgia.

Through the years, the car has changed hands a couple of times. It has made many appearances at nostalgic drag races and hot rod reunions that Hubert attended. The car is now owned by Kuck Motorsports in Lincoln, Nebraska.

***Just like in the 1960s, Hubert did not have a hair out of place. He loved the nostalgia drag racing events almost as much as racing. (Photo Courtesy Fred Simmons)***

*Hubert poses with the 427 FE at the NHRA Hot Rod Reunion in Bowling Green, Kentucky. He went to this event 10 years in a row from 2005 to 2014. (Photo Courtesy Fred Simmons)*

*Hubert hosted an annual car show that would bring more than 100 classics, customs, and race cars to his restaurant, the Sugar Hill Drive-In. The cars filled the restaurant parking lot and spilled over into the church parking lot across the street. (Photo Courtesy Fred Simmons)*

This tribute replica of Hubert's home-built long-nose Mustang was the first of many replicas in his honor. During the next two decades, drag racing enthusiasts would seemingly come out of the woodwork wanting Hubert's permission to duplicate his famous rides from back in the day. It also seemed to spark a treasure hunt for original *Georgia Shaker* race cars. Collectors often wanted Hubert to authenticate their finds. All of this was a joy to Hubert in his golden years. He loved working with collectors and builders, sharing all of his knowledge of these historical race cars.

## The Rebirth of the Thunderbolt

After Lee Malkemes purchased Hubert's Thunderbolt, he wrecked it in a match race versus Ronnie Sox in 1965. That accident resulted in a broken neck, and Lee parked the car for 26 years. The crash that totaled the T-Bolt was a violent rollover accident that happened at the end of the drag strip at high speed, so there wasn't really an unbent part on the body, and the hood, the roof, and the doors were all bent beyond repair.

Two and a half decades after that terrible crash, Lee decided it was time to get back on the horse that had bucked him off so many years ago. He brought in a 1964 Fairlane doner car and began the painstaking process of rebuilding the Thunderbolt. Full documentation and the use of every salvageable piece and part from the original car gained Lee the blessing of the American Thunderbolt Registry, and he was allowed to put the original VIN on the car. After two years of hard work, the car was completed. Lee had it painted exactly how it looked when he purchased it from Hubert.

*The rebuilt and restored Thunderbolt has a full roll cage so it can be raced in the modern era. Hubert and Lee Malkemes went to nostalgia drag events in the late 1990s, and Hubert made several passes in the T-bolt. He was glad to travel, show off the Thunderbolt, and reconnect with the other racers from back in the day, as well as fans new and old. (Photo Courtesy Fred Simmons)*

The *Little Georgia Shaker* was reborn, and Lee began to race it at nostalgia events. In July 1994, Lee and the T-Bolt were attending a Fun Ford Show event, a drag race and car show at Atlanta Dragway in Commerce, Georgia, and Lee invited Hubert. Hubert could not hide his enthusiasm for being reunited with his old ride. Hubert, now 63 years young, jumped into the driver's seat when Lee asked him if he would like to make a pass down the drag strip in the *Little Georgia Shaker*.

Lee had been racing the T-Bolt for several months now with a best ET of 11.43 at 121.03 mph. Hubert hadn't driven this car in 30 years and he hadn't driven a race car in 17 years, but on his first run he beat Lee's best ET with an 11.04 at 122.85 mph. When he returned to the pits, he told reporters on hand, "I'm ready to make a good run now! Just two more passes and it could run 10.80s." Lee and Hubert remained friends and toured together to some nostalgia drag events in the late 1990s.

Hubert drove the *Little Georgia Shaker* T-Bolt for the last time with sons Hubie and Allen watching from the starting line in 1998 at National Trail Dragway outside Columbus, Ohio. Lee sold the car to Johnny Kelley of Walhalla, South Carolina, who raced and showed the car for around eight years.

Johnny remembers the joy on the faces of fans when he would unload the car at events. He had many drag cars through the years, but he says it was a special thing to own the *Little Georgia Shaker* because of its history. He said, "Everywhere I went, people knew this car." In January 2006, Johnny decided to sell the T-Bolt, and he invited Hubert to join him, all expenses paid, in Scottsdale, Arizona, for the world-famous Barrett-Jackson auto auction. He knew Hubert's star power would help sell the car at the highest price possible. Hubert accepted the invitation and brought his friend and personal photographer Fred Simmons along for the ride.

Hubert and the car received a great response when the *Little Georgia Shaker* Thunderbolt went across the stage, and when the gavel fell, $150,000 was the highest and selling bid. Hubert couldn't believe that the used race car he sold 42 years before for around $4,000 just went to its fourth owner for that astronomical amount. Hubert said "Oh well, hindsight is 20-20." The happy new owner was Gary Kuck of Kuck Motorsports in Lincoln, Nebraska, a drag racer and auto enthusiast who has more than 120 cars in his collection, including the replica of Hubert's blue long-nose Mustang.

Johnny offered to fly Hubert home from Arizona, but Hubert wanted to ride back to Georgia in the truck so he could stop in El Paso, Texas, to buy some new cowboy boots.

### The Resurrection of the *Iowa Shaker*

In the mid-1970s, Mike Kerr was your average Chandler, Arizona, teenager with an old car he was trying to fix up. In his case, the car was a 1964 Ford Falcon Sprint that had a smashed quarter panel. Mike spent his evenings and weekends working on the car, which involved searching junkyards, body shops, and any old car graveyards, looking for cheap parts.

One such weekend while searching in nearby Gilbert, a neighboring town of Chandler, he came across a Falcon backed into the corner of an old body shop. He thought, *Finally, I've found the quarter panel I've been searching for!* After further inspection, he realized this was no ordinary Falcon. These quarter panels looked funny, the wheel wells had been moved forward. He wasn't sure what to make of the Falcon with all of its fiberglass parts and radical appearance, so he left the car and continued his search.

A year later while visiting a friend, he crossed paths with the funny Falcon again. To his surprise, his friend had bought the car. As he checked it out, he thought it was really a cool car. He began to wheel and deal with his friend to acquire the Falcon, but the friend was set on keeping it.

After graduation from high school in 1976, Mike continued to try to purchase the car. The friend had a Dodge Charger he was working on, and he needed some parts. Mike was working at a salvage yard at the time and was able to find just what was needed for the Charger: an automatic transmission with shifter and a Holley carburetor. Mike offered this as a trade, and the friend agreed. In 1977, the altered-wheelbase Falcon with no engine was finally his.

Mike didn't have a lot of extra money at the time, so the car sat patiently in his mom's backyard, awaiting its restoration. For the next five years, Mike slowly worked on the car, wondering all along about its history. In 1982, he contacted Brent Hajek of Ames, Oklahoma, a farmer and vintage race car collector with an extensive knowledge of drag racing history. Mike told him about the Falcon and asked if Brent may have a thought as to who owned or raced the car back in the day. Brent suggested it may be one of Hubert Platt's famous Falcons from the 1960s. He mailed Mike some 8x10 pictures of the *Georgia Shaker III*.

Mike noticed some differences in the photos compared to the Falcon he had been working on. His Falcon had a Mustang front gravel pan, but the one in the pictures did not. Also the rear wheel wells were a little different. He knew he had to dig deeper. He began to contact anyone who had anything to do with drag racing from

***Current owner Mike Kerr has owned the* Iowa Shaker *for more than 40 years. He restored the car himself and also painted and lettered the car.***

the 1960s and ask them questions about the history of this car. In 1985, he caught a break and was given Hubert Platt's phone number.

Hubert answered Mike's call, and the two talked for hours. Hubert explained that he had three different Falcons. The first one being the *Smallest Georgia Shaker*, which became the *Georgia Shaker III*, the second was the *Iowa Shaker*, and third was the one he built for Tommy McNeely. Hubert told Mike that the *Iowa Shaker* had a fiberglass dash and many other lightweight parts.

Everything Hubert told him matched his car. Hubert sent Mike pictures of the *Iowa Shaker*, and Mike immediately recognized his car with the unique Mustang front gravel pan. The wheel wells were the same, and he even noticed the misaligned fenders in the pictures like his car had. Mike had found and been holding on to a rare piece of drag racing history all along. Now that he knew what he had, he began the process of restoring this gem. Working little by little on a working man's budget, he took the next six years to bring the car back to its former glory. In January 1991, Mike painted the Falcon the beautiful shade of Ford blue again.

Mike devised a technique to recreate the 1960s custom lettering on the car. He covered the side with white butcher paper and used an overhead projector to project a photo of the original car at full size. Then, he traced the lettering onto the butcher paper with a pencil and made stencils to get the lettering the perfect size. This worked, and the paint job turned out beautifully, looking almost exactly like it had in the 1960s.

The finished car was debuted in Pomona, California, at the NHRA Winternationals in 1991, 25 years after it raced its way to the semifinals in 1966. Mike raced and showed the car at nostalgia drag events in California and Arizona for the next 13 years. He stopped racing the car in 2004, but he would still take it to local car shows in Arizona. Hubert attended several of these shows.

In April 2014, Mike brought Hubert and his son Allen to attend the Phoenix Drag Reunion in Phoenix, Arizona. Mike displayed the *Iowa Shaker,* and Hubert met with fans, signed autographs, and answered questions about the early days of drag racing. Allen had his picture taken beside the *Iowa Shaker* while holding a 1965 photo of himself by the car taken when he was only two years old.

## The Holy Grail Barn Find

In 1965, Hubert sold the *Georgia Shaker III* Falcon to Harold Pasley, who renamed the car the *Flying Falcon* and raced it into the 1966 season. Harold then sold the car to its cocreator, Hubert's partner Larry Yates. Larry raced the car for a while before selling it to a man named Willie from Macon, Georgia.

Stories from Macon tell of Willie racing the Falcon on the street in 1967 before falling ill and parking the car on its tow trailer behind his house. The car sat outside for so long the wooden floorboards of the trailer rotted and the Falcon actually fell through.

In the early 1980s, Willie was approached by Robert Lamb, who knew the history of the little Falcon and wanted to buy it. Robert and his father Bobby were car collectors from Georgia. For an unknown reason, Willie didn't want to sell to the Lambs, and he refused their offer.

Alvin Hutto, the owner of Performance Speed Shop in Macon, acted as a go-between and bought the Falcon from Willie. On the very same day, he sold it to Robert Lamb. Robert and his father contacted Hubert, telling him about their purchase of the car. He went to Hubert's home to look at pictures of the Falcon from its time on the drag strip and to hear the old stories Hubert had to tell. Robert was excited about restoring the classic drag car, and he began to take it apart and begin its restoration.

Soon after, Robert suffered an untimely death. After losing his son, Bobby lost interest and sold his entire car collection to Dwayne Reece and Tony Hogan. Dwayne and Tony were looking to flip the cars for a quick profit.

*Hubert stands with the* **Georgia Shaker** *Falcon barn find. The car is a time capsule, still having most all of its original parts from 1965. (Photo Courtesy Fred Simmons)*

Within 30 days of their purchase, they contacted auto enthusiast Tim Holland of Lawrenceville, Georgia. Tim came out to look at the collection, seeing many cars he was interested in.

As he looked around, Tim came across the Falcon. Seeing the rough shape it was in, he inquired about the vehicle to find out it was the famous *Georgia Shaker III*. Tim was a drag racing fan, and he got excited. A deal was made, and he left with a 1966 Shelby GT350-H, a 1967 Fairlane GT convertible, a 1961 Starliner, and the disassembled 1965 Falcon altered-wheelbase drag car complete with its original 427 injected powerplant.

Tim contacted Hubert and had him come out to see the find. Hubert was amazed when he saw his old car

*The Falcon still has the original tires and wheels all the way around.*

*The car has not been restored, although it does have a faux paint job lettered to match when Hubert last raced the car.*

*When Tim Holland began taking the Falcon around to car shows, people would always come up to see the car and say "Where's Hubert?" So he had these stickers made and would pass them out to everyone.*

in person for the first time in years. As he looked it over, he noticed one thing after another that confirmed that this was indeed the real car. From the straight-axle front end out of an Econoline van (which he had cut 6 inches out of the center and welded back together himself) to the one-of-a-kind custom pinstriping all across the top of the dashboard. The list went on and on.

Most drag cars that were sold after being campaigned by their first caretaker were raced for years and were modified and changed over time, but that was not the case with this car. It still had the original Goodyear racing slicks Hubert raced on so many years ago, as well as the custom headers made by Doug Thorley. Hubert was happy to authenticate this find, and he proudly stood beside it while his picture was taken. This photo was later featured *in Hot Rod* magazine, telling of this historical barn find.

When the car was found, you could still see where it said "Flying Falcon" on the quarter panel and Larry Yates on the door. Since this car was virtually a time capsule, the plan was to repair and reassemble it and get the engine running. The car had been taken apart after years of sitting outside, so putting it back together was somewhat of a rusty jigsaw puzzle. Many pieces had to be welded back together. After the car was back in one piece, the engine was rebuilt but not restored and put back in the car. Next, Tim had a faux paint job with patina put on the Falcon with lettering to look like it did when Hubert last raced it.

Hubert and Tim toured the Falcon barn find to nostalgia drag races and car shows for the next several years. It was amazing how many fans in their 60s would stand in line to get Hubert's autograph and tell him their account of when they were a teenager and saw this iconic car race.

### The Ford Drag Team Mustangs

In 1983, Bob Perkins of Perkins Restoration in Juneau, Wisconsin, was on his way to Carlisle, Pennsylvania, to attend the annual and world's largest all-Ford event

*The Ford Drag Team display at the MCACN 2017 in Rosemont, Illinois, was the first time the Ford Drag Team cars have been together in 47 years. The 12x12 booth is filled with Hubert "Georgia Shaker" Platt merchandise, and the clear-sided trailer in the back is the Ford Drag Team mobile museum of Bob Perkins.*

Hubert's Q-code 428 Cobra Jet Super Stock Mustang was restored to its original Platt & Payne paint scheme. It was back to the way it looked from January until September 1969, before it was relettered to read Ford Drag Team.

All of the Ford Drag Team, East Coast, West Coast, and Midwest team cars carried this large Ford banner on the decklid. Factory sponsorship is as good as it gets in motorsports. Racing these factory-backed cars was the pinnacle of Hubert's career.

The Ford Drag Team Super Stocks all proudly boasted in gold leaf on the hoods that there was a 428 Cobra Jet power-plant underneath. This was a successful engine for Ford and found its way into many different models.

*The restoration that has been done on Hubert's SOHC Mustang by Perkins Restoration is second to none. The car was restored to its 1969 match race version, which was the way it looked when Hubert raced it from October to December 1969. The total restoration process was done using no reproduction parts and the car won the Mustang Club of America's coveted Thoroughbred Gold Award in 2013. (Photos Courtesy Jerry Heasley)*

*Hubert and owner/restorer Bob Perkins show off the Best of the Best award given to the SOHC Ford Drag Team Mustang at the NHRA Hot Rod Reunion in 2013.*

*Hubert poses with sons Allen (left) and Hubie (right) at the 2012 MCACN show. Behind them is the SOHC Mustang and the Ford Drag Team mobile museum.*

when he stopped by the Sam Yanen Ford dealership in West Virginia. It was customary for Bob to stop at Ford dealerships any time he was on a trip and purchase any and all 1964–1973 "new old stock" Mustang parts for his Mustang restoration business.

At the Sam Yanen Ford dealership, Bob met the owner's son, Rick Yanen, who told him they had a warehouse close by where they stored the old parts. Bob accompanied Rick to the warehouse to find not only the parts but also a 1969 Mustang Super Stock drag car. Bob inquired about the old race car and Rick admitted he had raced it for a few years in the 1970s. Bob also found out that it was originally the Ford Drag Team Super Stock Cobra Jet Mustang that Hubert Platt campaigned the 1969 and 1970 race seasons.

Knowing the historical significance of this Mustang, Bob purchased it on the spot for $6,500. While attending the Carlisle Ford show the next day, Bob sold the Mustang to his best friend and fellow Mustang collector Jacky Jones, who owns a Ford dealership in Georgia and was personal friends with Hubert Platt.

Two years later in 1985, Jacky purchased the second Hubert Platt Ford Drag Team Mustang from Bob Oswald in Columbia, South Carolina. Oswald had found the car in Rock Hill, South Carolina, and bought it from Tom Sutton. Sutton purchased it from Hubert in 1970. It was the SOHC Mustang.

In 1986, Jacky sold the SOHC Mustang to Bob Perkins for $9,500. Ten years later in 1996, while acquiring parts to restore the SOHC Mustang, Perkins paid a visit to Tom Sutton, who still had the original fiberglass fenders, Grand National–style seat, tachometer, side glass, and headers for the SOHC. He sold all of it to Bob.

In 2006, more than 20 years after Bob Perkins sold the Super Stock Mustang to Jacky Jones, the restoration of that car began. Jacky chose to restore the classic Super Stock Mustang to the "Platt & Payne" paint scheme that it had campaigned in for first part of the 1969 season. Jacky Jones's restoration specialist, Mike Plott, worked on the project for more than a year and a half. When it was completed, Jacky debuted the car at the 2008 Georgia Racing Hall of Fame induction ceremony, which Hubert attended.

In 2010, 24 years after Bob bought the SOHC Mustang from Jacky, the restoration started on that car. At Perkins Restoration in Wisconsin, Bob chose to restore this car to its 1969 match race attire. For two years, Bob painstakingly restored the classic drag car back to its original livery with no reproduction parts. He even tracked down the original intake manifold and cylinder heads for the SOHC engine, which were stamped "PLATT" and "HP." This meticulous restoration was completed in 2012, and the car debuted that November at the Muscle Car and Corvette Nationals in Rosemont, Illinois. Hubert and his two sons were in attendance.

The next summer, Hubert, his sons, and two of his grandsons attended the NHRA Hot Rod Reunion, where the SOHC Mustang won the Best of the Best award and was invited to be displayed at the NHRA U.S. Nationals that September. The next year at the 2013 Mustang Club of America Nationals in Indianapolis, the restored SOHC Mustang won the Thoroughbred Gold award. This award is only given to Mustangs with no reproduction parts and this was the only time it was awarded to a race car.

In 2014 at the 50th Anniversary of the Mustang at Charlotte Motor Speedway, Bob displayed the SOHC

***This tribute replica of the East Coast Ford Drag Team truck is owned and was built by Ford Drag Team collector Luis Chanes from Newport Coast, California.***

***This tribute replica of the 1970 Ford Drag Team Maverick was commissioned by Hubert in 2013, but it wasn't completed until after his passing. It's owned by Elliot Sande of Ormond Beach, Florida, and was built by Bud McCauley.***

Mustang. Fans from around the world waited in line for up to two hours to get Hubert's autograph on a poster and buy a T-shirt from the legend.

Bob Perkins still owns the SOHC Mustang and takes it to major events yearly in a custom enclosed trailer with clear sides so you can see the car going down the highway. When the car is out and on display, the trailer doubles as a mobile museum filled with Hubert's racing jackets and Ford Drag Team memorabilia.

The Hubert Platt 1969 SOHC match race drag car is one of the most collectable Mustangs in the world with an estimated value at auction of more than $500,000. The 1969 Super Stock car is now owned by Gary Schwartz of Merrill, Wisconsin, who had been a partner in the car with Jacky Jones since the mid-1980s.

## The Shadrach Mustangs

In 2005, the all-new Mustangs came out that resembled the Fastback Mustangs from the 1960s. Blake Wilder, who had been building race cars and custom hot rods for 30 years, had the vision of honoring the 1969 Platt & Payne Ford Drag Team with a line of signature-series Mustangs. The plan was to build highly modified Mustangs bearing the Platt & Payne names along with "The Going Thing" logo from the 1969–1970 Ford Drag Team. Since Hubert and Randy both had such a deep racing history and a flashy paint job and racing stripes weren't going to be enough to honor these legends, the signature-series Mustangs were to be street-legal race cars.

Blake enlisted Mike Langston, a former ARCA racer, to help with some financial backing. The two men first received approval from Hubert and Randy and then started the search for five brand-new 2005, blue GT Mustangs, a task that turned out to be harder than they expected.

### *Jacky Jumps In*

The new Mustangs were in great demand, and dealers that did get one were selling them for $5,000 above sticker price. This looked as if it was going to be a major setback until Hubert got his friend Jacky Jones involved.

Jacky was a classic Mustang collector and owner of nine new car dealerships in Georgia, North Carolina, and Tennessee. He was able to pull some strings and got the five Mustangs the guys were looking for at list price. Jacky jump-started a program that was dead in the water before it had ever gotten off the ground.

Blake personally picked up the cars from different dealerships in Georgia, Florida, and North Carolina. Some of the dealers were so mad they wouldn't even speak to him because they didn't want to give up the highly sought after Mustangs at list price.

To have a facility large enough to take on a project of this size, Blake partnered with Seven Springs Church, which he attended in Powder Springs, Georgia. The church had a large shop. Youths from Blake's church were brought in to help with the builds as an outreach program focused on keeping kids out of trouble. In late January 2005, the first order of business was to strip and gut the five Mustangs.

The 4.6 V-8 engines were removed, and only the blocks and cylinder heads were used on the rebuilds. The crank, rods, pistons, and the complete valvetrain were all replaced with high-performance aftermarket parts. Kinsler made the stack fuel-injection system with 16 injectors

*Hubert poses at the NHRA Hot Rod Reunion with the Shadrach Mustang and daughter-in-law Anna Platt, Allen's wife.*

*Two of the different powerplants that were available in the Shadrach Mustangs are shown. Injected with twin turbos or a Boss 429 with two 4s; pick your poison!*

that had a custom billet hat on top. The twin-turbo setup was handmade by Blake himself.

The first two engines were set up by Steve Petty, a turbo expert and tuner from Pro-Line Racing. The built 4.6-liter Ford engine produced 700 hp for daily street driving but could be easily turned up to 1,100 hp on boost for racing.

The Mustangs were truly striped down to a shell. Every piece of Ford suspension was completely removed and replaced with custom one-off parts. The Mustangs were so new that aftermarket parts weren't yet available. Anthony Jones, founder of AJE, handmade the tube front suspensions, K-members, control arms, and spindles for the builds. Strange Engineering sent Blake a bare rear end housing to use as a mock-up. Blake customized it with all the brackets and mounts for the shocks and suspension and sent it back to them; they then finalized everything, adding axles, third member, and Detroit locker. Öhlins custom made adjustable shocks for the Mustangs that could be set up for road racing then easily adjusted on the car for drag racing.

The first Mustang was taken to the Öhlins shock factory and test facility, where it had the privilege of being put on the "Shake Rig" for a test and tune session. This was the very same rig used for NASCAR teams such as Rick Hendrick's.

World-class attention for a build like this doesn't come cheap. The custom Öhlins shocks for the Mustangs cost $6,000 per set of four! G-Force Transmissions made the 6-speed gearboxes, which was brand-new for them in 2005, and these 6-speed transmissions were the prototypes for the ones they would sell to the public the following year.

Weld Racing Wheels made the one-off 20-inch polished-aluminum deep dish racing wheels that had Toyo Proxes racing tires: 315/35R20 on the rear and 255/35R20 on the front. To slow everything down was a set of Brembo disc brakes all the way around.

In the interior, a four-point roll bar was installed, and the stock Ford seats were replaced with heated and air-conditioned Recaro racing seats front and back. The back of the front seats had custom embroidered stitching in them with flames that said Hubert Platt, Randy Payne Signature Edition.

The Mustangs were so new there weren't any aftermarket body kits available, so Blake and his crew mocked up ground effects to go all the way around the cars. They made a new front bumper with a large spoiler, custom flat bar grilles and fog lights, a new rear bumper with a modern Pro Stock–style rear spoiler, as well as a custom hood that had openings for the injection to peek through and forward-facing cold air scoops. They also made Shelby-style side scoops and rocker panel covers. All of these body parts were then sent to Hairy Glass in Jacksonville, Florida, where molds were made from all of the pieces. When the molds were finished, the body kits were completely made from carbon fiber.

Hairy Glass also made custom carbon fiber covers for parts of the dash and console. When the original car was finished, it had to be completely taken apart and sent out for bodywork, paint, and plating.

The plan was to debut the first Mustang at the NHRA Hot Rod Reunion in Bowling Green, Kentucky. Hubert and Randy would be attending on Saturday, June 18. The shell of the car and all the parts returned to the shop on Monday evening, June 13. Blake and his crew worked around the clock for the next four days while 25 volunteers from the church brought food and drinks to the shop to feed the workers three meals a day. The mechanics took short naps in the office, never going home during the rebuild.

The Seven Springs Church was so involved in making this dream a reality that they decided to give the build a biblical name. "Shadrach" was chosen and was painted on the hood, the rest of the car was painted to somewhat match the Platt & Payne Ford Drag Team cars from 1969 in beautiful blue with white stripes. Like the original, it had lettered "The Going Thing" in the inset of the stripe. Hubert and Blake had met with Ford to get its permission to use the company's slogan from the 1960s.

The completed Shadrach Mustang was awesome, to say the least. At 2 a.m. on Friday, the team headed north to Kentucky to get the car to Beech Bend Dragway for its Saturday debut. Hubert and Randy loved it, and they gave it their blessing by signing the dash with the inscription prototype #1.

On Labor Day weekend, the Shadrach was displayed at the NHRA U.S. Nationals in Indianapolis, Indiana, and then in October at the SEMA show in Las Vegas, Nevada. After the SEMA show, the Mustang was taken to MSD in El Paso, Texas, where it spent three days getting a custom ignition system installed.

After the number two car was finished, Al Moody Racing Engines from Mableton, Georgia, was brought on board to build the engines for Shadrachs numbers three and four. For the fifth Mustang, Gary Grimes (son of Hoyt Grimes, who was known as the "Granddaddy of Southeastern Drag Racing") built the engine: a Boss 429 with two 4s.

In August 2006, the number three Shadrach made the cover of *Modified Mustangs*, a performance magazine for Mustang enthusiasts. The cover headline read "Blue 'N

Bad 900HP Georgia Special." Inside was a nice article with pictures of Hubert and Randy with the Shadrach Mustang.

In 2008, this same Shadrach number three went across the block at the world famous Barrett-Jackson auction as a charity car, where a large portion of the sale goes to a charity. In this case, the charity was the Darrell Gwynn Foundation, a charity that helps people with paralysis. Darrell is a world champion Top Fuel Dragster driver who was paralyzed himself in a tragic accident in 1990. Hubert went to the auction to help boost the sale and even got on the auctioneer's microphone toward the end. He hyped up the crowd, saying, "Come on, get your money out; this is for charity!" The bid kept rising until it closed out at $190,000.

The next month, the Darrell Gwynn Foundation sent Hubert a small trophy with a star, thanking him for his help in selling the car. All five of the Shadrach Mustangs are in private collections today.

## 40th Anniversary of the Cobra Jet

Ford Motor Company realized that it didn't have current product in the NHRA sportsman classes, so it decided this would be perfect time to recreate its iconic drag car from 1968 with a 40th anniversary version of the Cobra Jet Mustang. Ford built 50 of the 2008 FR500CJ Cobra Jets, none of which were street legal. These were ready-to-drag-race production Mustangs, and when they went up for sale, all 50 sold out in just 10 days for $69,900 each!

The Cobra Jet Mustangs had 5.4L DOHC, supercharged engines that would power them to the first eight-second runs ever in NHRA Stock Eliminator. Brent Hajek bought the first 10.

With only a month before Winternationals, Brent called on Holzman Race Cars to help prepare the first four Cobra Jets for racing competitively in the NHRA. The first three 40th anniversary CJs were painted to match three of the original six from the 1968 Winternationals: Gas

***Brent Hajek of Ames, Oklahoma, stands with his 40th anniversary Cobra Jet display at the 2009 NHRA Winternationals with three of the five original drivers from the 1968 Winternationals. Pictured are (left to right): Gary Stinnett, Gas Ronda, Al Joniec, John Calvert, Brent Hajek, Hubert Platt, Jimmy Ronzello, Randy Richey, and Jim Waldo. Brent's tour bus pictured was originally used by legendary rock band the Grateful Dead in 1994.***

*After the 2009 NHRA Winternationals, Hubert had these promotional 8x10 photos made to commemorate the 40th anniversary of the Cobra Jet.*

*The 2008 Cobra Jet bearing Hubert's name went to many final rounds and was the NHRA record holder in 2009 and 2010.*

*The 2008 Cobra Jet bearing Hubert's name won its class at the 2009 NHRA U.S. Nationals with Jimmy Holzman driving. Team owner Brent Hajek stands to Hubert's right and driver Jimmy Holzman is on his left.*

Ronda/Russ Davis Ford, Hubert Platt/Paul Harvey Ford, and Al Joniec/Rice-Holman Ford.

Hubert was honored to be a part of this 40th anniversary of the Cobra Jet. He attended the Winternationals, as did Gas Ronda and Al Joniec. As fate would have it, the 2008 Cobra Jet painted as the Al Joniec–winning car from 1968 won the race driven by Stock Drag Champion John Calvert. Hajek Motorsports raced the 2008 Cobra Jets for the next few years, winning multiple NHRA national events and setting several national records.

Hubert was proud of the new Cobra Jet Mustang with his name on it, and he attended the NHRA U.S. Nationals in 2009, 2010, and 2011 to see it run. Hubert was especially thrilled in 2009 when it went to the U.S. Nationals winner's circle in AA/SA with Jimmy Holzman doing the driving. Hubert posed in the winner's circle photos with Jimmy, Brent, and the crews from Hajek Motorsports and Holzman Race Cars.

## Brannan/Platt Gold Long-Nose Mustang

In 2011, 45 years after the summer of 1966 when Hubert and Dick Brannan terrorized the drag strips across the country with a 427 SOHC long-nose Mustang, the two were reunited with that very car! Now owned by Brent Hajek of Oklahoma and restored by Holzman Race Cars, the famous Mustang redebuted at the NHRA Hot Rod Reunion in Bowling Green, Kentucky, in June.

To honor both of these men who famously campaigned this car, Brent had one side lettered to how it looked when Hubert drove the car for Dick and the other side to how it looked when Hubert drove it for Larry Coleman. The restored Mustang won its class in the Hot Rod Reunion car show and was featured with the other winners at that year's NHRA U.S. Nationals in Indianapolis, which Hubert also attended.

*Forty-five years after winning the NASCAR Sanctioned Summer Championship in West Salem, Ohio, Hubert and Dick Brannan were reunited with their famous Mustang at the 2011 NHRA Hot Rod Reunion.*

*The Holman & Moody-built gold long-nose Mustang was restored to honor both of the men who famously campaigned the car. The driver's side is painted the way it looked when Dick Brannan owned and Hubert drove the car in 1966 (top), and the passenger's side is painted the way it looked when Larry Coleman owned the car and Hubert drove it in 1967 (bottom).*

## He's Still Got It!

In 2012, Hubert was invited by his old friend and fellow drag racer Roy Hill to attend a session at his drag racing school in North Carolina. Hubert attended and hung out while Roy put some of his students through the paces.

Roy asked Hubert if he would like to renew his NHRA license (which expired in 1977) in one of the new Cobra Jet Mustangs. Hubert, with an "Of course I do" smile, quickly agreed. Hubert made three 9-second passes in a 2010 FR500CJ prototype Cobra Jet Mustang and renewed his competition license. Roy was shocked. At 80 years old, Hubert was driving like he had never retired.

Next Roy offered to let Hubert make a pass in one of the school's Pro Stock Ford Thunderbirds. Hubert accepted, jumped in, and ripped off a 165 mph run! Hubert was forever grateful to his old friend Roy for helping him relive his glory days, something most 80 year old's don't get to do.

*This is the 2010 Cobra Jet Mustang that Hubert used to renew his NHRA driver's license in 2012 at 80 years old. Isn't that when most men lose driving privileges?*

*When restoring an actual 1960s Funny Car, it can get pretty expensive, especially when the power is a rare injected 427 SOHC big-block Ford! As you can see, owner Brent Hajek of Ames, Oklahoma, spared no expense.*

*When looking at the unusual roll cage in the gold long-nose Mustang and comparing it to the pictures taken in 1967, there is no doubt that this is the actual car Hubert drove from August 1966 to May 1967.*

*The beautiful restoration of the gold long-nose Mustang was done by Holzman Race Cars of Wichita, Kansas. Holzman is a third-generation race car shop that worked closely with owner Brent Hajek on the build to return the car to the way it appeared in 1966–1967.*

*Nate Greco was commissioned to create artwork in 2012. Hubert picked his four favorite cars from his career. He made it clear that the gold Mustang was his favorite and the Falcon made him the most money.*

## GeorgiaShaker.Com

In June 2013, Hubert's son Allen launched the website GeorgiaShaker.com. It is an interactive site with videos and photos celebrating Hubert's legendary drag racing career. The site also hosts an online store, where you can shop for Hubert "Georgia Shaker" Platt merchandise, such as T-shirts, posters, diecast replicas, DVDs, and autographed pictures.

**The Little Georgia Shaker** ***Thunderbolt was made into a 1/64-scale electric slot car by Auto World. The details are amazingly accurate.***

***The GMP 1967 Fairlane 1/18-scale diecast is the most detailed of all the*** **Georgia Shaker** ***adult collectables. The windows actually roll up and down!***

***Fans sent Hubert diecast cars to autograph and send back. He always had time for his fans and never charged for an autograph.***

The Auto World 1/18-scale diecast of the 985 Cobra Jet Mustang has its original accurate paint scheme from the 1968 NHRA Winternationals.

The ACME 1/18-scale diecast of the 1964 Thunderbolt Little Georgia Shaker is one of the most popular Georgia Shaker adult collectables ever made, selling out all 1,000 units right after they were released in 2010.

The Racing Champions 1/18-scale diecast of the 984 Cobra Jet Mustang that came out in 2001 is neat but not very accurate. On the actual car, Hubert Platt and Tasca were lettered in red and the class was C/SA not SS/E.

The AMT 1/25-scale model kits of the Iowa Shaker and the Georgia Shaker III are unpainted, unassembled hobby kits for kids and adults alike.

This Revell 1/25-scale model kit has two different decal sheets and can be built to resemble Hubert's Little Georgia Shaker or the Thunderbolt of Phil Bonner.

The Johnny Lightning 1/64 scale diecast twin pack features both paint schemes of the 1969 Ford Drag Team Super Stock Mustang.

*Hubert's son Allen raced the tribute replica of the "Platt & Payne" Ford Drag Team Mustang at the 2017 FE Race and Reunion in Beaver Springs, Pennsylvania.*

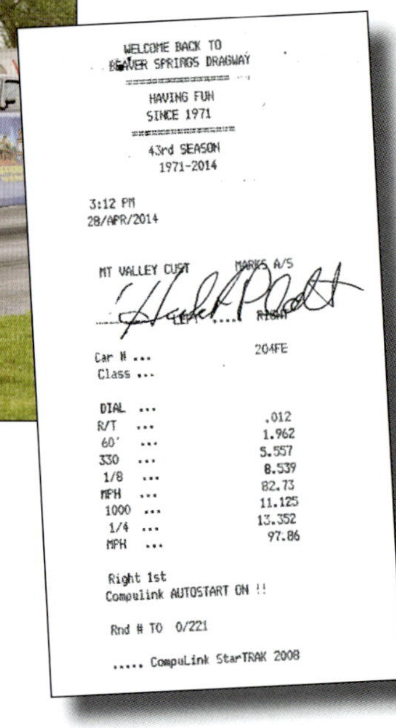

WELCOME BACK TO
BEAVER SPRINGS DRAGWAY

HAVING FUN
SINCE 1971

43rd SEASON
1971-2014

3:12 PM
28/APR/2014

MT VALLEY CUST MARKS A/S
LEFT ..... RIGHT

Car # ... 204FE
Class ...

DIAL ...
R/T ... .012
60' ... 1.962
330 ... 5.557
1/8 ... 8.539
MPH ... 82.73
1000 ... 11.125
1/4 ... 13.352
MPH ... 97.86

Right 1st
Compulink AUTOSTART ON !!

Rnd # TO 0/221

..... CompuLink StarTRAK 2008

*Hubert autographed the time slip from their run for Ford super fan Robert Gillespie. Robert is in the process of building a tribute replica of the blue and gold version of Hubert's Pro Stock Pinto, which will debut in 2019.*

## 1969 Platt & Payne Tribute Mustang

At the end of 2013, Andy Snetselaar, a Ford Drag Team fan from Ankeny, Iowa, had the idea of honoring the "Platt & Payne" Ford Drag Team of 1969 with a tribute replica. The plan was to have a running raceable tribute, not just a replica show car.

Andy purchased an IHRA legal Stock Eliminator 428 Cobra Jet 1969 Mustang that ran in B/SA (B/Stock Automatic). The car was almost exactly like the one Hubert raced: blue with black interior. Paying close attention to the old photographs of the Ford Drag Team from 1969, Andy painted the hood and decklid white as well as the area between the taillights. Next, the car was striped and lettered to match Hubert's Mustang from 1969. All period-correct contingency stickers were placed just as they were back in the day. To complete the recreation, Andy installed a set of Cragar chrome-reverse wheels just like the original.

The car turned out so well that when it was debuted at the 2014 FE Race and Reunion at Beaver Springs Dragway in Pennsylvania the first question out of the mouth of fans was: "Is this the real car?" Hubert was attending the reunion, and like the fans, he was thrilled to see the replica of his old ride from 45 years before. Fan after fan came up to Hubert and said, "I remember seeing you at the nationals in this car."

Hubert was so excited, he told Andy he wanted to drive the car. Andy obliged him and Ford super fan Robert Gillespie jumped into the passenger seat to go along for this once-in-a-lifetime ride. Andy was surprised when 82-year-old Hubert took the car straight to the starting line and made a 13-second, 97-mph pass with a reaction time of 0.012! Hubert said without a passenger he could have pushed the car to its full potential in the low 11s.

## The *Lil' General* Returns

In 2014, Platt family friend Mike Thomas of Augusta, Georgia, built a tribute replica of Hubert's 1962 Chevy Biscayne 409 SS/S, the *Lil' General*. Hubert spent a lot of time at Mike's shop overseeing the meticulous work that was done to recreate the factory drag car and make it look brand new like went Hubert first raced it in 1962.

Hubert was on hand that June for the debut at the NHRA Hot Rod Reunion in Bowling Green, Kentucky. Many of Hubert's fans never knew he got his start driving Chevys until seeing this tribute replica.

## The Last Build

At the end of 2014, Tom Krull of Cumming, Georgia, enlisted Hubert's help in building a tribute replica of his record-setting 1967 Fairlane. Tom wanted Hubert to be involved in every part of this process, and Hubert drove hundreds of miles around the Southeast looking at potential donor cars until finally finding the right one.

Hubert spent countless hours on the phone, calling old contacts and looking for period-correct performance parts to make the build as authentic as possible. In December, at Hubert's 83rd birthday party, all he could talk about was the Fairlane they were building, where they had to go to get all the parts, and how much everything cost. He was like a 16-year-old kid talking about

## Old Friends

Hubert was a special guy, and his outgoing personality gained him many lifelong friends. At reunions, he would run into folks he hadn't seen in years and pick up right where they left off, talking about old times like they never missed a beat. Hubert had a way of making a lasting impression on people. If someone met him, chances were they didn't forget it. He was generally a fun guy to be around, the type of person who never met a stranger and always had a little joke or something funny to say.

*Hubert and old friend Doug Thorley reunited at the 2000 NHRA California Hot Rod Reunion in Bakersfield. The two talked about the glory days and posed with Doug's recreation of his famous Chevy 2 Much A/FX Nova.*

*Hubert and "Ohio" George Montgomery met at the 2012 NHRA U.S. Nationals and talked about racing Gassers together down in Georgia some 52 years earlier in 1960.*

*Hubert and close friend Linda Vaughn reconnected at the MCACN in 2012. This is when we missed our chance to recreate their famous interior photo from 1969!*

*Randy "Mr. Big Stuff" Payne, Hubert "Georgia Shaker" Platt, and Phil "Daddy Warbucks" Bonner posed together at the 2010 NHRA Hot Rod Reunion in Bowling Green, Kentucky.*

*Hubert and Connie Kalitta had a long-running tradition they started in the 1960s. When they would see one another at the drag races, without speaking, they would each pull out a quarter and flip them, one calling "odd or even." The winner would get $100! The high rollers always impressed the fans that would crowd around to see the game.*

*Hubert stood by the tribute replica of his 409 1962 Biscayne, the* **Lil' General** *in 2014. This was Hubert's last trip to the NHRA Hot Rod Reunion in Bowling Green, Kentucky. Hubert welcomed recreations of his old race cars and liked to help out on the builds. He spent many hours and late nights at Mike Thomas's shop in Augusta, Georgia, when this tribute replica of his Biscayne was being built. Hubert was close friends with Mike's father, national champion mud racer Ennis Thomas.*

his first hot rod; he wouldn't shut up! Hubert's family all agreed that they hadn't seen him this excited in a while.

In the beginning of 2015, Hubert started to not feel like his old self. Normally vibrant and full of energy, he was feeling tired and having pains. He had his physician run tests while he continued working on the build and going to drag race reunions around the country. He once again attended the FE Race and Reunion in Beaver Springs, where he posed in the winner's circle with the tribute replica of his 1969 Platt & Payne Mustang when owner Andy Snetselaar won the Cool FE Class.

Hubert was on top of the world, traveling the country and going to nostalgia drag races and car shows. He enjoyed all of the attention from his fans and working on replica builds when he got the results back from his doctor. Hubert had liver cancer.

*Hubert loved going to events with his son Allen. Selling* **Georgia Shaker** *merchandise, talking with fans, and signing autographs was a joy to him. He was constantly planning and looking forward to the next event. This photo was taken at the Southeastern International Dragway Reunion in 2015, six months before his passing.*

Eight and a half weeks later, on the morning of September 26, 2015, Hubert passed away peacefully in his sleep in hospice care.

Tom Krull finished the 1967 Fairlane build the next year, and the car was displayed at the 2016 NHRA U.S. Nationals and the North Georgia Moonshine Festival in Hubert's honor. The Fairlane was later sold at the Barrett-Jackson auction and is now in a private collection.

### The Revival of the Grudge Matches

In October 2015, one month after Hubert's passing, Sonee Hall, an engineer and drag racer from East Tennessee, approached Hubert's son Allen about building a tribute replica of his father's most iconic ride: the *Georgia Shaker III* 1965 Falcon. The plan was to build an exact replica of Hubert's car and have Allen drive it in exhibition match races versus his cousin Rocky Platt (Huston's son) driving a tribute replica of Huston's 1965 Chevy II Fastback *Dixie Twister*.

This sounded like a fantasy to Allen. It was something he had dreamed of his entire life, and he eagerly agreed. The build began. In the next few months, cousin Rocky began to drive the A/FX Fastback Chevy II, preparing for the match races. Then in April 2017, Allen attended the FE Race and Reunion in Beaver Springs, driving the same 1969 Platt & Payne tribute replica his father had three years earlier, getting his feet wet in a drag car for the first time.

Sonee and friend Kelvin Cannon (owner of the *Dixie Twister* Fastback) built the Falcon in eight months. The completed car debuted in June at the 2016 NHRA Hot Rod Reunion in Kentucky.

*The 1967 Fairlane tribute replica was displayed at the 2016 Mountain Moonshine Festival in Dawsonville, Georgia. This was the last build Hubert got to work on.*

After months of test and tune to get the Falcon "dialed in," Allen and Rocky began to recreate the grudge matches: Ford-versus-Chevy, brother-versus-brother, two-out-of-three match races like their fathers had more than 50 years before. The vision of Sonee Hall and Kelvin Cannon had been realized, and Allen and Rocky are eternally grateful to these two men for helping them celebrate their fathers' racing careers on this incredible level.

In February 2018, Sonee Hall sold the *Georgia Shaker III* tribute replica to Allen just before passing away from recurring heart problems. Allen, Rocky, and Kelvin continue Sonee's mission to keeping drag racing history alive by racing the cars on tour with the Southeast Gassers Association, which is the most period-correct nostalgia drag racing organization in the United States.

## Drag Racing Hall of Fames

Hubert traveled the country for more than 20 years from the early 1990s until his passing in 2015. He attended nostalgia drag races, car shows, and hot rod reunions and was inducted into 10 drag racing halls of fame.

In 2005 at the NHRA Hot Rod Reunion, Hubert received his most prestigious trophy: the coveted NHRA Lifetime Achievement Award. The Wally trophy reads, "For his years of faithful dedication to serving the interests of others on the behalf of the entire hot rod fraternity, NHRA Lifetime Achievement Award, Presented with gratitude from a thankful sport on June 18, 2005, at Beech Bend Raceway Park, Bowling Green, Kentucky."

Hubert Platt was a pioneer and a legend in the sport of drag racing. His charming persona endured him to fans, many of whom called him their hero. After racing, Hubert was a union millwright for many years. After retiring from commercial construction, he was the owner and operator of a small diner in Buford, Georgia, called the Sugar Hill Drive-In.

To date, 7 of Hubert's actual race cars have resurfaced and 15 tribute cars have been built in his honor. These cars are either on tour or in private collections today.

Hubert remained a lifelong advocate and spokesman for the sport of drag racing. He and son Allen toured the country coast to coast, attending nostalgia drag races and racer reunions for more than 20 years, from the early 1990s until his passing in 2015. Hubert remained energetic, hale and hearty up until the end of his life, always eager to go to events and reminisce about the glory days of drag racing. Everywhere he went the shouts of "Hu-Baby!" would always bring a smile to his face, and he never tired of meeting, talking with fans, and signing autographs.

*Huston's son Rocky Platt and Hubert's son Allen Platt battle it out in tribute replicas of their dads' cars from 1965 at Shadyside Dragway in Shelby, North Carolina, in April 2018. Rocky and Allen are on a mission to keeping drag racing history alive and well!*

*Allen Platt launched the Falcon at Mooresville Dragway in North Carolina. The* Georgia Shaker III *tribute replica and the recreation of the grudge matches was the vision of Sonee Hall and Kelvin Cannon of East Tennessee. Kelvin owns the Fastback Chevy II* Dixie Twister *tribute replica and was the builder of both cars. (Photo Courtesy Tom Hassell)*

*Cousins Rocky Platt and Allen Platt match race their AWB, alcohol-injected, A/FX tribute replicas of their dads' cars on tour with the Southeast Gassers Association, which is the most period-correct nostalgia drag racing organization in the country. (Photo Courtesy Caleb Sewell)*

*Hubert is shown here doing what he loved most. This was at the 2014 Mountain Moonshine Festival in Dawsonville, Georgia. Tim Holland, owner of the* Georgia Shaker III *barn find (left), is with Hubert (seated) and son Allen Platt (right).*

*Hubert received the coveted NHRA Lifetime Achievement Award "Wally" in 2005 at the NHRA Hot Rod Reunion in Bowling Green, Kentucky.*

| Hubert Platt Drag Racing Hall of Fame Inductions | |
|---|---|
| 1986 | NHRA Division 2 Hall of Fame, Atlanta, Georgia |
| 1993 | Pro Stock Legends Hall of Fame, Sikeston, Missouri |
| 1995 | Super Stock Hall of Fame, Richmond, Virginia |
| 1998 | Supercar Showdown Legend Hall of Fame, National Trail Raceway, Columbus, Ohio |
| 2002 | East Coast Drag Times Hall of Fame, Henderson, North Carolina |
| 2003 | Georgia Auto Racing Hall of Fame, Middle, Georgia Chapter 1 |
| 2003 | Old Drag Racers Reunion Hall of Fame, Panama City, Florida |
| 2006 | Georgia Racing Hall of Fame, Dawsonville, Georgia |
| 2012 | AIRPS Hall of Fame, Augusta International Raceway Preservation Society |
| 2018 | North Carolina Drag Racing Hall of Fame, Kernersville, North Carolina |

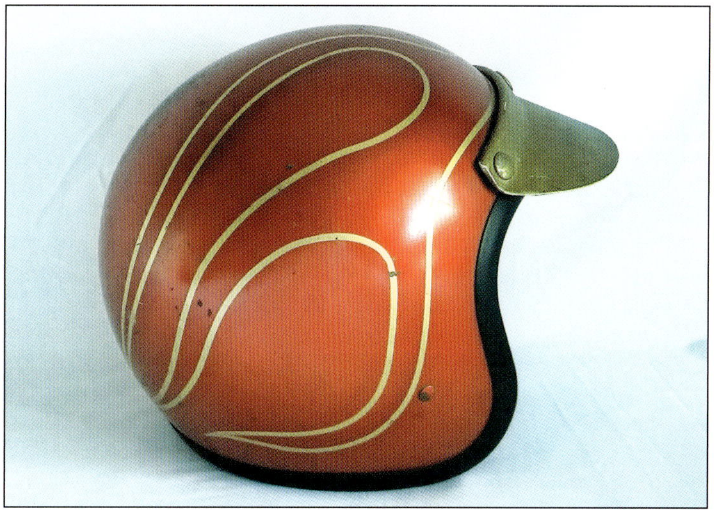

This was Hubert's last helmet, which he used in his Pro Stock Pinto.

Hubert received his NHRA Lifetime Achievement Award from legendary NHRA announcer Dave McClelland at the 2005 NHRA Hot Rod Reunion.

The walls of Hubert's pool room were covered with hall of fame plaques and awards from his drag racing days.

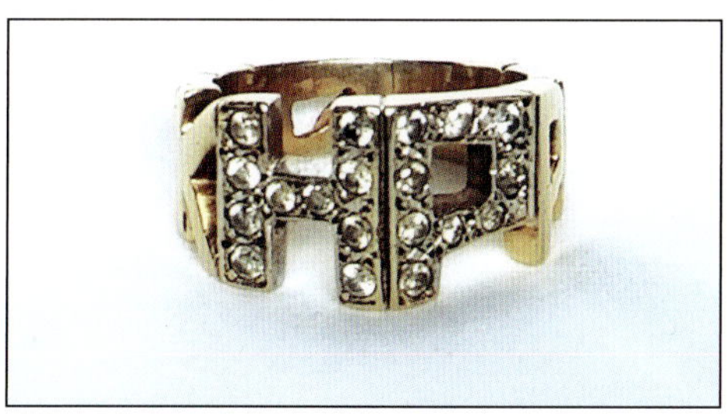
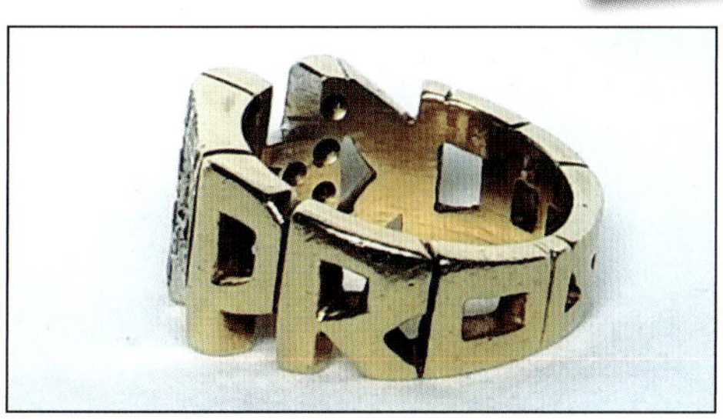
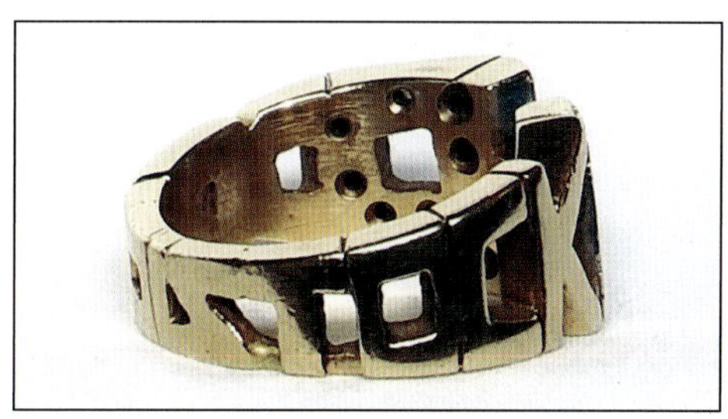

Hubert bought a gold and diamond HP ring in the 1960s and wore it up until the 1990s, when he gave it to son Hubie. He had a new custom HP ring made for himself (shown). The band of the new ring reads Pro Stock to commemorate being one of the pioneers of the class.

# INDEX

1320 Dragway 102
1938 Chevy 20–24, 26
1939 Ford Coupe 9
1950 Olds 12
1953 Firedome DeSoto 13
1955 Chevy 22, 23
1958 Ford Custom 300 Tudor Sedan 18
1961 Pontiac 23
1962 Biscayne *Lil' General* 26, 28, 32, 184, 186
1962 Super Sport Impala 29, 30
1964 Falcon 34, 41–45, 47–49, 52, 53, 55, 57, 59, 61, 63–66, 68, 69, 94, 127, 151, 166–169, 181, 187, 188
1965 Falcon Sprint 127
1967 drag car 163
1967 Ford Fairlane 29, 34, 40, 41, 87–93, 96, 97, 102, 103, 106, 109, 165, 168, 182, 184, 187
1968 Shelby GT500KR 163
1968 Torino Cobra 106–111, 113–115, 122, 124, 127, 135, 136
1969 match-race Mustang 133
1969 Mustang Mach I 113
1969 Super Stock Mustang 137
1970 Pro Stock Mustang 136, 137

**A**

*ABC's Wide World of Sports* 95
AHRA Winternationals 81, 85, 99
Allen, Kenneth 163
Allie, Bill 103
Anderson, Bob 142
Aquasco Dragway 47, 77, 84
Arons, Dick 89, 102, 103
Arrington, Lew 84
Ashville-Hendersonville Dragway 24
Atco Dragway 78, 154, 155
AWB long-nose Mustang 49, 55–57, 59–61, 64, 66, 68–71, 75–80, 83–85, 151, 164–166, 178–180

**B**

Bagshaw, Bill 142
Bell, Wally 39
Big Race, The 13, 101
Blanding, Bill 143
Booth, Wally 102, 146, 169
*Bounty Hunter* 29, 30
Boyd, Bobby 109
Brantley, Bruce 6, 20, 23, 38, 39
Brantmeier, Jon 6, 123, 127, 136
Brewer, Donnie 148
Bristol International Dragway 84, 87
Brown, Prescott 17, 18, 23, 26, 136, 148, 154
Brown, Sammy 148, 149, 154
Butler, Anthony 109

**C**

Campbell, Willie "Camrod" 6, 154, 155
Cannon, Kelvin 187, 188
*Car Craft* magazine 123
Carlton, Don 131, 146
Carman, Chuck 66
Carpenter, Al 8, 146
Chadwick, Kelly 69, 71
Chamblee Carburetor & Electric 19, 20, 38, 39, 144, 149, 155, 157
Champion Spark Plugs 33
Chesser, Ronald "Slick" 14, 22, 28, 29, 32, 41, 44, 52, 127, 144, 148
Cobra Jet Mustang 98, 100–103, 106, 108, 113, 117, 121, 123, 127, 131, 139, 163, 172, 176, 178, 180, 183
Coleman, Larry 6, 79, 81, 82, 87, 117, 178, 179
Coley, Jerry 6, 133, 136, 141–143
Crutchfield, Tom 103
Cumming Dragway 50, 93, 155

**D**

Dallafior, John 85
Daytona Winter Drags 44
Denby, Billy 140
Detroit Dragway 75, 76, 78, 83
Dixie Southland Dragstrip 52
*Dixie Twister* 30, 34, 41, 44, 54, 72, 77, 85, 93, 187, 188
Drag City Dragway 147
*Drag Racing* magazine 50, 61
*Drag Speed Illustrated* 41
Dunbar, Jerry 103
Durbin, John 109, 110
Durham, Malcolm 83
Dutton, Harold 89, 90, 105

**E**

*Esquire* 139
Everett, Ronald 148

**F**

Faubel, Bud 77
Flegel, Ponnie 6, 12
Fons, Mike 146
Fontana Dragway 53
Ford Drag Clubs 112, 123, 124, 127, 129, 136, 137
Ford Drag Racing 6, 75, 81, 111, 123
Ford Drag Teams 112, 116, 120, 121, 123, 124, 131, 136, 137, 140, 141
Ford Racing Division 87
Foster, Pat 69, 70
Foster, Sidney 85, 117
Foulger, Chuck 101, 104, 105, 108–111, 113, 117, 119
Frank Vego Ford 38, 39
Funny Car 38, 58, 61, 69–79, 81, 83, 85–88, 93, 95, 117, 122, 136, 137, 180
Funny Car Bash 83

**G**

Gapp, Wayne 146
Garlits, "Big Daddy" Don 30, 140
Gates, Pete 77, 142
*Georgia Shaker* 6, 32–34, 37–40, 60, 61, 65, 66, 71, 89, 90, 92–95, 103–105, 107, 109, 132–134, 136, 139, 142–144, 146–148, 157, 164, 165, 168, 182, 183
*Georgia Shaker III* 44, 48–50, 52, 53, 55, 60, 61, 63–66, 68, 94, 166–168, 183, 187–189
Gilbert, Bill 97, 166
Gillis, Rusty 6, 106, 130, 131, 135
Glidden, Bob 157, 159
Gowland, Bruce 102
Greer, Shirl 41, 94
Grotheer, Don 136, 145, 146

**H**

Hajek, Brent 6, 166, 176, 178, 180
Hall, Sonee 187, 188
Harrell, Dick "Mr. Everything" 29, 52, 60, 62, 63, 66
Hart, C.J. "Pappy" 53, 60, 61, 66
Harvey, Paul 79, 82–84, 89, 90, 93, 100, 101, 104–106, 129, 155–157, 178
Heath, Dave 30
Henderson, Don 102
Hernandez, Fran 34, 69
Hill, Roy 180
*Hi-Performance Cars* 85
Holland, Tim 6, 168, 169, 189
Holzman, Jimmy 176–178, 180
*Hot Rod* magazine 102, 112, 119, 123, 139, 169
*Hotrod Parts Illustrated* 73
Hubert Platt Texaco 19–22
Hurley, Frank 124
Huszar, Frank 69
Hut, The 12, 13, 19

**I**

*Iowa Shaker* 64–66, 68, 69, 166, 167, 183
Irwindale Raceway 66

**J**

Jacobs, Billy 52
Jenkins, Bill "Grumpy" 29, 102, 103, 146, 158
Jenkins, Larry 94, 95
Johnson, Roosevelt 148, 149, 153, 154, 161
Jones, Jacky 172, 173, 175
Joniec, Al 100, 101, 137, 176, 178

**K**

Kelley, Johnny 166
Kerr, Mike 6, 166, 167
Kirby, Don 70
Knoxville Dragway 33
Krull, Tom 184, 187
Kruse, Doug 70
Kuck, Gary 164, 166

L

Lambeck, Bob 110
Lamb, Robert 168
Landy, "Dandy" Dick 87, 90, 102, 106, 110, 140, 146
Lassiter Mountain Raceway 45–47
Leal, Bill "Butch" 29, 35
Leong, Roland 137
Lindamood, Roger 78, 83
Lions Drag Strip 53, 57, 60–62, 65, 66, 71, 81, 84, 85, 99
*Little Georgia Shaker* 35–43, 60, 166, 182, 183
Livingston, John 84
Loehr, Dick 77, 81, 82, 85, 123, 136, 139
Loflin, Gene 69
Lorenzen, Fred 75
Los Angeles County Fairgrounds 98, 101, 120, 121, 142
Louisa Drag Strip 38
Lyles, Ronnie 146

M

Maddox, Bob 23, 105
Malkemes, Lee 41, 165
Manassas Drag Strip 15
Marshall, Jim 16, 142
Martin, Buddy 17, 29, 90, 100, 101, 106, 116, 131, 143, 146, 148
Matthews, Banjo 19
Mazmanian, Big John 117
McCandless, Herb 6, 146
McCants, Paul 11
McClure, Captain Jack 34
McDull, Billy 77
McEwen, Tom "the Mongoose" 81, 137
McNeely, Tommy 68, 167
Miller, Ed 102
Mirarcki, Rich 143, 146
*Modern Rod* magazine 61
Montgomery International Terminal Drag-strip 102
moonshine 10, 12, 13, 16, 187, 189
Motor City Dragway 69, 85
Mount Lassiter Dragway 83
Mustang Funny Car 69, 71, 86
Myrtle Beach Dragway 89

N

Nabors, Calvin 148
Nalley-Nicholson Dyno Shop 26, 28, 30
Nalley Race Team 26
Nance, Robert 155
NASCAR Drag Racing Championships 22
NASCAR Drag Racing Series Winter Championships 122
NASCAR Summer Championships 77
National Trail Dragway 166
Neal, Howard 37
New England Dragway 135
NHRA Lifetime Achievement Award 188, 189
NHRA Nationals 29, 30, 35, 63, 90–92, 94, 96, 127–130, 137, 139, 140, 157–159, 172, 175, 177, 178, 184, 185, 187
NHRA Springnationals 89, 127
NHRA Winternationals 99, 101

O

Old Dominion Speedway 75
Ongais, Danny 137
Orangeburg Drag Strip 33
Orange County International Raceway 110, 116, 117

P

Palm Beach International Dragway 83
Pasley, Howard 61, 168
Passino, Jacque 109, 110
*Performance on the Line* 116
Perkins, Bob 6, 169, 171–173
Petty, Richard 45, 46
Phenix City Dragway 83
Phoenix Drag Reunion 167
Pike, Buck 141, 148, 149
Platt, Allen 4, 39, 188, 189
Platt Brothers Automotive Speed Shop 157, 163
Platt, Huston 8, 9, 11, 14, 19–21, 26, 28–30, 34, 39, 41, 44, 53, 54, 71, 72, 77, 78, 83–85, 93, 95, 107, 122, 144, 148, 153, 157, 187, 188
Platt, Ray 6, 8, 19, 107
Platt, Rocky 187, 188
Poole, Barrie 102
*Popular Hot Rodding* 157, 158
Pro Stock Pinto 155–159, 184, 190
Prudhomme, Don "the Snake" 123, 137, 140

R

Raceway Park 89, 154, 189
Reeves, Donnie 164
Renfroe, Bogan 94
Renzler, Bobby 30
Reyes, Larry 6, 143
Ritchey, Les 64, 65
Robinson, Pete 142
Ronda, Gas 35, 100, 102, 117, 176, 178
Rupp, Maynard 85

S

Schartman, Ed "Fast Eddie" 69, 83, 85, 146
Schumacher, Don 117
Shahan, Shirley "Drag-On-Lady" 52, 63
Simmons, Fred 164–166, 168
Skelton, Ed 137, 141
*Smallest Georgia Shaker* 42–49, 53, 60, 167
Snetselaar, Andy 184, 186
*Southeastern Drag News* 24
Southeastern Dragway 83, 94, 153
Sox & Martin 29, 90, 100, 101, 106, 116, 131, 146, 148
*Speed and Supercar* 106
Sportman's Park Dragstrip 34
Spruce Creek Airport 37
Stardust Dragway 142
Strickler, Dave 29, 146
Suffolk International Raceway 71
*Super Stock & Drag Illustrated* 136
*Super Stock* magazine 44, 136, 157
*Super Stock News* 41, 71
*Super Thrill* 136, 137
Sutton, Tom 172

T

*Tach* magazine 61
Tampa Dragway 28, 34
Tanner, Bill 122
Tasca, Bob 34, 97, 100, 101, 105, 106, 126, 183
Terminal Transport Racing Division 22, 23, 26
Terry, Ed 102, 112, 113, 115–118, 121, 124, 130, 146, 149, 150, 154
Thomas, Bill 29, 53
Thompson, Tim 107, 143, 144, 149, 153
Thunderbolt Raceway 47
Turner, Al 69
Turner, Curtis 75

U

Union Hill Drag Strip 37
United States Racing Team (USRT) 146, 147
US Army 14

V

Vanek, Jerry 102
Vanke, Arlen 91, 101, 146

W

Walden, Lamar 29
Wallace, "Pee Wee" 38
Walters, Dick 60, 64–66, 69, 71, 77
Warner Robins Dragway 89, 161, 162
Warren, George 103, 149, 161
Weis, Joe 78
West Salem Dragway 42 77
Whisnant, Reid 140, 148
White, Dan 130-131
*White Lightning* 34, 37
Wilder, Blake 53, 75, 173
Wood, Bobby 83
Wood, Dick 112, 113, 137

Y

Yates, Larry 6, 46, 49, 52, 56, 61, 151, 168, 169
Yellow River Dragstrip 7, 94, 122
Yow, Melvin 140, 141

Z

Z11 30, 32-35, 37–40
Zimmerman, Frank 34

# Additional books that may interest you...

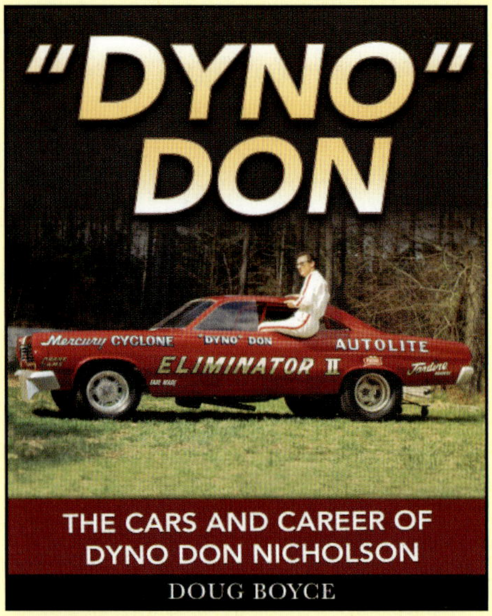


**DYNO DON**: The Cars and Career of Dyno Don Nicholson *by Doug Boyce*
If you are a fan of a certain era of racing, a Ford fan, or certainly a "Dyno" Don fan this book will be a welcome addition to your library. Follow his Hall of Fame career on the match race circuit. Softbound, 8.5 x 11 inches, 176 pages, 330 photos. **Part # CT631**

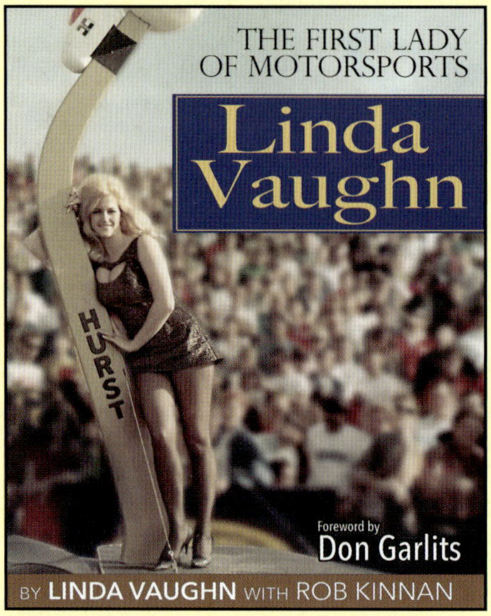


**LINDA VAUGHN:** The First Lady of Motorsports
*by Rob Kinnan and Linda Vaughn*
This is the most comprehensive gathering of photography ever assembled on Linda Vaughn. Through her 50-plus years in motorsports, Linda has lived it all, been everywhere, and met everyone. Whether you are simply a fan of Linda or a collector of Linda Vaughn memorabilia, this will be the premier piece in your collection. Hardbound, 8.5 x 11 inches, 224 pages, 350 photos. **Part # CT555**

**MATCH RACE MAYHEM:** Drag Racing's Grudges, Rivalries and Big-Money Showdowns
*by Doug Boyce*
Veteran drag race author Doug Boyce tells the tale of the history of match racing through the cars, the drivers, the events, the classes, the rivalries, and everything else that was fun about match racing during the golden era. It's all here, complemented by wonderful vintage photography provided by fans and professionals in attendance. Softbound, 8.5 x 11 inches, 176 pages, 297 photos. **Part # CT582**

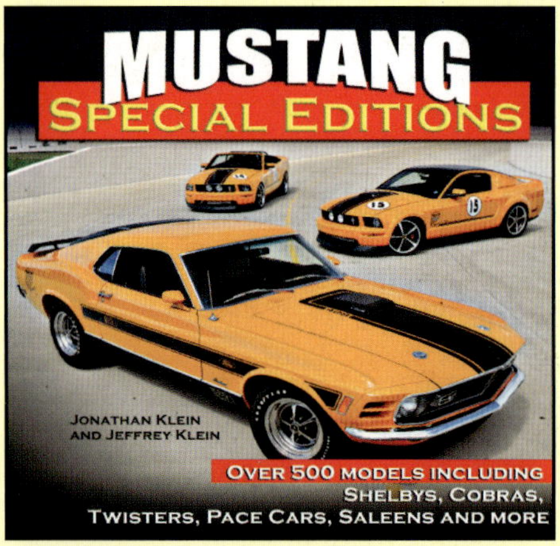


**MUSTANG SPECIAL EDITIONS**: More Than 500 Models Including Shelbys, Cobras, Twisters, Pace Cars, Saleens, and More
*by Jonathan Klein & Jeffrey Klein*
This book examines more than 500 special-edition Mustangs from 1964 through today. Coverage includes factory offerings such as the 2001 Bullitt and SVT Cobras, regional promotions including the Twister Special, third-party tuners such as Roush and Saleen, and factory race cars including the 1968 Cobra Jets and the 2000 Cobra-R. Hardbound, 10 x 10 inches, 192 pages, 509 photos. **Part # CT632**

*Check out our website:*

## CarTechBooks.com

✓ Find our newest books before anyone else

✓ Get weekly tech tips from our experts

✓ Featuring a new deal each week!

**Exclusive Promotions and Giveaways at www.CarTechBooks.com!**

**www.cartechbooks.com or 1-800-551-4754**